# ALL ASIA COOKBOOK

CAVENDISH HOUSE

Edited by Isabel Moore
and Jonnie Godfrey

Published by Marshall Cavendish Books Limited
58 Old Compton Street
London W1V 5PA

© Marshall Cavendish Limited, 1978, 1979, 1983

This material was previously published
as Foods of the Orient: South-East Asia and
Japan and Korea

First printing 1983

Printed and bound by Koon Wah Printing Pte Ltd, Singapore

ISBN 0 86307 152 X

# CONTENTS

# INTRODUCTION Derek Davies

# TO JAPAN & KOREA

Neither Japanese nor Korean cuisine is much known outside its own shores, although with increasing travel, especially to Japan, this will probably change. Those lucky enough to have tasted food from Japan and Korea know them to be delicious and unique, but the majority, who have not, assume them to be more or less the same and both rather poor relations of the magnificent cuisine of China. Nothing could be farther from the truth for while there are similarities (many ingredients are common to all three, they all use chopsticks and rice is the basic staple), there are also enormous differences (methods of preparation and cooking, the flavours preferred). They are related to one another, in fact, only as the French, British and Spanish cuisines are inter-related.

In general, Japanese food is delicate and refined, with an emphasis on freshness and clean, sharp, natural tastes: hot, spicy flavourings, popular in India and Malaysia are not used. Many ingredients, fish in particular, are eaten uncooked, and dipping sauces are used extensively to enhance the flavours. Not only are subtleties of taste all important, but the appearance of the dish should satisfy the eye just as much as the flavours satisfy the palate. Korean food, with a strong, rather spicy character of its own, also 'borrows' what is considered to be the best of neighbouring cuisines – so you will find Chinese noodles happily married to a dish containing Japanese soy sauce, and even a dish called 'curry', which turns out to be hot and spicy and with a chilli base.

The two most important ingredients in both cuisines are rice and soya beans. Plain rice is served with all meals. In Japan it has an almost religious significance and shrines to the rice god, *Inari*, can be seen throughout the country. Historically, it was used as a unit of taxation and as a measure of man's wealth; even today, so important is its preparation, that a women's skill at cooking is judged according to how well she makes it. Rice is also used to make wine: in Korea, known as *mah koli*, and in Japan, *sake* and *mirin*, not only drunk but also used extensively in cooking.

The versatile soya bean makes its appearance in several forms: it is the basic ingredient of soy sauce, which is the foundation of all Korean and Japanese cooking (it is used not only as a dipping sauce and as a seasoning, but as part of the base mixture in which many ingredients are cooked); it is con-verted into the white, jelly-like bean curd cake called *tofu* in Japan, which turns up in all sorts of dishes and in many different forms; and it is made into *miso*, a fermented paste used to marinate and dress fish and vegetables, and as a base for a whole range of soups.

Meat has always been part of the Korean diet, if something of a luxury, and several national dishes boast beef in various guises, but the Japanese ate it only rarely until about a hundred years ago. Partly, this was the result of Buddhist proscriptions against eating anything that had 'received the breath of life' and partly because the mountainous islands of Japan lacked suitable grazing land for the breeding of cattle. At the end of the nineteenth century, however, Japan was opened to the West after more than 200 years of isolation and the diet, among many other things, changed dramatically. As part of the general adoption of Western ways, people were positively encouraged to eat meat. Most Japanese meat dishes, in fact, date from this time, including the popular *sukiyaki*. Reservations about meat do still remain in respect to lamb, which is rarely eaten.

For both the Japanese and Koreans, the most important source of protein is the sea. Favourable currents in the surrounding waters, long coastlines and numerous islands endow both with a wealth of marine life. The Japanese eat more fish per head of the population than any other people in the world: nearly half a kilo or a pound each per week. They also eat a wide variety including, on occasions, strange species such as sea-urchins and deadly blow-fish (*fugu*). (Blow-fish are prepared in restaurants specially licensed to remove the poison – but even so a number of Japanese people die from *fugu* poisoning each year.) The Japanese are particuarly ingenious at cooking and preparing fish and shell-fish: an old text describes a hundred ways of preparing one fish alone, the *tai*, or sea bream, much appreciated by the Japanese and always eaten on festive occasions.

Fish is not the only seafood eaten in Japan, however, seaweeds – or more accurately sea vegetables such as *nori* (laver) and *kombu* (kelp) – are used extensively. They are eaten primarily for their flavour which is rich and subtle, but they also contain a high proportion of iodine and vitamins, which makes them beneficial to health as well. *Nori* is specially prepared in thin, dried sheets which

*Seaweed is a very
important part of the
Japanese diet.*

can be used as a sort of delicate wrapping material for many foods, or as a garnish for soups and rice dishes. Its flavour is enhanced when heated until dry and brittle, and then it is quite delicious simply dipped in a soy sauce and eaten with rice. *Kombu* is also dried into sheets, but thicker and harder ones than *nori* and they are used mainly in soups and stocks – Japanese *dashi* (stock) is made from *kombu* and the flakes of dried bonito fish (*katsuobushi*). In contrast, the Koreans usually make soups and stocks with a meat base. Seaweed is not part of their diet, though it is cultivated for export to Japan.

Apart from their great range of seafoods, Japan and Korea also possess a wealth of fruit and vegetables. Korea is a mainly agricultural country where most of the world's common vegetables are grown, as well as some unusual roots, leaves and edible mosses. Koreans say that without vegetables, no meal is complete. As for Japan, the sheer length of the country – over a thousand miles from north to south – as well as a varied topography and pronounced seasons, create climatic differences conducive to great variety.

In keeping with their love of nature, the Japanese pay great attention to seasonal changes. Not only do fruit and vegetables have their seasons, but even cakes and tea.

Winter is the time for tangerines, hot noodles and warming one-pot dishes cooked on the table; in February the world's largest and most succulent strawberries make their appearance; with the spring and the first sound of the nightingale come cakes shaped like nightingales; and as the cherry blossom begins to flower, cakes flavoured with cherry blossoms also appear. Spring is also the time for tender bamboo shoots and the mellow flavour of new tea, *shincha*.

May sees the opening of the season for the *ayu*, a small, delicious and delicately flavoured river trout. In one part of Japan, Gifu, there is an ingenious method of catching *ayu*: cormorants tethered to fishing boats snatch the fish from the water, and are then pulled back on to the boats by the fishermen where they disgorge their catch. Summer is also the time for chilled noodles, chilled *tofu* and hot eels.

Autumn (fall) is the season for pickle making. In Korea, the markets are laden with large, white radishes, Chinese cabbages, hot red peppers and dozens of other vegetables that go into the many varieties of *kim chee*. All domestic activity centres on the business of chopping and sorting vegetables and filling the pickle pots for winter. 'When the

*Fish and octopus on sale
in a seafood market in
Korea.*

kim chee is prepared for the winter,' they say, 'half the harvest is done.' The Japanese also make and eat many pickles, although generally they are gentler than the Korean variety. In Japan, autumn is also the season for what are said to be the world's most delicious mushrooms, the *matsutake*. During the season, city dwellers equipped with cooking gear converge on the forests where the mushrooms grow to picnic on them.

One of the great pleasures of travelling in both countries is the variety of their regional specialities. Each town or area has its own products, from handicrafts such as lacquerware or pottery, to various foods, such as cakes, pickles and fish. A Japanese island might be noted for abalone (*awabe*), which is collected from the seabed by specially-trained diving girls; or a mountain village might be famous for its young fern shoots (*warabi*). But apart from such special products, the taste of food varies from region to region. In Japan, the food of Kyoto tends to be lighter and more subtle than that of Tokyo, reflecting perhaps the tastes of the old Kyoto court. With its many Buddhist temples, Kyoto is also famous for its vegetarian dishes, while Tokyo, with its huge fish market, is known for the flavour of its seafood. The long trading history of Nagasaki in the southern island has left strong Chinese influences on the food of that region.

It was in the imperial courts of Kyoto and Nara that the tea ceremony was developed from its Chinese origins into a stylized ritual. Today, the tea ceremony is still widely practised, and knowledge of it is considered to be an important qualification for prospective Japanese brides. Essentially, the tea ceremony is the art of preparing tea as gracefully as possible, but the manner in which it is done is highly formalized. Practitioners must strictly observe the correct procedures, such as how to pour the water and hold the tea bowl. Tea ceremony food, *kaiseki*, is the most refined of the Japanese cuisine, with great emphasis being placed upon simplicity and harmony. The tastes, textures and colours of the food should balance one another, and the containers in which it is served should enhance its appearance. *Kaiseki* food reflects the seasons and, if possible, is locally produced; it should not be expensive or extravagant, but should be imaginative and in good taste. The tea used for the tea ceremony is a special type of powdered green tea, *matcha*. After adding hot water to the powder, it is whipped with a bamboo whisk which looks rather like a shaving brush. The taste is bitter, but refreshing.

The Koreans have no equivalent of the Japanese tea ceremony, though they are enthusiastic tea drinkers. They do, however, have a special tea made from the roots of the *ginsing* plant. *Ginsing* tea is rich to taste and is reputed to have many medicinal properties. They also make a rice tea from the grains remaining in the saucepan after the rice has been cooked.

To describe the ingredients of a nation's cooking, particularly when many of them are strange to the western palate, can be misleading – the thought of eating uncooked fish, for example, is repugnant to many, but when it is eaten absolutely fresh, in the Japanese manner, you can almost forget that it is fish at all; the tastes and textures might best be compared to chilled, very tender, rare beef. And many who have tried uncooked fish dishes, such as *sushi* and *sashimi*, consider them to be among the greatest delicacies in Japan's vast cuisine.

Other dishes are less difficult: *tempura*, for example, deep-fried vegetables and fish in the lightest of batters, is popular throughout the world. Properly prepared, it is succulent and crisp with only the slightest hint of oil. Strangely enough although it is one of the country's best-known dishes, it is not strictly speaking Japanese at all – but an adaptation of a Portuguese dish. (It arrived with Western traders and missionaries over four hundred years ago and the name itself comes from the Latin word for time – a reference to those certain days of the year on which the Portuguese, as good Catholics, could not eat meat.) Another dish easy to appreciate is *sukiyaki*, thinly sliced beef cooked in one-pot style on the table.

*Sukiyaki* and *tempura* are served both at home and in restaurants, or are delivered from the restaurants to the home – a common practice in Japan. This is because, on the whole, restaurants are better equipped to prepare the food properly – the cutting of the fish for *sushi*, for example, requires great skill, and *sushi* cooks are required to spend many years in apprenticeship. Some restaurants serve only one type of food, such as *tempura*, *noodles* or *sushi*, and there are even some which serve only *tofu* dishes. The Japanese never drink without eating and many dishes can therefore be regarded primarily as snacks with alcohol – even the smallest bars serve their own specialities. The Koreans also make many snack dishes to be served with drinks, some of them quite unusual – bulls' testicles, which are thought to be a powerful aphrodisiac, are very popular!

For both Japanese and Korean meals, the dishes are not served consecutively in courses as they are in the West, but are placed together on the table. The Koreans arrange the dishes on low tables in the kitchen and then carry them to the eating area. Almost invariably every Japanese and Korean meal includes rice and soup, perhaps a main dish of meat or fish, dipping sauces and various side dishes. Usually there will be separate dishes and bowls for each person. There are no rules about the order in which the food is eaten, though it is customary to sip a little of the soup first. Some hot dishes, such as *tempura* or *shin-sol-lo* should be eaten as soon as they are served. Very often, if people are drinking *sake* with the meal, they will not eat rice until they

*Dinner – in the traditional Japanese way, cross-legged on the floor below a low table.*

have finished drinking. The meal is usually completed by rice, pickles and tea. Desserts are not a part of either Japanese or Korean cooking, though sometimes fresh fruit will be served at the end of a meal.

The style of a one-pot meal is somewhat different, however, for all the ingredients are prepared in the kitchen in advance and the cooking done on a portable burner on the centre of the dining table. Each person selects what he or she wants from the plates of uncooked ingredients and places them in the communal pot. After brief cooking, the food is transferred to a dipping sauce before eating. The cooking time is so short that the flavour, texture and essential nutrients of the ingredients are not destroyed. A one-pot meal is ideal for dinner parties since it does not take long to prepare or cook, and is informal to eat. A selection of ingredients to make up a first batch to be put in the pot, is put on the table and, when these are eaten, there is traditionally a pause while conversation and drinking take over from food. Later, more rounds can be cooked, with further rests between them. The portable burner may be of any type, so long as it is powerful enough to bring the cooking liquid to boiling point. The Japanese have a variety of dishes known as *nabes* (pots), after which many one-pot dishes are named, but any type of flameproof pot, or fondue pot is equally suitable. The Koreans have a special charcoal stove, called *shin-sol-lo*, used to cook their national dish. It is shaped rather like a hat: the charcoal is placed in the middle and the cooking liquid in the surrounding brim.

In spite of the emphasis that is placed on appearance, it is a mistake to assume that Japanese and Korean food is expensive to prepare at home. Elaborate garnishes and beautiful pottery are not necessary, and more often than not they can be omitted from home cooking: you can improvise very well with soup or cereal bowls, or even decorative ashtrays. Many of the ingredients are relatively cheap, though obviously some special ones are necessary for certain dishes. Very often substitutes are quite acceptable, while other dishes can be made from ingredients commonly available at grocery stores and supermarkets. But it is advisable for someone interested in making Japanese and Korean food to stock up with some standard items, such as soy sauce – for Japanese dishes, make sure it is the Japanese variety — *mirin* (sweet

*A family from the Ainu, an important sub-group from the northern archipelago of Japan.*

cooking wine), *sake* (dry rice wine), *miso* paste and perhaps sesame oil. All can be kept for long periods, and can be obtained from Japanese food stores; some are stocked by general Oriental or Chinese stores.

The preparation of Japanese and Korean food is not as difficult as it might seem: the cutting of vegetables, particularly, is considered to be very important and something of an art form. There are no set rules for menus: but dishes are usually chosen to give variety in taste and colour. Remember that in Japanese and Korean meals the side dishes might not seem very substantial, but the volume is made up with rice; about half a cup of uncooked rice is usually allowed for each person.

Do not be afraid to vary the proportions of ingredients in the recipes which follow, or to adapt them to your own requirements. The important thing is to find the tastes which suit you best — and the recipes you enjoy most.

*The face of Japan is delicate, beautiful and full of ceremony and grace.*

# SOUPS & NOODLES

# Dashi

(Basic Stock)

*Dashi is used extensively in Japanese cooking, and is the base for almost every soup and noodle dish. There are several types, but the simplest way to make it is with instant dashi powder (dashi-no-moto), which is obtainable from Japanese and some general Oriental stores. If all else fails, a chicken stock (bouillon) cube can be used as a substitute – although this does of course affect the authenticity (not to mention the taste) of the cooked dish.*

| Metric/Imperial | American |
| --- | --- |
| ⅓ tsp. instant dashi powder (dashi-no-moto) | ⅓ tsp. instant dashi powder (dashi-no-moto) |
| 250ml./8fl.oz. water | 1 cup water |

Add the dashi powder to boiling water and set over moderately low heat. Boil for about 1 minute, stirring gently to blend. Remove from the heat and use as described in the various recipes.
*Makes 250ml./8fl. oz. (1 cup) stock*
Preparation and cooking time: 2 minutes

# Kombo to Katsuobushi no Dashi

(Home-made Stock)

*If you prefer to make your own dashi, the recipe which follows is one version. Kombo (dried kelp) and katsuobushi (dried bonito fish [tunaj]) are essential ingredients and both can be bought in Japanese or Oriental stores, or in the case of kombu, in many health food stores. Kombu is sold in sheets and the katsuobushi either in flakes or in a solid block, which then has to be flaked.*

| Metric/Imperial | American |
| --- | --- |
| 5cm./2in. piece of kombu | 2in. piece of kombu |
| 250ml./8fl.oz. water | 1 cup water |
| 1 tsp. katsuobushi | 1 tsp. katsuobushi |

Put the kombu and water into a small saucepan and bring to the boil, stirring constantly to release the flavour of the kelp. Remove from the heat and drain the water into a second saucepan, discarding the kombu pieces. Add the katsuobushi flakes and set the saucepan over moderate heat. Bring to the boil and boil for 1 minute. Remove the pan from the heat and set aside until the flakes settle. Strain the liquid, discarding the flakes.
The stock is now ready to use.
*Makes 250ml./8fl.oz. (1 cup) stock*
Preparation and cooking time: 5 minutes

*Oysters fresh from the sea, still in the half shell. They can be used as a substitute for clams in the recipe for Hamaguri Sumashi-Juri given on this page.*

# Hamaguri Sumashi-Jiru

(Clam and Mushroom Soup)

*Oysters can be substituted for the clams in this recipe. If used, omit the soaking period and add straight to the water.*

| Metric/Imperial | American |
|---|---|
| 8 clams, soaked in salt water for 3 hours and drained | 8 clams, soaked in salt water for 3 hours and drained |
| salt | salt |
| 8 small button mushroom caps | 8 small button mushroom caps |
| 8 watercress sprigs | 8 watercress sprigs |
| 1 tsp. soya sauce | 1 tsp. soy sauce |
| monosodium glutamate (optional) | MSG (optional) |
| 125ml./4fl.oz. sake or dry sherry | ½ cup sake or dry sherry |
| 4 pieces of lemon rind | 4 pieces of lemon rind |

Put the clams and about 900ml./1½ pints (3¾ cups) of water into a large saucepan. Bring to the boil, then continue to boil until the shells open. Discard any that do not open. Remove any scum which rises to the surface and stir in salt to taste, the mushroom caps and watercress. Cook for 1 minute. Stir in soy sauce, monosodium glutamate to taste and the sake or sherry and return the soup to the boil.

Put one piece of lemon rind into each of four serving bowls, then divide the soup among the bowls. Serve at once.

*Serves 4*
Preparation and cooking time: 3¼ hours

# Yakinasu no Miso Shiru

(Miso Soup with Fried Aubergine [Eggplant])

| Metric/Imperial | American |
|---|---|
| 125ml./4fl.oz. vegetable oil | ½ cup vegetable oil |
| 2 medium aubergines, sliced and dégorged | 2 medium eggplants, sliced and dégorged |
| 1.2l./2 pints dashi | 5 cups dashi |
| 4 Tbs. miso paste | 4 Tbs. miso paste |
| 2 mint leaves, thinly sliced | 2 mint leaves, thinly sliced |
| mustard to taste | mustard to taste |

Heat the oil in a frying-pan. When it is hot, add the aubergine (eggplant) slices and fry over moderately high heat until the skin begins to burn and peel. Remove from the heat and transfer the aubergines (eggplants) to a chopping board. Carefully peel off the skin and chop the flesh into bite-sized pieces. Divide the pieces among 4 to 6 soup bowls and keep hot.

Heat the dashi in a saucepan until it comes to the boil. Stir in the miso paste until it melts, forming a suspension in the liquid.

Pour the liquid over the aubergine (eggplant) pieces and add some mint leaf slices and mustard to taste to each bowl. Serve at once.

*Serves 4–6*
Preparation and cooking time: 35 minutes

# Iwashi no Tsumire Jiru

(Clear Soup with Sardine Balls)

| Metric/Imperial | American |
| --- | --- |
| 5 fresh sardines, cleaned and with the heads removed | 5 fresh sardines, cleaned and with the heads removed |
| 2 Tbs. miso paste | 2 Tbs. miso paste |
| 1cm./½in. piece of fresh root ginger, peeled and grated | ½in. piece of fresh green ginger, peeled and grated |
| 1 Tbs. flour | 1 Tbs. flour |
| 1.2 l./2 pints water | 5 cups water |
| 2 Tbs. soya sauce | 2 Tbs. soy sauce |
| ¼ tsp. salt | ¼ tsp. salt |
| 1 medium turnip, thinly sliced then quartered | 1 medium turnip, thinly sliced then quartered |
| 4 small pieces of lemon rind | 4 small pieces of lemon rind |

Remove the main bones from the sardines and clean them in salted water. Dry on kitchen towels and chop into small pieces. Put the sardines into a blender and blend until smooth. Alternatively, pound in a mortar with a pestle until smooth. Stir the miso paste, grated ginger and flour into the sardines and beat until they are thoroughly combined. Using the palm of your hands, gently roll small pieces of the mixture into balls.

Bring the water to the boil in a large saucepan. Drop in the fish balls and cook until they rise to the surface. Using a slotted spoon, transfer the fish balls to a plate and strain the liquid into a fresh pan. Stir in the soy sauce and salt.

In the meantime, cook the turnip in boiling water for about 5 minutes, or until the pieces are crisp. Drain and reserve.

Reheat the strained soup liquid and add the fish balls. Bring to the boil, then stir in the turnip.

Transfer to soup bowls and garnish with lemon rind.

*Serves 4–6*

Preparation and cooking time: 40 minutes

# Tofu no Miso Shiru

(Bean Paste Soup with Bean Curd)

| Metric/Imperial | American |
| --- | --- |
| 1.2 l./2 pints dashi | 5 cups dashi |
| 4 Tbs. miso paste | 4 Tbs. miso paste |
| 2 bean curd cakes (tofu), cut into small cubes | 2 bean curd cakes (tofu), cut into small cubes |
| 2 spring onions, finely chopped | 2 scallions, finely chopped |

Put the dashi into a large saucepan and set over moderate heat. Stir in the miso paste until it melts. Raise the heat to high and add the bean curd pieces. Boil until the bean curd rises to the surface of the liquid.

Serve at once, garnished with the spring onions (scallions).

*Serves 4–6*

Preparation and cooking time: 10 minutes

# Kong-Na-Mool Kuk

(Bean Sprout Soup)                                                    (Korea)

| Metric/Imperial | American |
|---|---|
| 225g./8oz. lean beef, cut into thin strips | 8oz. lean beef, cut into thin strips |
| 2 garlic cloves, crushed | 2 garlic cloves, crushed |
| 2 tsp. roasted sesame seeds, ground | 2 tsp. roasted sesame seeds, ground |
| 2 spring onions, green part only, finely chopped | 2 scallions, green part only, finely chopped |
| salt and pepper | salt and pepper |
| 3 Tbs. soya sauce | 3 Tbs. soy sauce |
| 1½ Tbs. sesame oil | 1½ Tbs. sesame oil |
| 700g./1½lb. bean sprouts | 3 cups bean sprouts |
| 1.751./3 pints water | 1½ quarts water |

Mix the beef, garlic, sesame seeds, half the spring onions (scallions), the salt and pepper and half the soy sauce together. Heat the oil in a saucepan. When it is hot, add the meat and stir-fry until it is evenly browned .Stir in the bean sprouts and stir-fry for a further 3 minutes.

Pour in the water and remaining soy sauce and bring to the boil. Cover and simmer for 30 minutes. Stir in the remaining spring onion (scallion) and simmer for a further 5 minutes.

*Serves 4–6*
Preparation and cooking time: 40 minutes

# Sumashi Jiru

(Chicken and Noodle Soup)

*The type of noodle most commonly used in this soup is* udon, *which somewhat resembles spaghetti in appearance. If* udon *is not available, then spaghetti vermicelli or any similar noodle may be substituted.*

| Metric/Imperial | American |
|---|---|
| 350g./12oz. udon | 12oz. udon |
| 1 large chicken breast, skinned, boned and cut into thin strips | 1 large chicken breast, skinned, boned and cut into thin strips |
| 1.21./2 pints dashi | 5 cups dashi |
| 6 dried mushrooms, soaked in cold water for 30 minutes, drained and sliced | 6 dried mushrooms, soaked in cold water for 30 minutes, drained and sliced |
| 2 tsp. soya sauce | 2 tsp. soy sauce |
| 2 spring onions, chopped | 2 scallions, chopped |
| 6 strips of lemon rind | 6 strips of lemon rind |

Cook the noodles in boiling salted water for 5 to 12 minutes, or until they are just tender. Drain and keep hot.

Put the chicken meat strips into a large saucepan and pour over the dashi. Bring to the boil, then reduce the heat to moderate. Cook for 3 minutes. Add the mushrooms and soy sauce and cook for a further 2 minutes. Stir in the udon and return to the boil. Cook for 1 minute, then remove the pan from the heat.

Pour the soup either into a large warmed tureen, or into six individual small soup bowls. Garnish with spring onions (scallions) and lemon before serving.

*Serves 6*
Preparation and cooking time: 1 hour

*Tofu No Ankake (Bean Curd Soup) and Chawan Mushi (Chicken and Steamed Vegetables in Egg) are both served as soup·courses in Japan – although Chawan Mushi is also a popular breakfast dish.*

# Tofu no Ankake

(Bean Curd Soup)

| Metric/Imperial | American |
|---|---|
| 1.2 l./2 pints dashi | 5 cups dashi |
| 3 Tbs. soya sauce | 3 Tbs. soy sauce |
| ½ tsp. salt | ½ tsp. salt |
| 2 Tbs. mirin or sweet sherry | 2 Tbs. mirin or sweet sherry |
| 2 Tbs. cornflour, mixed to a paste with 2 Tbs. water | 2 Tbs. cornstarch, mixed to a paste with 2 Tbs. water |
| 2 Tbs. water | 2 Tbs. water |
| 4 dried mushrooms, soaked in cold water for 30 minutes, drained and sliced | 4 dried mushrooms, soaked in cold water for 30 minutes, drained and sliced |
| 350g./12oz. bean curd cakes (tofu), diced | 2 cups diced bean curd cakes (tofu) |
| 1cm./½in. piece of fresh root ginger, peeled and grated | ½in. piece of fresh green ginger, peeled and grated |

Put the dashi, soy sauce, salt, mirin or sherry, cornflour (cornstarch) mixture and mushrooms into a large saucepan and bring to the boil, stirring constantly. Reduce the heat to low, cover and simmer the soup for 15 minutes. Stir in the bean curd and simmer for a further 5 minutes.

Ladle the soup into individual soup bowls, dividing the bean curd pieces equally among them. Garnish each bowl with a little grated ginger and serve.

*Serves 4–6*
Preparation and cooking time: 1 hour

# Chawan Mushi

(Chicken and Steamed Vegetables in Egg)

| Metric/Imperial | American |
|---|---|
| 1 small chicken breast, boned and diced | 1 small chicken breast, boned and diced |
| soya sauce | soy sauce |
| 50g./2oz. firm white fish, skinned and cut into 4 pieces | 2oz. firm white fish, skinned and cut into 4 pieces |
| salt | salt |
| 8 prawns, shelled | 8 shrimp, shelled |
| 4 mushrooms caps, quartered | 4 mushroom caps, quartered |
| 50g./2oz. French beans, thinly sliced and parboiled | ⅓ cup green beans, thinly sliced and parboiled |
| EGG MIXTURE | EGG MIXTURE |
| 900ml./1½ pints dashi | 3¾ cups dashi |
| 1½ tsp. salt | 1½ tsp. salt |
| 1½ tsp. soya sauce | 1½ tsp. soy sauce |
| monosodium glutamate (optional) | MSG (optional) |
| 1 tsp. mirin or sweet sherry | 1 tsp. mirin or sweet sherry |
| 4 eggs, plus 2 egg yolks, lightly beaten | 4 eggs, plus 2 egg yolks, lightly beaten |

Sprinkle the chicken pieces with soy sauce and set aside for 5 minutes. Sprinkle the fish pieces with salt and set aside.

Meanwhile, to make the egg mixture, mix the dashi, salt, soy sauce, mono-sodium glutamate to taste and mirin or sherry together. Pour the beaten eggs slowly into the mixture, stirring gently. Set aside.

Divide the chicken dice, fish pieces, prawns or shrimp and mushrooms among four small ovenproof bowls. Pour the egg mixture on top and cover, leaving the covers slightly ajar.

Arrange the bowls in the top of a double boiler and half fill the bottom with boiling water. (If you do not have a double boiler, improvise by using a small baking dish set in a deep roasting pan. Fill the pan with water until it comes halfway up the sides of the baking dish.) Steam the mixture for 25 minutes, or until the eggs have set. (The surface should be yellow not brown and although the egg will be set on the outside it should still contain some liquid inside.)

About 5 minutes before the end of the cooking time, remove the covers from the bowls and garnish with the sliced beans. Serve hot, either as a soup course or as a breakfast dish.

*Serves 4*
Preparation and cooking time: 1¼ hours

# Mandoo

(Meat Dumpling Soup)                                                    (Korea)

| Metric/Imperial | American |
|---|---|
| SOUP | SOUP |
| 1.75 l./3 pints beef stock | 7½ cups beef stock |
| 2 Tbs. soya sauce | 2 Tbs. soy sauce |
| 1 Tbs. roasted sesame seeds, ground | 1 Tbs. roasted sesame seeds, ground |
| 1 large spring onion, chopped | 1 large scallion, chopped |
| DUMPLING DOUGH | DUMPLING DOUGH |
| 350g./12oz. flour | 3 cups flour |
| 250ml./8fl.oz. water | 1 cup water |
| DUMPLING FILLING | DUMPLING FILLING |
| 2 Tbs. vegetable oil | 2 Tbs. vegetable oil |
| 225g./8oz. minced beef | 8oz. ground beef |
| 1 onion, finely chopped | 1 onion, finely chopped |
| 1 garlic clove, crushed | 1 garlic clove, crushed |
| 50g./2oz. button mushrooms, chopped | ½ cup chopped button mushrooms |
| 225g./8oz. bean sprouts, chopped | 1 cup chopped bean sprouts |
| 2 spring onions, finely chopped | 2 scallions, finely chopped |
| 2 Tbs. soya sauce | 2 Tbs. soy sauce |
| 1 Tbs. roasted sesame seeds, ground | 1 Tbs. roasted sesame seeds, ground |
| ½ tsp. salt | ½ tsp. salt |

First make the dumpling dough. Put the flour into a mixing bowl and make a well in the centre. Gradually pour in the water, beating with a wooden spoon until the mixture forms a smooth dough. Turn the dough out on to a lightly floured board and knead for 5 minutes. Return to the bowl, cover with a damp cloth and set aside to 'rest' for 15 minutes while you prepare the filling.

Heat the oil in a frying-pan. When it is hot, add the beef, onion and garlic and fry for 5 minutes, stirring occasionally, or until the beef loses its pinkness. Stir in the mushrooms, bean sprouts, half the spring onions (scallions), soy sauce, sesame seeds and salt and bring to the boil. Cook for 1 minute, stirring frequently, then remove the pan from the heat.

To make the soup, pour the stock and soy sauce into a large saucepan and bring to the boil. Reduce the heat to moderately low and stir in the sesame seeds. Cook for 10 minutes.

Meanwhile, assemble the dumplings. Roll out the dough very thinly, then, using a 7.5cm./3in. pastry cutter, cut into circles. Spoon about 1 tablespoonful of filling on to the lower half of the circle, then fold over to make a semi-circle, pressing the edges firmly together so that the filling is completely enclosed.

Carefully add the dumplings to the soup and continue to cook until they come to the surface. Cook for 2 minutes longer, then transfer the mixture to a warmed tureen or ladle into individual soup bowls. Garnish the soup with the remaining chopped spring onion (scallion) before serving.

Serves 6–8

Preparation and cooking time: 45 minutes

# Kitsune Donburi

('Fox' Noodles)

*The unusual name of this dish (kitsune is the Japanese word for fox) comes about because, so folklore has it, the fox is very partial to bean curd which, with udon noodles, is the main ingredient of the dish. Udon noodles greatly resemble spaghetti in shape and texture though they are lighter coloured – spaghetti, or even vermicelli or tagliatelle can therefore be substituted if Japanese-style noodles are not available.*

| Metric/Imperial | American |
| --- | --- |
| BEAN CURD | BEAN CURD |
| 175g./6oz. bean curd cakes (tofu), cut into six pieces | 6oz. bean curd cakes (tofu), cut into six pieces |
| 125ml./4fl.oz. dashi | ½ cup dashi |
| 75ml./3fl.oz. soya sauce | ⅓ cup soy sauce |
| 2 Tbs. mirin or sweet sherry | 2 Tbs. mirin or sweet sherry |
| 2 Tbs. sugar | 2 Tbs. sugar |
| ¼ tsp. monosodium glutamate (optional) | ¼ tsp. MSG (optional) |
| NOODLES | NOODLES |
| 1.2 l./2 pints water | 5 cups water |
| 1 tsp. salt | 1 tsp. salt |
| 225g./8oz. udon | 8oz. udon |
| KAKEJIRU SOUP | KAKEJIRU SOUP |
| 1.2 l./2 pints dashi | 5 cups dashi |
| 125ml./4fl.oz. soya sauce | ½ cup soy sauce |
| 125ml./4fl.oz. mirin or sweet sherry | ½ cup mirin or sweet sherry |
| ½ tsp. salt | ½ tsp. salt |
| ¼ tsp. monosodium glutamate | ¼ tsp. MSG |
| 2 spring onions, thinly sliced | 2 scallions, thinly sliced |

To make the bean curd, put the bean curd, dashi, soy sauce, mirin or sherry, sugar and monosodium glutamate into a saucepan and bring to the boil, stirring occasionally. Reduce the heat to low and simmer for 20 to 25 minutes, or until the bean curd has absorbed most of the liquid.

Meanwhile, prepare the noodles. Cook the udon in boiling, salted water for 10 to 12 minutes, or until they are just tender. Drain and return them to the saucepan. Set aside and keep hot.

To make the soup, put the dashi, soy sauce, mirin or sherry, salt, monosodium glutamate and spring onions (scallions) into a second large saucepan. Bring to the boil, reduce the heat to low and simmer the soup for 10 minutes.

To serve, divide the noodles between individual soup bowls. Place some bean curd on top and spoon over any remaining bean curd liquid. Pour over the soup, then serve at once.

*Serves 6–8*
Preparation and cooking time: 1 hour

# Wu-Dung

(Fried Noodles)                                                                                    (Korea)

*Chinese rice noodles would probably be the most authentic type of pasta to use in this dish, but if they are unavailable, egg noodles or vermicelli can be substituted.*

| Metric/Imperial | American |
|---|---|
| 350g./12oz. rice vermicelli | 12oz. rice vermicelli |
| 50ml./2fl.oz. vegetable oil | ¼ cup vegetable oil |
| 225g./8oz. rump steak, cut into strips | 8oz. rump steak, cut into thin strips |
| 3 spring onions, chopped | 3 scallions, chopped |
| 1 garlic clove, crushed | 1 garlic clove, crushed |
| 125g./4oz. button mushrooms, sliced | 1 cup sliced button mushrooms |
| 125g./4oz. peeled prawns | 4oz. peeled shrimp |
| 1 bean curd cake (tofu), chopped | 1 bean curd cake (tofu), chopped |
| 2 Tbs. soya sauce | 2 Tbs. soy sauce |
| 1 tsp. sugar | 1 tsp. sugar |
| 1 Tbs. roasted sesame seeds, ground | 1 Tbs. roasted sesame seeds, ground |

Cook the vermicelli in boiling, salted water for 5 minutes. Drain and keep warm.

Heat the oil in a large, deep frying-pan. When it is hot, add the steak strips and stir-fry until they lose their pinkness. Add the spring onions (scallions) and garlic to the pan and stir-fry for 2 minutes. Add the mushrooms, prawns (shrimp) and bean curd and stir-fry for a further 2 minutes. Add the soy sauce, sugar and sesame seeds, then stir in the vermicelli. Cook the mixture for a further 2 minutes, or until the vermicelli is heated through.

Transfer the mixture to a warmed serving bowl and serve at once.
*Serves 4*
Preparation and cooking time: 20 minutes

# Hiyashi Somen

(Iced Noodles)

| Metric/Imperial | American |
|---|---|
| 450g./1lb. somen or noodles | 1lb. somen or noodles |
| 2 hard-boiled eggs, thinly sliced | 2 hard-cooked eggs, thinly sliced |
| 2 tomatoes, thinly sliced | 2 tomatoes, thinly sliced |
| ⅓ medium cucumber, peeled and cubed | ⅓ medium cucumber, peeled and cubed |
| 175g./6oz. lean cooked ham, cubed | 1 cup lean cooked ham cubes |
| 4 mint leaves, cut into strips | 4 mint leaves, cut into strips |

SAUCE

| | |
|---|---|
| SAUCE | SAUCE |
| 900ml./1½ pints dashi | 3¾ cups dashi |
| 150ml.5fl.oz. soya sauce | ⅔ cup soy sauce |
| 2 Tbs. sugar | 2 Tbs. sugar |
| 150ml./5fl.oz. sake or dry sherry | ⅔ cup sake or dry sherry |
| monosodium glutamate (optional) | MSG (optional) |
| 2 dried mushrooms, soaked in cold water for 30 minutes, drained and chopped | 2 dried mushrooms, soaked in cold water for 30 minutes, drained and chopped |

Cook the somen or noodles in boiling salted water for 5 minutes, or until they are just tender. Drain and rinse under cold running water. Transfer to a bowl and put into the refrigerator for 30 minutes.

Meanwhile, make the sauce. Put the dashi into a large saucepan and add all the remaining sauce ingredients. Bring to the boil and cook briskly for 8 minutes. Remove from the heat and set aside to cool.

Arrange the eggs, tomatoes, cucumber and ham decoratively on a large serving platter and sprinkle over the mint strips.

To serve, put the somen noodles over a bed of ice cubes, or sprinkle them with ice chips. Pour the sauce mixture into individual serving bowls. Traditionally, each guest helps himself to a portion of each dish, dipping the noodles into the sauce before eating.

*Serves 6*
Preparation and cooking time: 1¼ hours

# Buta Udon

(Noodles with Pork)

| Metric/Imperial | American |
|---|---|
| 1.2l./2 pints dashi | 5 cups dashi |
| 275g./10oz. lean pork meat, cut into thin strips | 10oz. lean pork meat, cut into thin strips |
| 2 leeks, cleaned and cut into 2½cm./1in. lengths | 2 leeks, cleaned and cut into 1in. lengths |
| 150ml./5fl.oz. soya sauce | ⅔ cup soy sauce |
| 1½ Tbs. sugar | 1½ Tbs. sugar |
| ½ tsp. monosodium glutamate (optional) | ½ tsp. MSG (optional) |
| salt | salt |
| 350g./12oz. udon or spaghetti | 12oz. udon or spaghetti |
| 2 spring onions, finely chopped | 2 scallions, finely chopped |
| paprika or hichimi togarashi | paprika or hichimi togarashi |

Pour the dashi into a large saucepan and bring to the boil. Add the pork strips and leeks and cook the meat for 5 to 8 minutes, or until they are cooked through. Remove the pan from the heat and stir in the soy sauce, sugar and monosodium glutamate. Keep hot.

Meanwhile, cook the noodles in boiling salted water for 5 to 12 minutes, or until they are just tender. Drain and stir them into the soup. Return to moderate heat and bring to the boil.

To serve, divide the soup among 4 to 6 serving bowls and garnish with spring onions (scallions) and paprika or hichimi togarashi to taste.

Serve at once.

*Serves 4–6*
Preparation and cooking time: 30 minutes

# RICE

# Gohan

(Plain Boiled Rice, Japanese Style)

*Short-grain rice is the closest Western equivalent to Japanese rice and has therefore been suggested here; long-grain can, of course, be substituted, but the texture will be a little different. The proportion of water to rice is always vital in rice cooking but it does tend to vary a little according to the age and quality of the rice grains. The amounts given below, therefore, are approximate and should be taken as a guide only. The finished product should be white, shiny, soft and moist; never wet and sticky.*

| Metric/Imperial | American |
| --- | --- |
| 450g./1lb. short-grain rice | 2⅔ cups short-grain rice |
| 600ml./1 pint water | 2½ cups water |

Wash the rice to remove the starch, under cold running water. Alternatively, put the rice into a bowl, add water and stir and drain. Repeat two or three times until the water is almost clear.

Put the rice into a large, heavy saucepan and pour over the water. Bring to the boil, cover the pan and reduce the heat to low. Simmer for 15 to 20 minutes, or until the rice is cooked and the liquid absorbed. Reduce the heat to an absolute minimum and leave for 15 minutes. Turn off the heat but leave the saucepan on the burner for a further 10 minutes.

Transfer to a warmed serving bowl. The rice is now ready to serve.

*Serves 4-6*
Preparation and cooking time: 1 hour

# Kuri Gohan

(Chestnut Rice)

| Metric/Imperial | American |
| --- | --- |
| 450g./1lb. short-grain rice | 2⅔ cups short-grain rice |
| ½kg./1lb. chestnuts | 2⅔ cups chestnuts |
| 900ml./1½ pints water | 3¾ cups water |
| 1½ Tbs. sake or dry sherry | 1½ Tbs. sake or dry sherry |
| 1 tsp. salt | 1 tsp. salt |

Wash the rice, then soak it for 1 hour.

Meanwhile, put the chestnuts into a saucepan and pour over the water. Bring to the boil, then parboil for 15 minutes. Drain and remove the skins from the chestnuts. Quarter them if they are large; keep them whole if they are not.

Add the chestnuts, sake or sherry and salt to the drained rice and cook, following the instructions given in *Gohan*.

Serve at once.

*Serves 4-6*
Preparation and cooking time: 1¾ hours
**Note:** You can cheat on this recipe by substituting a 450g./1lb. can of whole chestnuts for the fresh chestnuts above. In this case, the parboiling can be omitted and the chestnuts should be added straight to the rice.

# Maze Gohan

(Mixed Vegetables and Rice)

| Metric/Imperial | American |
|---|---|
| 1 large dried mushroom, soaked in cold water for 30 minutes, drained and finely chopped | 1 large dried mushroom, soaked in cold water for 30 minutes, drained and finely chopped |
| 2 carrots, sliced | 2 carrots, sliced |
| 2½cm./1in. piece of fresh root ginger, peeled and chopped | 1in. piece of fresh green ginger, peeled and chopped |
| 12 tinned ginko nuts, drained | 12 canned ginko nuts, drained |
| 2 celery stalks, chopped | 2 celery stalks, chopped |
| 2 Tbs. soya sauce | 2 Tbs. soy sauce |
| 1 Tbs. sake or dry sherry | 1 Tbs. sake or dry sherry |
| ½ tsp. salt | ½ tsp. salt |
| 700g./1½lb. short-grain rice, soaked in cold water for 1 hour and drained | 4 cups short-grain rice, soaked in cold water for 1 hour and drained |
| 900ml./1½ pints water | 3¾ cups water |
| 125g./4oz. green peas, weighed after shelling | ½ cup green peas, weighed after shelling |
| 125g./4oz. shelled shrimps | ½ cup shelled shrimp |

*Maze Gohan is a superb mixture of rice, peas, carrots, peas and shrimps, delicately flavoured with ginger, sake and ginko nuts.*

Put the mushroom, carrots, ginger, ginko nuts, celery, soy sauce, sake, salt and rice into a large, heavy saucepan. Pour over the water and bring to the boil. Cover the pan, reduce the heat to low and simmer the rice for 15 to 20 minutes, or until it is cooked and the water absorbed.

Stir in the peas and shrimps and simmer for a further 10 minutes. (If the mixture becomes a little dry during this period add a tablespoonful or two of water.)

Transfer to a warmed serving dish and serve at once.

*Serves 4*
Preparation and cooking time: 1½ hours

# Song i Pahb

(Rice and Mushrooms)                                                    (Korea)

| Metric/Imperial | American |
| --- | --- |
| 1 Tbs. sesame oil | 1 Tbs. sesame oil |
| 4 spring onions, chopped | 4 scallions, chopped |
| 225g./8oz. mushrooms, thinly sliced | 2 cups thinly sliced mushrooms |
| 175g./6oz. lean cooked meat, very finely chopped | 1 cup very finely chopped lean cooked meat |
| 2 Tbs. soya sauce | 2 Tbs. soy sauce |
| 2 tsp. roasted sesame seeds, ground | 2 tsp. roasted sesame seeds, ground |
| salt and pepper | salt and pepper |
| 350g./12oz. long-grain rice, soaked in cold water for 30 minutes and drained | 2 cups long-grain rice, soaked in cold water for 30 minutes and drained |
| 725ml./1¼ pints water | 3 cups water |

Heat the oil in a large frying-pan. When it is hot, stir in the spring onions (scallions), mushrooms, meat, soy sauce, sesame seeds and salt and pepper, and cook for 3 minutes, stirring constantly. Stir the mixture into the rice and transfer to a saucepan. Pour over the water and bring to the boil. Cover, reduce the heat to very low and simmer for 30 minutes, or until the rice is very dry and fluffy and the liquid completely absorbed; do not remove the lid during the cooking period.
*Serves 4-6*
Preparation and cooking time: 1 hour

# Katsudon

(Pork Cutlets with Rice)

| Metric/Imperial | American |
| --- | --- |
| 450g./1lb. short-grain rice | 2⅔ cups short-grain rice |
| 600ml./1 pint water | 2½ cups water |
| 575g./1¼lb. pork fillet, cut into 4 cutlets | 1¼lb. pork tenderloin, cut into 4 cutlets |
| 4 eggs, lightly beaten | 4 eggs, lightly beaten |
| 50g./2oz. flour | ½ cup flour |
| 75g./3oz. dry breadcrumbs | 1 cup dry breadcrumbs |
| vegetable oil for deep-frying | vegetable oil for deep-frying |
| 650ml./1¼ pints dashi | 3 cups dashi |
| 150ml./5fl.oz. soya sauce | ⅔ cup soy sauce |
| 1½ Tbs. mirin or sweet sherry | 1½ Tbs. mirin or sweet sherry |
| 2 medium onions, thinly sliced into rings | 2 medium onions, thinly sliced into rings |

Cook the rice, following the instructions given in *Gohan*.

Meanwhile, coat the pork cutlets first in half the eggs, then in the flour and finally in the breadcrumbs, coating thoroughly and shaking off any excess.

Fill a large saucepan one-third full with oil and heat until it is very hot. Carefully lower the cutlets, two at a time, into the oil and fry until they are golden brown. Drain on kitchen towels. Set aside and keep hot.

Put the dashi, soy sauce and mirin into a pan and bring to the boil. Reduce the heat to low, add the onion rings and simmer for 10 minutes, or until the rings are soft. When the pork is cool enough to handle, slice into thin strips and add to the saucepan with the onion rings. Pour in the remaining beaten egg and simmer the mixture gently for 3 minutes. Remove from the heat.

Transfer the cooked rice into individual serving bowls. Top with the egg, onion and pork mixture and pour over any remaining liquid from the pan. Serve at once.
*Serves 4*
Preparation and cooking time: 50 minutes

# Tendon

(Tempura with rice)

*The 'tempura' offerings in Tendon always include fish and/or seafood but other than this, can be tailored to suit your taste and purse! The items listed below are therefore suggestions rather than ethnically essential.*

| Metric/Imperial | American |
|---|---|
| 450g./1lb. short-grain rice | 2⅔ cups short-grain rice |
| 600ml./1 pint water | 2½ cups water |
| TEMPURA | TEMPURA |
| 4 large Dublin Bay prawns, shelled | 4 large Gulf shrimp, shelled |
| 3 small plaice fillets, quartered | 3 small flounder fillets, quartered |
| 1 red pepper, pith and seeds removed and cut into squares | 1 red pepper, pith and seeds removed and cut into squares |
| 6 button mushrooms | 6 button mushrooms |
| 50g./2oz. flour | ½ cup flour |
| 75ml./3fl.oz. water | ⅓ cup water |
| 1 small egg, lightly beaten | 1 small egg, lightly beaten |
| vegetable oil for deep-frying | vegetable oil for deep-frying |
| SAUCE | SAUCE |
| 175ml./6fl.oz. dashi | ¾ cup dashi |
| 3 Tbs. sake or dry sherry | 3 Tbs. sake or dry sherry |
| 3 Tbs. soya sauce | 3 Tbs. soy sauce |
| ½ tsp. sugar | ½ tsp. sugar |
| monosodium glutamate (optional) | MSG (optional) |
| 1cm./½in. piece of fresh root ginger, peeled and grated | ½in. piece of fresh green ginger, peeled and grated |
| 2 spring onions, chopped (to garnish) | 2 scallions, chopped (to garnish) |

Cook the rice, following the instructions given in *Gohan*.

Meanwhile, prepare the tempura. Arrange the seafood and vegetables on a platter. Beat the flour, water and egg together to make a light, thin batter, then dip the seafood and vegetable pieces into it to coat them thoroughly. Set aside.

Fill a large deep-frying pan about one-third full of vegetable oil and heat it until it is very hot. Carefully lower the seafood and vegetable pieces into the oil, a few at a time, and fry until they are crisp and golden brown. Using a slotted spoon, transfer the pieces to kitchen towels to drain, then keep hot while you prepare the sauce.

Put the dashi, sake or dry sherry, soy sauce, sugar and monosodium glutamate to taste into a saucepan and gently bring to the boil, stirring until the sugar has dissolved. Stir in the grated ginger and remove from the heat.

To serve, transfer the rice to a warmed serving bowl and arrange the tempura pieces decoratively over the top. Pour over the sauce and garnish with the chopped spring onions (scallions) before serving.
*Serves 4-6*
Preparation and cooking time: 1 hour

*(See previous page)* The translation of Mi-Iro Gohan is 'three-coloured rice'—so called because of the pretty pattern made by the three main ingredients, the rice, minced (ground) beef and green peas.

# Mi-Iro Gohan

(Three-Coloured Rice)

| Metric/Imperial | American |
|---|---|
| 450g./1lb. short-grain rice | 2⅔ cups short-grain rice |
| 225g./8oz. green peas, weighed after shelling | 1 cup green peas, weighed after shelling |
| MEAT | MEAT |
| 275g./10oz. minced beef | 10oz. ground beef |
| 3 Tbs. soya sauce | 3 Tbs. soy sauce |
| 1 tsp. salt | 1 tsp. salt |
| 3 Tbs. sugar | 3 Tbs. sugar |
| 150ml./5fl.oz. dashi | ⅔ cup dashi |
| 4 Tbs. sake or dry sherry | 4 Tbs. sake or dry sherry |
| EGGS | EGGS |
| 5 eggs, lightly beaten | 5 eggs, lightly beaten |
| 1 Tbs. sugar | 1 Tbs. sugar |
| 1 Tbs. vegetable oil | 1 Tbs. vegetable oil |
| ¼ tsp. salt | ¼ tsp. salt |

Cook the rice, following the instructions given in *Gohan*.

Meanwhile, prepare the meat. Combine all the meat ingredients in a small saucepan and set over moderate heat. Cook, stirring constantly, until the meat loses its pinkness and is broken up into small grains. Cook for a further 5 minutes, or until the meat is cooked through. Remove from the heat and keep hot.

Beat all the egg ingredients together and put into a small saucepan. Set over low heat and cook, stirring constantly, until the eggs scramble and become dry. Remove from the heat and keep hot.

Cook the peas in boiling salted water for 5 minutes, or until they are just cooked. Remove from the heat, drain and set aside.

To assemble, fill individual serving bowls with rice. Level the top and arrange the meat mixture, egg mixture and peas decoratively on top, in three sections. Pour over any juices from the meat bowl and serve at once.

*Serves 4-6*
Preparation and cooking time: 1 hour

# Iwashi no Kabayaki

(Sardines with Rice)

| Metric/Imperial | American |
|---|---|
| 450g./1lb. short-grain rice, soaked in cold water for 1 hour and drained | 2⅔ cups short-grain rice, soaked in cold water for 1 hour and drained |
| 12 sardines, cleaned, gutted and with the head removed | 12 sardines, cleaned, gutted and with the head removed |
| 3 Tbs. soya sauce | 3 Tbs. soy sauce |
| 4cm./1½in. piece of fresh root ginger, peeled and grated | 1½in. piece of fresh green ginger, peeled and grated |
| 50g./2oz. cornflour | ½ cup cornstarch |
| 50ml./2fl.oz. vegetable oil | ¼ cup vegetable oil |
| 225g./8oz. cooked green peas, weighed after shelling | 1 cup cooked green peas, weighed after shelling |

SAUCE

| | |
|---|---|
| SAUCE | SAUCE |
| 150ml./5fl.oz. soya sauce | $\frac{2}{3}$ cup soy sauce |
| 4 Tbs. mirin or sweet sherry | 4 Tbs. mirin or sweet sherry |
| 2 Tbs. sugar | 2 Tbs. sugar |
| 3 Tbs. water | 3 Tbs. water |
| monosodium glutamate (optional) | MSG (optional) |
| 2 tsp. miso paste | 2 tsp. miso paste |

Cook the rice, following the instructions given in *Gohan*.

Meanwhile, remove the main bones from the sardines and splay open. Wash in lightly salted water then transfer to a shallow dish. Pour over the soy sauce and ginger and set aside at room temperature for 20 minutes, turning the fish from time to time. Remove the fish from the marinade and pat dry with kitchen towels.

Dip the fish in the cornflour (cornstarch), shaking off any excess. Heat the oil in a large frying-pan. When it is hot, add the sardines, in batches, and fry for 6 to 8 minutes or until they are golden and the flesh flakes.

Meanwhile, combine all the sauce ingredients, except the miso paste, and bring to the boil. Stir in the miso paste and continue cooking until it melts. Remove from the heat.

Pour off the oil from the sardines and add the sauce mixture. Bring to the boil then remove from the heat.

When the rice is cooked, arrange in deep serving bowls and top with the sardines. Pour over the soy sauce mixture and garnish with cooked green peas. Serve at once.

*Serves 4*

Preparation and cooking time: $1\frac{3}{4}$ hours

# Nigiri Zushi

(Rice and Fish 'Sandwiches')

| Metric/Imperial | American |
|---|---|
| 700g./1½lb. short-grain rice | 4 cups short-grain rice |
| 8 large prawns, in the shell | 8 large shrimp, in the shell |
| 1 lemon sole fillet, skinned | 1 lemon sole fillet, skinned |
| 1 mackerel fillet, skinned | 1 mackerel fillet; skinned |
| 40g./1½oz. smoked salmon | $\frac{1}{6}$ cup smoked salmon |
| 1 medium squid, cleaned, skinned and boned | 1 medium squid, cleaned, skinned and boned |
| 3 tsp. green horseraish (wasabi), mixed to a paste with 1 Tbs. water | 3 tsp. green horseradish (wasabi), mixed to a paste with 1 Tbs. water |
| parsley or mint | parsley or mint |
| 350ml./12fl.oz. soy sauce | 1½ cups soy sauce |
| VINEGAR SAUCE | VINEGAR SAUCE |
| 125ml./4fl.oz. white wine vinegar | ½ cup white wine vinegar |
| 1½ Tbs. sugar | 1½ Tbs. sugar |
| 1½ tsp. salt | 1½ tsp. salt |
| monosodium glutamate (optional) | MSG (optional) |

Cook the rice, following the instructions given in *Gohan*. Transfer the drained rice to a warmed bowl and set aside. To make the vinegar sauce, combine the vinegar, sugar, salt and monosodium glutamate to taste, then pour the mixture over the rice. Stir gently with a wooden spoon and set aside to cool at room temperature.

Cook the prawns (shrimp) in boiling water until they turn pink. Drain and

remove the shell and heads. Gently cut along the underside of the prawns (shrimp) and splay them open. Set aside. Sprinkle the sole with salt, then neatly cut the flesh into rectangles about 5cm by 2½cm./2in. by 1in. and just under 1cm./½in. thick. Cut the mackerel, smoked salmon and boned squid into pieces about the same size as the sole.

Using the palm of your hand, gently shape about 1 tablespoon of the rice mixture into a wedge, about the size of your thumb. Smear a small amount of horseradish paste on to the middle of one piece of fish and press the fish and rice gently together to form a 'sandwich', with the horseradish in the centre. Continue this procedure, using up the remaining fish pieces and the remaining rice, but omitting the horseradish mixture for the prawns (shrimp). (You will probably find that the rice will stick to your hands slightly, so rinse them regularly in a bowl of water to which a dash of vinegar has been added.)

When the 'sandwiches' have been made, arrange them decoratively on a large flat dish and garnish with parsley or mint. Pour the soy sauce into individual small dipping bowls, and dip the 'sandwiches' into the soy sauce before eating. This is usually served as a snack or hors d'oeuvre in Japan.

*Serves 6-8*
Preparation and cooking time: 1 hour

# Sashimi Gohan

(Prepared Fish and Rice)

| Metric/Imperial | American |
|---|---|
| 1 large mackerel, cleaned, gutted, then filleted | 1 large mackerel, cleaned, gutted, then filleted |
| 1 tsp. salt | 1 tsp. salt |
| 450ml./15fl.oz. white wine vinegar | 2 cups white wine vinegar |
| 350g./12oz. short-grain rice, soaked in cold water for 1 hour and drained | 2 cups short-grain rice, soaked in cold water for 1 hour and drained |
| 600ml./1 pint water | 2½ cups water |
| GARNISH | GARNISH |
| 4cm./1½in. piece of fresh root ginger, peeled and grated | 1½in. piece of fresh green ginger, peeled and grated |
| 5 spring onions, finely chopped | 5 scallions, finely chopped |
| 350ml./12fl.oz. soya sauce | 1½ cups soy sauce |
| 2 tsp. green horseradish (wasabi), mixed to a paste with 2 tsp. water | 2 tsp. green horseradish (wasabi), mixed to a paste with 2 tsp. water |

Sprinkle the mackerel fillets with salt and put into the refrigerator to chill for 1 hour. Remove from the refrigerator and soak in the vinegar for a further 1 hour.

Meanwhile, put the rice into a saucepan and cover with the water. Bring to the boil, reduce the heat to low and cover the pan. Simmer for 15 to 20 minutes, or until the rice is cooked and the water absorbed. Remove from the heat and transfer to a warmed serving bowl. Set aside and keep hot.

Remove the fish from the vinegar and pat dry with kitchen towels. Cut vertically into 1cm./½in. pieces, removing any bones. Arrange the fish decoratively on a serving dish and surround with the grated ginger and spring onions (scallions). Pour the soy sauce into small, individual dipping bowls and serve individual portions of the horseradish mixture.

To eat, mix horseradish to taste into the soy sauce and dip the mackerel pieces into the sauce before eating with the rice.

*Serves 4*
Preparation and cooking time: 2½ hours

*Sashimi Gohan (Sliced Raw Fish with Rice) is so popular in Japan that there are restuarants devoted exclusively to preparing it. This version is simplicity itself, and the result is guaranteed to make a convert of even the most doubtful eater of uncooked fish!*

35

# Seki Han

(Red Cooked Rice)

*This special festival dish is most authentic when the small red Japanese azuki beans are used. They can be obtained from many health food stores and oriental delicatessens. However, if they are not available, dried red kidney beans can be substituted successfully.*

| Metric/Imperial | American |
| --- | --- |
| 275g./10oz. dried azuki beans, soaked overnight in cold water | 1½ cups dried azuki beans, soaked overnight in cold water |
| 350g./12oz. short-grain rice | 2 cups short-grain rice |
| 1 tsp. salt | 1 tsp. salt |
| 2 Tbs. sake or dry sherry | 2 Tbs. sake or dry sherry |
| 1 Tbs. soya sauce | 1 Tbs. soy sauce |

Put the beans and their soaking liquid into a saucepan and bring to the boil (top up with water if necessary, so that the beans are completely covered). Cover the pan, reduce the heat to low and cook the beans for 1 hour, or until they are just tender. Remove the pan from the heat and drain and reserve the bean cooking liquid. Transfer the beans to a bowl and set aside and keep hot.

Cook the rice, following the instructions given in *Gohan*, except that instead of using all water to cook the rice, use the bean cooking liquid and make up any extra liquid needed with water.

About 5 minutes before the rice is ready to serve, stir in the reserved beans, the salt, sake or sherry and soy sauce and cook until they are all heated through.

Transfer the mixture to a warmed serving bowl and serve at once.
*Serves 3-4*
Preparation and cooking time: 14 hours

# Nori Maki

(Rice Rolls Wrapped in Seaweed)

| Metric/Imperial | American |
| --- | --- |
| 900g./2lb. short-grain rice | 5⅓ cups short-grain rice |
| 1.2l./2 pints water | 5 cups water |
| ¼ large mackerel, filleted | ¼ large mackerel, filleted |
| 150ml./5fl.oz. white wine vinegar | ⅔ cup white wine vinegar |
| 1 Tbs. kanpyo, soaked in cold salted water for 1 hour and drained | 1 Tbs. kanpyo, soaked in cold salted water for 1 hour and drained |
| 1 Tbs. soya sauce | 1 Tbs. soy sauce |
| 50ml./2fl.oz. water | ¼ cup water |
| 2 tsp. sugar | 2 tsp. sugar |
| ½ cucumber | ½ cucumber |
| 125g./4oz. fresh tuna fish | 4oz. fresh tuna fish |
| 4 sheets of nori (seaweed) | 4 sheets of nori (seaweed) |
| 3 tsp. green horseradish (wasabi), mixed to a paste with 1 Tbs. water | 3 tsp. green horseradish (wasabi), mixed to a paste with 1 Tbs. water |
| 350ml./12fl.oz. soya sauce | 1½ cups soy sauce |

VINEGAR SAUCE
125ml./4fl.oz. white wine vinegar
1½ Tbs. sugar
1½ tsp. salt
monosodium glutamate (optional)

VINEGAR SAUCE
½ cup white wine vinegar
1½ Tbs. sugar
1½ tsp. salt
MSG (optional)

Cook the rice, following the instructions given in *Gohan*. Transfer the drained rice to a warmed bowl and set aside. To make the vinegar sauce, combine the vinegar, sugar, salt and monosodium glutamate to taste, then pour the mixture over the rice. Stir gently with a wooden spoon and set aside to cool at room temperature.

Meanwhile, soak the mackerel in the vinegar for 1 hour. Put the kanpyo into a saucepan and just cover with water. Bring to the boil and cook briskly until it is just tender. Drain then return the kanpyo to the saucepan and add the soy sauce, water, and sugar. Cook over moderate heat for 10 minutes, to ensure that the flavours are absorbed into the kanpyo. Set aside.

Remove the mackerel from the vinegar and pat dry on kitchen towels. Cut the flesh vertically into long strips. Slice the cucumber and tuna fish into long thin strips, about the same length as the nori. Set aside.

Preheat the grill (broiler) to moderately high. Place the nori sheets on the rack and grill (broil) until it is crisp on one side. Remove from the heat and cut each sheet into half.

Place one half nori sheet on a flexible bamboo mat or heavy cloth napkin. Spread a handful of sushi rice over the top of the nori, to within about 5cm./2in. of all the edges. Smear a little horseradish over the sushi. Arrange two or three strands of mackerel across the centre of the rice and roll up the mat or napkin gently but firmly so that the mixture will stick together and form a long cylinder. Remove the mat and, in the same way, make cylinders of the remaining nori, sushi rice and fish. Omit the horseradish from the kanpyo mixture.

When all the cylinders have been formed, gently slice across them to form sections about 2½cm./1in. wide.

Pour the soy sauce into small individual dipping bowls and dip the nori sections into the sauce before eating.

Serve the nori maki either on its own as an hors d'oeuvre or as a light snack, or with nigiri zushi as a light meal.

*Serves 8*
Preparation and cooking time: 2½ hours

# Chirashi Zushi

(Rice Salad with Fish)

| Metric/Imperial | American |
| --- | --- |
| 125g./4oz. French beans, sliced | ⅔ cup sliced green beans |
| 2 sheets of nori (seaweed) | 2 sheets of nori (seaweed) |
| sprinkling of shredded ginger | sprinkling of shredded ginger |
| MACKEREL | MACKEREL |
| 1 small mackerel, filleted | 1 small mackerel, filleted |
| 1 Tbs. salt | 1 Tbs. salt |
| 450ml./15fl.oz. white wine vinegar | 2 cups white wine vinegar |
| RICE | RICE |
| 450g./1lb. short-grain rice, soaked in cold water for 1 hour and drained | 2⅔ cups short-grain rice, soaked in cold water for 1 hour and drained |

| | |
|---|---|
| 75ml./3fl.oz. white wine vinegar | ⅓ cup white wine vinegar |
| 1½ Tbs. sugar | 1½ Tbs. sugar |
| 1 Tbs. salt | 1 Tbs. salt |
| KANPYO | KANPYO |
| handful of kanpyo, soaked in cold, salted water for 1 hour and drained | handful of kanpyo, soaked in cold, salted water for 1 hour and drained |
| 3 Tbs. soya sauce | 3 Tbs. soy sauce |
| 2 Tbs. sugar | 2 Tbs. sugar |
| 250ml./8fl.oz. water | 1 cup water |
| MUSHROOMS | MUSHROOMS |
| 5 dried mushrooms, soaked in 450ml./15fl.oz. cold water for 30 minutes, stalks removed and caps sliced | 5 dried mushrooms, soaked in 2 cups cold water for 30 minutes, stalks removed and caps sliced |
| 1½ Tbs. soya sauce | 1½ Tbs. soy sauce |
| 3 Tbs. sugar | 3 Tbs. sugar |
| 1½ Tbs. sake or dry sherry | 1½ Tbs. sake or dry sherry |
| ½ tsp. salt | ½ tsp. salt |
| CARROTS | CARROTS |
| 1 large carrot, sliced | 1 large carrot, sliced |
| 2 tsp. sugar | 2 tsp. sugar |
| ¼ tsp. salt | ¼ tsp. salt |
| EGGS | EGGS |
| 3 eggs, lightly beaten | 3 eggs, lightly beaten |
| few drops soya sauce | few drops soy sauce |
| ½ tsp. salt | ½ tsp. salt |
| ½ Tbs. vegetable oil | 2 Tbs. vegetable oil |

Sprinkle the mackerel fillets with salt and put into the refrigerator to chill for 1 hour. Remove from the refrigerator and soak in the vinegar for a further 1 hour.

Cook the rice, following the instructions given in *Gohan*. Transfer the drained rice to a warm bowl and set aside. To make the vinegar sauce, combine the vinegar, sugar and salt, then pour the mixture over the rice. Stir gently with a wooden spoon and set aside to cool at room temperature.

Put the kanpyo into a saucepan and just cover with water. Bring to the boil and cook briskly until it is just tender. Drain, then return to the saucepan with the soy sauce, sugar and water. Cook over moderate heat for 10 minutes, to ensure that the flavours are absorbed into the kanpyo. Set aside.

Reserve the mushroom draining liquid and add to a small saucepan with the soy sauce, sugar, sake or sherry and salt. Stir in the mushroom pieces and bring to the boil. Cook over moderate heat for 15 minutes, then transfer the mushrooms to a plate with a slotted spoon. Add the carrots to the saucepan, with the sugar and salt. Reduce the heat to low and simmer until all of the sauce has evaporated. Remove from the heat and set aside.

Beat the eggs, soy sauce and salt together. Heat a little of the oil in a small frying-pan. When it is hot, add some of the egg mixture and fry until it forms a wafer-thin pancake. Using a spatula, carefully remove from the pan. Continue to cook the egg mixture in this way until it is all used up. When all the pancakes are cooked, roll them up together and slice them into thin strips. Set aside.

Cook the beans in boiling salted water for 5 minutes, or until they are just tender. Drain and set aside.

Remove the mackerel fillets from the vinegar and pat dry on kitchen towels. Cut vertically into thin strips and set aside.

Preheat the grill (broiler) to moderately high. Place the nori sheets on the rack and grill (broil) until crisp on both sides. Remove from the heat and set aside.

To assemble, arrange the rice in a large serving bowl. Combine the mushrooms, carrots and kanpyo and stir gently into the rice. Arrange the beans, eggs and sliced mackerel on top and sprinkle over the ginger. Crumble over the nori and serve at once.

*Serves 4-6*

Preparation and cooking time: 2¾ hours

*Zushi rice (rice mixed with vinegar and sugar) forms the basis of Chirashi Zushi. It is garnished with nori, a type of seaweed popular in Japan.*

# Oyako Donburi

(Chicken and Eggs with Rice)

| Metric/Imperial | American |
|---|---|
| 450g./1lb. short-grain rice, soaked in cold water for 1 hour and drained | 2⅔ cups short-grain rice, soaked in cold water for 1 hour and drained |
| 3 Tbs. vegetable oil | 3 Tbs. vegetable oil |
| 2 small chicken breasts, skinned, boned and cut into thin strips | 2 small chicken breasts, skinned, boned and cut into thin strips |
| 2 medium onions, thinly sliced | 2 medium onions, thinly sliced |
| 4 eggs, lightly beaten | 4 eggs, lightly beaten |
| 2 sheets of nori (seaweed) | 2 sheets of nori (seaweed) |
| SAUCE | SAUCE |
| 4 Tbs. water | 4 Tbs. water |
| 4 Tbs. soya sauce | 4 Tbs. soy sauce |
| 4 Tbs. dashi | 4 Tbs. dashi |

Cook the rice, following the instructions given in *Gohan*.

Meanwhile, heat the oil in a frying-pan. When it is hot, add the chicken pieces and fry until they are just cooked through. Remove from the heat and, using a slotted spoon, transfer to a plate.

Combine the sauce ingredients together.

Put about a quarter of the sauce mixture into a small frying-pan and bring to the boil. Add about a quarter of the onions and fry briskly for 3 minutes. Add quarter of the chicken slices and quarter of the eggs. Reduce the heat to low and stir once. Leave until the egg has set then cover the pan and steam for 1 minute.

Spoon about a quarter of the rice into an individual serving bowl and top with the egg mixture. Repeat this process three more times, using up the remaining ingredients.

Meanwhile, preheat the grill (broiler) to moderately high. Place the nori on the rack of the grill (broiler) pan and grill (broil) until it is crisp. Remove from the heat and crumble over the rice and egg mixture. Serve at once.
*Serves 4*
Preparation and cooking time: 1¾ hours

# Oboro

(Chicken and Rice)

| Metric/Imperial | American |
|---|---|
| 450g./1lb. short-grain rice | 2⅔ cups short-grain rice |
| 6 dried mushrooms, soaked in cold water for 30 minutes and drained | 6 dried mushrooms, soaked in cold water for 30 minutes and drained |
| 75ml./3fl.oz. soya sauce | ⅓ cup soy sauce |
| 75ml./3fl.oz. sake or dry sherry | ⅓ cup sake or dry sherry |
| 1 tsp. sugar | 1 tsp. sugar |
| 2 chicken breasts, skinned, boned and cut into strips | 2 chicken breasts, skinned, boned and cut into strips |
| 225./8oz. frozen green peas | 1 cup frozen green peas |
| 50ml./2fl.oz. vegetable oil | ¼ cup vegetable oil |
| 2 eggs, beaten | 2 eggs, beaten |

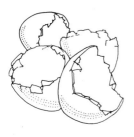

Cook the rice, following the instructions given in *Gohan*.

Remove the stalks from the mushrooms and cook the caps in boiling water for 5 minutes, drain then cut into slices. Set aside.

Put the soy sauce, sake or sherry and sugar into a large saucepan and bring to the boil, stirring constantly until the sugar has dissolved. Add the chicken strips and peas to the pan and reduce the heat to low. Cover and simmer for 5 minutes, or until the chicken strips are cooked. Remove from the heat and set aside.

Heat the oil in a small frying-pan. When it is hot, add the eggs and cook for 2 minutes, or until the bottom has set and is browned. Turn over the omelet and cook for 2 minutes on the other side. Slide the omelet on to a plate and cut into strips. Set aside.

When the rice is cooked, transfer it to a warmed serving bowl. Arrange the chicken strips and peas on top and pour over the chicken cooking liquid. Scatter over the mushrooms and omelet strips and serve at once.

*Serves 4–6*
Preparation and cooking time: 1 hour

# Gyu Donburi

(Beef on Rice)

| Metric/Imperial | American |
|---|---|
| 450g./1lb. short-grain rice, soaked in cold water for 1 hour and drained | $2\frac{2}{3}$ cups short-grain rice, soaked in cold water for 1 hour and drained |
| 175ml./6fl.oz. soya sauce | $\frac{3}{4}$ cup soy sauce |
| 175ml./6fl.oz. dashi | $\frac{3}{4}$ cup dashi |
| 3 Tbs. sugar | 3 Tbs. sugar |
| $\frac{1}{2}$kg./1lb. rump steak, thinly sliced | 1lb. rump steak, thinly sliced |
| 50ml./2fl.oz. vegetable oil | $\frac{1}{4}$ cup vegetable oil |
| 2 green peppers, pith and seeds removed and cut into bite-sized pieces | 2 green peppers, pith and seeds removed and cut into bite-sized pieces |
| $\frac{1}{2}$kg./1lb. leeks, cleaned and cut diagonally into 1cm./$\frac{1}{2}$in. lengths | 1lb. leeks, cleaned and cut diagonally into $\frac{1}{2}$in. lengths |
| 4cm./$1\frac{1}{2}$in. piece of fresh root ginger, peeled and grated | $1\frac{1}{2}$in. piece of fresh green ginger, peeled and grated |

Cook the rice, following the instructions given in *Gohan*.

Meanwhile, combine the soy sauce, dashi and sugar together in a large shallow dish. Add the beef slices and set aside to marinate at room temperature for 15 minutes, basting occasionally. Remove from the marinade and pat dry with kitchen towels. Reserve the marinade.

Heat half the oil in a large frying-pan. When it is hot, add the beef slices and cook for 2 minutes on each side. Reduce the heat to moderately low and cook for a further 2 minutes on each side. Stir in the reserved marinade and remove from the heat. Keep hot.

Heat the remaining oil in a second frying-pan. When it is hot, add the peppers and leeks and fry gently for 8 to 10 minutes, or until they are just cooked. Remove from the heat and set aside.

When the rice is cooked, transfer it to individual serving bowls. Either cut the beef into thin strips or serve it as it is. Arrange the peppers and leeks and beef to make three sections on top of the rice. Pour over the meat cooking juices and sprinkle with grated ginger.

Serve at once.

*Serves 4*
Preparation and cooking time: 1 hour

# MEAT & POULTRY

# Kushi Dango

(Meatballs)

| Metric/Imperial | American |
|---|---|
| 575g./1¼lb. minced beef | 1¼lb. ground beef |
| 4 spring onions, finely chopped | 4 scallions, finely chopped |
| 4cm./1½in. piece of fresh root ginger, peeled and grated | 1½in. piece of fresh green ginger, peeled and grated |
| 3 Tbs. flour | 3 Tbs. flour |
| 1 Tbs. soya sauce | 1 Tbs. soy sauce |
| 3 eggs, lightly beaten | 3 eggs, lightly beaten |
| monosodium glutamate (optional) | MSG (optional) |
| vegetable oil for deep-frying | vegetable oil for deep-frying |

Combine the beef, spring onions (scallions), ginger, flour, soy sauce, eggs and monosodium glutamate to taste in a large bowl. Using the palm of your hands, gently shape the mixture into small balls, about 2½cm./1in. in diameter.

Fill a large deep-frying pan about one-third full with vegetable oil and heat it until it is very hot. Carefully lower the meatballs, a few at a time, into the hot oil and fry until they are golden brown. Using a slotted spoon, remove the meatballs from the pan and drain on kitchen towels. Keep hot while you fry the remaining meatballs in the same way.

To serve, thread three or four meatballs each on to short skewers and serve as an hors d'oeuvre.

*Serves 4–6*
Preparation and cooking time: 40 minutes

# San Juhk

(Beef Kebabs)                                                                          (Korea)

| Metric/Imperial | American |
|---|---|
| ½kg./1lb. rump steak, cut into 5cm./2in. strips | 1lb. rump steak, cut into 2in. strips |
| 1 green pepper, pith and seeds removed and cut into strips | 1 green pepper, pith and seeds removed and cut into strips |
| 4 spring onions, cut into 2½cm./1in. lengths | 4 scallions, cut into 1in. lengths |
| 2 eggs, beaten | 2 eggs, beaten |
| 50g./2oz. flour | ½ cup flour |
| 125ml./4fl.oz. vegetable oil | ½ cup vegetable oil |
| MARINADE | MARINADE |
| 2 Tbs. soya sauce | 2 Tbs. soy sauce |
| 1 Tbs. sesame oil | 1 Tbs. sesame oil |
| 1 garlic clove, crushed | 1 garlic clove, crushed |
| 1 tsp. sugar | 1 tsp. sugar |
| 1 Tbs. roasted sesame seeds, ground | 1 Tbs. roasted sesame seeds, ground |

First, make the marinade. Put the soy sauce, sesame oil, garlic clove, sugar and half the ground sesame seeds into a large, shallow bowl. Add the beef strips to the bowl and turn to baste thoroughly. Set aside at room temperature for 30 minutes. Remove the strips from the bowl and pat dry with kitchen towels. Discard the marinade.

Thread the beef on to skewers, alternating them with the pepper and spring onion (scallion) pieces. Carefully dip the skewers into the beaten eggs, then coat in the flour, shaking off any excess.

Heat the oil in a large frying-pan. When it is hot, carefully arrange the skewers in the pan. Fry, turning the skewers occasionally, for 8 to 10 minutes, or until the beef is brown and crisp. Remove from the heat and drain on kitchen towels.

Transfer the skewers to a warmed serving dish, sprinkle over the remaining sesame seeds and serve at once.

*Serves 4*
Preparation and cooking time: 1 hour

# Gyuniku no Amiyaki

(Steak Marinated in Sesame)

| Metric/Imperial | American |
|---|---|
| 4 x 225g./8oz. rump steaks | 4 x 8oz. rump steaks |
| MARINADE | MARINADE |
| 1½ Tbs. sesame seeds | 1½ Tbs. sesame seeds |
| 1 garlic clove, crushed | 1 garlic clove, crushed |
| 1½ Tbs. soya sauce | 1½ Tbs. soy sauce |
| 1 Tbs. sake or dry sherry | 1 Tbs. sake or dry sherry |
| 1 tsp. sugar | 1 tsp. sugar |
| DIPPING SAUCE | DIPPING SAUCE |
| 2 spring onions, finely chopped | 2 scallions, finely chopped |
| 4cm./1½in. piece of fresh root ginger, peeled and grated | 1½in. piece of fresh green ginger, peeled and grated |
| ½ tsp. paprika or hichimi togarashi | ½ tsp. paprika or hichimi togarashi |
| 150ml./5fl.oz. soya sauce | ⅔ cup soy sauce |
| 2 Tbs. dashi | 2 Tbs. dashi |

First make the marinade. Fry the sesame seeds gently in a small frying-pan until they begin to 'pop'. Transfer them to a mortar and crush with a pestle to release the oil. Put the crushed seeds into a large shallow bowl and mix thoroughly with all the remaining marinade ingredients. Add the steaks to the dish and baste thoroughly. Set aside to marinate at room temperature for 30 minutes, turning the steaks and basting them occasionally.

Meanwhile, prepare the dipping sauce by mixing all the ingredients together. Pour the sauce into individual dipping bowls and set aside.

Preheat the grill (broiler) to moderately high.

Remove the steaks from the marinade and arrange on the rack of the grill (broiler). Grill (broil) for 2 minutes on each side, then reduce the heat to moderate. Grill (broil) for a further 2 minutes on each side for rare steaks; double the cooking time for medium.

Remove the steaks from the heat, transfer to a chopping board and carefully cut into strips. Arrange the strips on individual serving plates. Serve at once, with the dipping sauce.

*Serves 4*
Preparation and cooking time: 1 hour

# Bul-Ko-Kee

(Barbecued Beef)                                                      (Korea)

| Metric/Imperial | American |
| --- | --- |
| ½kg./1lb. topside of beef, very thinly sliced into strips | 1lb. top round of beef, very thinly sliced into strips |
| 3 Tbs. soft brown sugar | 3 Tbs. soft brown sugar |
| 125ml./4fl.oz. soya sauce | ½ cup soy sauce |
| salt and pepper | salt and pepper |
| 5 Tbs. roasted sesame seeds, ground | 5 Tbs. roasted sesame seeds, ground |
| 50ml./2fl.oz. sesame oil | 4 Tbs. sesame oil |
| 1 garlic clove, crushed | 1 garlic clove, crushed |
| 2 spring onions, green part only, finely chopped | 2 scallions, green part only, finely chopped |
| ½ tsp. monosodium glutamate (optional) | ½ tsp. MSG (optional) |

Mix the beef, sugar, soy sauce, salt and pepper to taste, half the sesame seeds, the oil, garlic, spring onions (scallions) and monosodium glutamate together. Set aside at room temperature for 2 hours, basting and turning the meat from time to time.

Preheat the grill (broiler) to hot.

Lay the beef strips on the lined grill (broiler) pan and grill (broil) for 5 to 8 minutes, or until the strips are cooked through and evenly browned. (If you prefer, the beef can be fried quickly in a little sesame oil until browned.)

Remove from the heat, sprinkle over the remaining sesame seeds and serve at once.

*Serves 4*
Preparation and cooking time: about 2¼ hours

*Bul-Ko-Kee, a succulent mixture of beef strips, first marinated then barbecued and sprinkled with sesame seeds, is almost the Korean national dish. It is served here with Kim Chee, a popular Korean version of pickled cabbage.*

# Yuk-Kae-Jang-Kuk

(Beef Stew with Peppers)                                              (Korea)

| Metric/Imperial | American |
| --- | --- |
| 1kg./2lb. braising steak, cut into thin strips | 2lb. chuck steak, cut into thin strips |
| 3 green peppers, pith and seeds removed and cut into strips | 3 green peppers, pith and seeds removed and cut into strips |
| 3 red peppers, pith and seeds removed and cut into strips | 3 red peppers, pith and seeds removed and cut into strips |
| 3 spring onions, chopped | 3 scallions, chopped |
| ½ tsp. sugar | ½ tsp. sugar |
| ½ tsp. salt | ½ tsp. salt |
| 125ml./4fl.oz. soya sauce | ½ cup soy sauce |
| 175ml./6fl.oz. water | ¾ cup water |

Put all the ingredients into a heavy-bottomed saucepan and bring to the boil. Cover and simmer for 2 to 2½ hours, or until the beef is very tender. (Do not add any more liquid – enough is produced by the ingredients.)

Transfer to a warmed serving dish before serving.

*Serves 4–6*
Preparation and cooking time: 3 hours

# Gyuniku no Kushiyaki

(Beef Kebabs with Green Pepper)

*This dish is a sort of Japanese shashlik and the 'extra' fillings can be varied according to taste. The combination used here is particularly colourful, but you could substitute small whole onions, tomatoes, or mushrooms if you prefer.*

| Metric/Imperial | American |
|---|---|
| ½kg./1lb. rump steak, cut into bite-sized cubes | 1lb. rump steak, cut into bite-sized cubes |
| 1 large green pepper, pith and seeds removed and cut into pieces about the same size as the meat cubes | 1 large green pepper, pith and seeds removed and cut into pieces about the same size as the meat cubes |
| 1 large red pepper, pith and seeds removed and cut into pieces about the same size as the meat cubes | 1 large red pepper, pith and seeds removed and cut into pieces about the same size as the meat cubes |
| 50g./2oz. flour | ½ cup flour |
| 2 eggs, beaten | 2 eggs, beaten |
| 75g./3oz. fine dry breadcrumbs | 1 cup fine dry breadcrumbs |
| vegetable oil for deep-frying | vegetable oil for deep-frying |
| MARINADE | MARINADE |
| 75ml./3fl.oz. soya sauce | ⅓ cup soy sauce |
| 3 Tbs. mirin or sweet sherry | 3 Tbs. mirin or sweet sherry |
| 2 spring onions, chopped | 2 scallions, chopped |
| 1 tsp. sugar | 1 tsp. sugar |
| ½ tsp. hichimi togarishi or paprika | ½ tsp. hichimi togarishi or paprika |

First, make the marinade. Put all the ingredients into a large, shallow dish and mix until they are thoroughly blended.

Thread the meat and pepper pieces on to skewers then arrange them carefully in the marinade mixture. Set aside at room temperature for at least 1 hour, turning the skewers from time to time so that all sides of the mixture become coated in the marinade. Remove from the marinade, then discard the marinade. Pat the cubes dry with kitchen towels and dip lightly in the flour, shaking off any excess. Dip the skewers into the beaten eggs, then coat thoroughly with the breadcrumbs, shaking off any excess.

Fill a large deep-frying pan about one-third full with vegetable oil and heat until it is very hot. Carefully lower the skewers, a few at a time, into the oil and fry the beef and peppers until they are crisp and golden brown. Remove from the oil and drain on kitchen towels.

Serve at once, piping hot.

*Serves 4*
Preparation and cooking time: 1½ hours

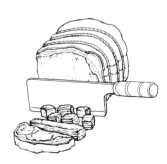

# Bulgalbi

(Marinated Beef Spareribs)                                                    (Korea)

| Metric/Imperial | American |
|---|---|
| 1kg./2lb. beef spareribs, cut into 7½cm./3in. pieces | 2lb. beef spareribs, cut into 3in. pieces |
| 1 Tbs. peanut oil | 1 Tbs. peanut oil |
| MARINADE | MARINADE |
| 4 Tbs. soya sauce | 4 Tbs. soy sauce |

| Metric/Imperial | American |
|---|---|
| 3 garlic cloves, crushed | 3 garlic cloves, crushed |
| 2 Tbs. sake or dry white wine | 2 Tbs. sake or dry white wine |
| 4 Tbs. water | 4 Tbs. water |
| 2 tsp. roasted sesame seeds, ground | 2 tsp. roasted sesame seeds, ground |
| 2 Tbs. sugar | 2 Tbs. sugar |
| 1 tsp. black pepper | 1 tsp. black pepper |
| 4 spring onions, chopped | 4 scallions, chopped |
| 1 onion, chopped | 1 onion, chopped |
| 1 large ripe pear, peeled and cored | 1 large ripe pear, peeled and cored |

First prepare the spareribs. Using a sharp knife, carefully open out the flesh to make three 'wings', then criss-cross all of the meat (and bone) with small, deep incisions, taking care not to cut through the meat entirely.

To make the marinade, combine all the ingredients, except the pear, in a large, shallow dish. Chop the pear roughly so that the flesh is crumbling, and stir into the marinade mixture. Add the ribs and set aside to marinate overnight at room temperature.

Preheat the grill (broiler) to moderately high.

Remove the beef from the marinade and transfer to the rack of the grill (broiler). Brush lightly with the oil. Grill (broil) the meat for 15 minutes, or until it is cooked through and golden brown.

Remove from the heat and serve at once.

*Serves 4*

Preparation and cooking time: 13 hours

# Oyi Jim

(Beef with Cucumbers)                                                    (Korea)

| Metric/Imperial | American |
|---|---|
| 50ml./2fl.oz. vegetable oil | ¼ cup vegetable oil |
| 350g./12oz. rump steak, cut into thin strips | 12oz. rump steak, cut into thin strips |
| 2 medium cucumbers, halved lengthways with the seeds removed, then cut into 1cm./½in. slices | 2 medium cucumbers, halved lengthways with the seeds removed, then cut into ½in. slices |
| 1 red chilli, finely chopped | 1 red chilli, finely chopped |
| 1 Tbs. roasted sesame seeds, ground | 1 Tbs. roasted sesame seeds, ground |
| MARINADE | MARINADE |
| 1 Tbs. sesame oil | 1 Tbs. sesame oil |
| 1 Tbs. soya sauce | 1 Tbs soy sauce |
| 1 garlic clove, crushed | 1 garlic clove, crushed |
| ½ tsp. sugar | ½ tsp. sugar |

First, prepare the marinade. Combine all the ingredients together, beating until they are thoroughly blended. Arrange the beef strips in the marinade and baste and turn until they are covered. Set aside at room temperature for 15 minutes, turning the strips from time to time.

Heat the oil in a large frying-pan. When it is hot, add the beef mixture and stir-fry for 1½ minutes. Add the cucumbers and chilli and stir-fry for a further 2 minutes, or until the cucmbers are cooked but still crisp.

Transfer the mixture to a warmed serving dish and sprinkle over the ground sesame seeds before serving.

*Serves 3–4*

Preparation and cooking time: 35 minutes

# Beef Teriyaki I

| Metric/Imperial | American |
|---|---|
| 1kg./2lb. fillet steak, cut into ½cm./¼in. slices | 2lb. fillet steak, cut into ¼in. slices |
| MARINADE | MARINADE |
| 2½cm./1in. piece of fresh root ginger, peeled and chopped | 1in. piece of fresh green ginger, peeled and chopped |
| 2 garlic cloves, crushed | 2 garlic cloves, crushed |
| 4 spring onions, finely chopped | 4 scallions, finely chopped |
| 25g./1oz. soft brown sugar | 2 Tbs. soft brown sugar |
| 250ml./8fl.oz. soya sauce | 1 cup soy sauce |
| 125ml./4fl.oz. sake or dry sherry | ½ cup sake or dry sherry |
| salt and pepper | salt and pepper |

Combine all the marinade ingredients in a large shallow dish. Put the steak pieces into the marinade and set aside at room temperature to marinate for 2 hours, basting occasionally.

Preheat the grill (broiler) to high.

Remove the steaks from the marinade and arrange them on the rack of the grill (broiler). Brush them generously with the marinade mixture and grill (broil) for 2 minutes. Remove from the heat, turn the steak and brush with the marinade. Grill (broil) for a further 2 minutes. These will give you rare steaks; double the cooking time for medium.

Transfer the steaks to warmed serving dishes and either serve at once, or cut into thin strips before serving.

*Serves 6*

Preparation and cooking time: 2¼ hours

# Beef Teriyaki II

| Metric/Imperial | American |
|---|---|
| 4 small fillet steaks, cut ½cm./¼in. thick | 4 small fillet steaks, cut ¼in. thick |
| 3 Tbs. vegetable oil | 3 Tbs. vegetable oil |
| MARINADE | MARINADE |
| 50ml./2fl.oz. sake or dry sherry | ¼ cup sake or dry sherry |
| 2 Tbs. soya sauce | 2 Tbs. soy sauce |
| 1 garlic clove, crushed | 1 garlic clove, crushed |
| 50ml./2fl.oz. dashi | ¼ cup dashi |

Combine all the marinade ingredients in a large, shallow dish. Arrange the steaks in the mixture and set aside at room temperature to marinate for 1 hour, basting occasionally. Remove the steaks from the marinade, drying on kitchen towels, and reserve the marinade.

Heat the oil in a large frying-pan. When it is hot, add the steaks and fry for 1 minute on each side. Pour off all but a thin film of fat from the pan and add the marinade. Cook the steaks for a further 3 minutes on each side, basting them occasionally with the pan juices. These times will give rare steaks; double the cooking time for medium.

Transfer the steaks to warmed individual serving plates and either serve as they are or cut them into thin strips. Pour a little of the pan juices over the meat before serving.

*Serves 4*

Preparation and cooking time: 1¼ hours

# Juhn Kol

(Mixed Meats and Vegetables cooked at the Table) (Korea)

*This popular dish has Japanese origins still represented today since the hibachi-type grill (broiler) plate on the table is a favourite way to present it. This is also a particularly suitable dish for barbecuing. The meats and vegetables suggested below are typical but any can be omitted or added to – the choice is yours.*

*Serve this superb Beef Teriyaki I with rice and bean sprouts for a delicious Japanese meal. If you wish to use chopsticks, you should cut the beef into thin strips before eating, as the Japanese do.*

| Metric/Imperial | American |
| --- | --- |
| ½kg./1lb. rump steak or pork fillet<br>  (or a mixture of the two),<br>  cut into thin squares | 1lb. rump steak or pork tenderloin<br>  (or a mixture of the two),<br>  cut into thin squares |
| 2 large onions, sliced | 2 large onions, sliced |
| 3 celery stalks, cut into 2½cm./1in. lengths | 3 celery stalks, cut into 1in. lengths |
| 125g./4oz. small button mushrooms | 1 cup small button mushrooms |
| 2 carrots, thinly sliced diagonally | 2 carrots, thinly sliced diagonally |
| MARINADE | MARINADE |
| 125ml./4fl.oz. soya sauce | ½ cup soy sauce |
| 50g./2oz. sugar | ¼ cup sugar |
| 2 Tbs. vegetable oil | 2 Tbs. vegetable oil |
| 2 garlic cloves, crushed | 2 garlic cloves, crushed |
| 1 spring onion, finely chopped | 1 scallion, finely chopped |
| 1 chilli, finely chopped | 1 chilli, finely chopped |
| 1 Tbs. roasted sesame seeds, ground | 1 Tbs. roasted sesame seeds, ground |

First, prepare the marinade. Put all the marinade ingredients into a shallow mixing bowl and beat well until they are thoroughly blended. Add the meat squares to the mixture and baste well to cover them completely. Set aside for 2 hours, turning the squares from time to time.

Meanwhile, arrange all the vegetables attractively on a large platter and set on the table. Put the burner or electric plate on the table and warm up.

The meal is now ready to be cooked, ingredients requiring most cooking to be cooked first. The meat is first seared then cooked with enough of its marinade to keep from burning.

Serve hot.

*Serves 4*
Preparation and cooking time: 2½ hours

# Binatok

(Dried Green Pea Pancake with Filling)                                      (Korea)

| Metric/Imperial | American |
|---|---|
| 450g./1lb. dried split peas | 2⅔ cups dried split peas |
| 175g./6oz. long-grain rice | 1 cup long-grain rice |
| 2 garlic cloves, crushed | 2 garlic cloves, crushed |
| 2 spring onions, finely chopped | 2 scallions, finely chopped |
| 1 small onion, finely chopped | 1 small onion, finely chopped |
| 1 carrot, grated | 1 carrot, grated |
| Water | Water |
| 4 Tbs. peanut oil | 4 Tbs. peanut oil |
| FILLING | FILLING |
| 125g./4oz. rump steak, cut into thin strips | 4oz. rump steak, cut into thin strips |
| 3 spring onions, cut into 2½cm./1in. lengths | 3 scallions, cut into 1 in. lengths |
| 2 carrots, thinly sliced on the diagonal | 2 carrots, thinly sliced on the diagonal |
| 1 red or green pepper, pith and seeds removed and cut into strips | 1 red or green pepper, pith and seeds removed and cut into strips |
| 1 dried red chilli, crumbled | 1 dried red chilli, crumbled |
| black pepper | black pepper |
| DIPPING SAUCE | DIPPING SAUCE |
| 250 ml./8fl.oz. soya sauce | 1 cup soy sauce |
| 2 spring onions, very finely chopped | 2 scallions, very finely chopped |

Put the split peas and rice into a large bowl and just cover with water. Set aside to soak overnight. Drain, then put the mixture into a blender. Grind until smooth. Transfer the mixture to a large bowl. Stir in the garlic, spring onions (scallions), onion and carrot until they are well blended, then stir in enough water to form a thick batter. Set aside to 'rest' at room temperature for 30 minutes.

Meanwhile, assemble the filling ingredients on a large plate, in the order of cooking, that is those to be cooked longest first.

Heat quarter of the oil in a small saucepan. When it is very hot, add about a quarter of the batter and fry until the edges curl slightly. Arrange about a quarter of the meat over the batter and cook for 1 minute. Arrange a quarter of the spring onions (scallions), carrots, pepper and chilli, with pepper to taste, in the same way. Cook for 3 minutes, carefully working around the edges occasionally with a spatula, or until the bottom is brown. Carefully turn the pancake over and fry on the other side until it is golden brown.

Slide the pancake on to a warmed serving plate and keep hot while you cook the remaining batter and the remaining filling ingredients in the same way.

To make the dipping sauce, combine the soy sauce and spring onions (scallions) and pour into small, individual dipping bowls. Serve at once, with the bintatok.
*Serves 4*
Preparation and cooking time: 12¾ hours

# Kan Juhn

(Fried Liver)                                                                                            (Korea)

| Metric/Imperial | American |
|---|---|
| ½kg./1lb. lamb's liver, thinly sliced | 1lb. lamb's liver, thinly sliced |
| 1 large garlic clove | 1 large garlic clove |
| salt and pepper | salt and pepper |
| 50g./2oz. flour | ½ cup flour |
| 2 eggs, lightly beaten | 2 eggs, lightly beaten |
| 50ml./2fl.oz. sesame oil | ¼ cup sesame oil |
| SAUCE | SAUCE |
| 125ml./4fl.oz. soya sauce | ½ cup soy sauce |
| 125ml./4fl.oz. wine vinegar | ½ cup wine vinegar |
| 1 Tbs. soft brown sugar | 1 Tbs. soft brown sugar |
| 2 tsp. chopped pine nuts | 2 tsp. chopped pine nuts |

Rub the liver gently with the garlic, then discard the clove. Sprinkle with salt and pepper to taste. Dip the slices in flour, shaking off any excess, then in the beaten eggs.

Heat the oil in a large frying-pan. When it is hot, add the liver slices and fry for 3 to 4 minutes on each side (depending on thickness), or until the meat is just cooked through.

Meanwhile, make the sauce by combining all the ingredients in a screw-top jar until they are thoroughly blended. Pour into a shallow dipping bowl.

Transfer the liver slices to a warmed serving platter and serve at once, with the dipping sauce.
*Serves 4*
Preparation and cooking time: 20 minutes

# Buta no Kakuni

(Pork Cooked with Sake)

| Metric/Imperial | American |
|---|---|
| 575g./1¼lb. lean pork meat, cut into 4 pieces | 1¼lb. lean pork meat, cut into 4 pieces |
| 4cm./1½in. piece of fresh root ginger, peeled and sliced | 1½in. piece of fresh green ginger, peeled and sliced |
| 2 garlic cloves, sliced | 2 garlic cloves, sliced |
| 450ml./15fl.oz. sake or dry sherry | 2 cups sake or dry sherry |
| 4 Tbs. sugar | 4 Tbs. sugar |
| 5 Tbs. soya sauce | 5 Tbs. soy sauce |
| ½ tsp. salt | ½ tsp. salt |
| 1 Tbs. mustard | 1 Tbs. mustard |

Put the pork into a medium saucepan and just cover with water. Add the ginger and garlic. Bring to the boil, reduce the heat to low and simmer for 1 hour. Remove from the heat, cool, then skim any fat from the surface of the liquid. Add the sake or sherry and sugar and continue to simmer for about 1½ hours, or until the meat is so tender that it is almost coming apart. Stir in the soy sauce and salt and remove the pan from the heat.

To serve, put one piece of pork on four individual, deep serving plates and pour over the cooking liquid. Add a dash of mustard to each piece of meat and serve at once.

*Serves 4*
Preparation and cooking time: 3½ hours

# Ton-Yuk-Kui

(Korean Pork Fillets)

*Ton-Yuk-Kui is a Korean dish of lean pork fillet (tenderloin), first marinated then baked until it is tender. It is tradionally served with a sauce made from the delicious marinade.*

| Metric/Imperial | American |
| --- | --- |
| 1kg./2lb. pork fillet, thinly sliced | 2lb. pork tenderloin, thinly sliced |
| 2 Tbs. sesame oil | 2 Tbs. sesame oil |
| MARINADE | MARINADE |
| 125ml./4fl.oz. soya sauce | ½ cup soy sauce |
| 50 ml./2fl.oz. water | ¼ cup water |
| 3 Tbs. sugar | 3 Tbs. sugar |
| 2 spring onions, finely chopped | 2 scallions, finely chopped |
| 2 garlic cloves, crushed | 2 garlic cloves, crushed |
| 5cm./2in. piece of fresh root ginger, peeled and finely chopped | 2in. piece of fresh green ginger, peeled and finely chopped |
| salt and pepper | salt and pepper |

Combine all the marinade ingredients in a shallow dish and add the pork slices. Baste well, then set aside at room temperature for 2 hours, basting occasionally.

Preheat the oven to fairly hot 190°C (Gas Mark 5, 375°F).

Remove the pork from the marinade and dry on kitchen towels. Reserve the marinade.

Coat the bottom and sides of a baking dish with the oil. Arrange the pork slices in the dish, in one layer. Cover and bake the meat for 45 minutes to 1 hour, or until it is tender.

Meanwhile, pour the marinade into a saucepan and bring to the boil. Reduce the heat to low and simmer for 10 to 15 minutes, or until it has reduced slightly.

Remove the meat from the oven and arrange it on a warmed serving dish. Pour the cooking juices into the saucepan with the marinade and bring to the boil again. Pour a little over the pork and serve the rest with the meat.

*Serves 4–6*

Preparation and cooking time: 3¼ hours

# Tonkatsu

(Japanese Pork Schnitzel)

*The schnitzels are divided into thin strips before serving in the recipe below to enable chop-stick users to pick up the meat easily. If you plan to eat your meal with a knife and fork, this step can be omitted.*

| Metric/Imperial | American |
|---|---|
| 6 large slices of pork fillet, beaten thin | 6 large slices of pork tenderloin, beaten thin |
| 2 eggs, beaten | 2 eggs, beaten |
| 2 Tbs. finely chopped spring onion | 2 Tbs. finely chopped scallion |
| 125g./4oz. soft white breadcrumbs | 2 cups soft white breadcrumbs |
| 75ml./3fl.oz. vegetable oil | ⅓ cup vegetable oil |
| hichimi togarishi or paprika (to garnish) | hichimi togarishi or paprika (to garnish) |
| MARINADE | MARINADE |
| 6 Tbs. soya sauce | 6 Tbs. soy sauce |
| 4 Tbs. mirin or sweet sherry | 4 Tbs. mirin or sweet sherry |
| 2 garlic cloves, crushed | 2 garlic cloves, crushed |
| 1 tsp. hichimi togarishi or paprika | 1 tsp. hichimi togarishi or paprika |

To make the marinade, combine the soy sauce, mirin or sherry, garlic and hichimi togarishi or paprika together, beating until they are thoroughly blended. Arrange the pork slices in the marinade and set aside at room temperature for 20 minutes, basting and turning the pork occasionally. Remove from the marinade and pat dry with kitchen towels. Discard the marinade.

Beat the eggs and spring onion (scallion) together in a shallow bowl. Dip the pork, first in the egg then in the breadcrumbs, shaking off any excess. Arrange the coated pork pieces on a plate and chill in the refrigerator for 2 hours.

Heat the oil in a large frying-pan. When it is hot, add the schnitzels and fry for 3 to 4 minutes on each side, or until they are golden brown and crisp. Remove from the heat and drain on kitchen towels.

Cut the schnitzels, crosswise, into thin strips, then carefully reassemble into the schnitzel shape. Serve at once, garnished with hichimi togarishi to taste.

*Serves 4*

Preparation and cooking time: 2½ hours

# Kulbi Jim

(Spareribs with Sesame Seed Sauce)                                (Korea)

*This is a very basic version of a very popular dish. If you wish, vegetables can be added to the mixture – some sliced carrots or mushrooms, for instance, or even water chestnuts.*

| Metric/Imperial | American |
|---|---|
| 3 Tbs. vegetable oil | 3 Tbs. vegetable oil |
| 1½kg./3lb. American-style spareribs, cut into 5cm./2in. pieces | 3lb. spareribs, cut into 2-rib serving pieces |
| 2 Tbs. sugar | 2 Tbs. sugar |
| 2 Tbs. sesame oil | 2 Tbs. sesame oil |
| 4 Tbs. soya sauce | 4 Tbs. soy sauce |
| 3 spring onions, chopped | 3 scallions, chopped |
| 2 garlic cloves, crushed | 2 garlic cloves, crushed |
| 2½cm./1in. piece of fresh root ginger, peeled and chopped | 1in. piece of fresh green ginger, peeled and chopped |
| 3 Tbs. roasted sesame seeds, ground | 3 Tbs. roasted sesame seeds, ground |
| 300ml./10fl.oz. water | 1¼ cups water |

Heat the oil in a large, shallow saucepan or frying-pan. When it is hot, add the spareribs and fry until they are evenly browned. (If necessary, fry the ribs in two or three batches.)

Stir in the sugar, sesame oil, soy sauce, spring onions (scallions), garlic, ginger and 2 tablespoons of the sesame seeds until they are thoroughly blended. Pour over the water and bring to the boil. Reduce the heat to low, cover the pan and simmer the mixture for 50 minutes, or until the spareribs are cooked and crisp.

Transfer the mixture to a warmed serving dish and sprinkle over the remaining roasted sesame seeds before serving.

*Serves 6–8*
Preparation and cooking time: 1½ hours

# Seekumche Kuk

(Spinach with Pork)                                                (Korea)

*Many Korean dishes, like most Chinese ones, are geared to make comparatively little meat go quite a long way – and this dish is a particularly good example. If you prefer, lean beef, such as rump steak, can be substituted for the pork.*

| Metric/Imperial | American |
|---|---|
| 1kg./2lb. spinach, washed thoroughly and chopped | 2lb. spinach, washed thoroughly and chopped |
| 1 tsp. salt | 1 tsp. salt |
| 3 Tbs. vegetable oil | 3 Tbs. vegetable oil |
| 225g./8oz. pork fillet, cut into bite-sized pieces | 8oz. pork tenderloin, cut into bite-sized pieces |
| 1 garlic clove, crushed | 1 garlic clove, crushed |
| ¼ tsp. cayenne pepper | ¼ tsp. cayenne pepper |
| 2 spring onions, chopped | 2 scallions, chopped |
| 2 Tbs. soya sauce | 2 Tbs. soy sauce |
| ½ tsp. sugar | ½ tsp. sugar |
| 2 Tbs. roasted sesame seeds, ground | 2 Tbs. roasted sesame seeds, ground |

Put the spinach into a large saucepan with the salt and cook gently for 8 to 10 minutes, or until it is just tender. (Do not add water – there should be enough clinging to the leaves to provide moisture for cooking.) Drain, then transfer the spinach to a plate. Keep hot.

Heat the oil in a large frying-pan. When it is hot, add the pork pieces and garlic and stir-fry for 2 minutes. Stir in the cayenne, spring onions (scallions), soy sauce and sugar and continue to stir-fry for a further 2 minutes. Stir in the chopped spinach and heat it through.

Transfer the mixture to a warmed serving dish and sprinkle over the roasted sesame seeds before serving.

*Serves 3–4*
Preparation and cooking time: 25 minutes

# Yakibuta

(Basted Pork)

| Metric/Imperial | American |
| --- | --- |
| 1kg./2lb. boned leg or loin of pork | 2lb. boned leg or loin of pork |
| 3 garlic cloves, crushed | 3 garlic cloves, crushed |
| 4cm./1½in. piece of fresh root ginger, peeled and sliced | 1½in. piece of fresh green ginger, peeled and sliced |
| 150ml./5fl.oz. sake or dry sherry | ⅔ cup sake or dry sherry |
| 150ml./5fl.oz. soya sauce | ⅔ cup soy sauce |
| 2 Tbs. sugar | 2 Tbs. sugar |
| 1½ tsp. salt | 1½ tsp. salt |

Put the pork piece in a large saucepan and just cover with water. Add the garlic and ginger. Bring to the boil, then cook over moderate heat for 1 hour, or until the water has evaporated and the oil on the bottom of the saucepan begins to bubble. Pour off the oil and turn the meat in the pan, slightly burning the outside.

Warm the sake or sherry to tepid then add to the saucepan. Continue cooking until the sake has boiled away. Turn the meat again, basting with the pan juices. Stir in the remaining ingredients and cook for a further 10 minutes.

Serve either hot or cold.

*Serves 6–8*
Preparation and cooking time: 1¾ hours

# Goma Yaki

(Chicken with Sesame Seeds)

| Metric/Imperial | American |
| --- | --- |
| 2 large chicken breasts, skinned, boned and halved | 2 large chicken breasts, skinned boned and halved |
| 3 Tbs. sesame oil | 3 Tbs. sesame oil |
| 2 Tbs. roasted sesame seeds | 2 Tbs. roasted sesame seeds |
| MARINADE | MARINADE |
| 75ml./3fl.oz. sake or dry sherry | ⅓ cup sake or dry sherry |
| 2 tsp. soya sauce | 2 tsp. soy sauce |
| monosodium glutamate (optional) | MSG (optional) |
| ¼ tsp. hichimi togarishi or paprika | ¼ tsp. hichimi togarishi or paprika |

First, prepare the marinade. Combine all the ingredients in a medium-sized shallow bowl, beating until they are thoroughly blended. Add the chicken pieces and baste well. Set aside at room temperature for 20 minutes, turning and basting the chicken from time to time.

Heat the oil in a large frying-pan. When it is hot, add the chicken pieces and fry for 5 minutes on each side. Sprinkle over half the sesame seeds and stir and turn until the chicken is coated. Reduce the heat to low and cook the chicken for a further 6 to 8 minutes, or until the pieces are cooked through and tender.

Transfer the mixture to a warmed serving dish and sprinkle over the remaining sesame seeds before serving.

*Serves 2-4*

Preparation and cooking time: 50 minutes

# Dak Jim

(Steamed Chicken and Vegetables)                                    (Korea)

| Metric/Imperial | American |
|---|---|
| 1 x 2kg./4lb. chicken, cut into 8 or 10 serving pieces | 1 x 4lb. chicken, cut into 8 or 10 serving pieces |
| 2 carrots, cut into thin strips | 2 carrots, cut into thin strips |
| 3 dried mushrooms, soaked in cold water for 30 minutes, drained and thinly sliced | 3 dried mushrooms, soaked in cold water for 30 minutes, drained and thinly sliced |
| 1 bamboo shoot, sliced | 1 bamboo shoot, sliced |
| 2 spring onions, thinly sliced | 2 scallions, thinly sliced |
| 2 garlic cloves, crushed | 2 garlic cloves, crushed |
| 1 tsp. ground ginger | 1 tsp. ground ginger |
| 50g./2oz. walnuts, chopped | $\frac{1}{3}$ cup chopped walnuts |
| 50ml./2fl. oz. soya sauce | $\frac{1}{4}$ cup soy sauce |
| 2 Tbs. soft brown sugar | 2 Tbs. soft brown sugar |
| 1 Tbs. roasted sesame seeds, ground | 1 Tbs. roasted sesame seeds, ground |
| salt and pepper | salt and pepper |
| GARNISH | GARNISH |
| 2 eggs, separated | 2 eggs, separated |

Put the chicken pieces into a saucepan and cover with water. Bring to the boil, cover and simmer for 1 to 1½hours, or until the chicken is tender. Drain and reserve the stock. When the meat is cool enough to handle, cut the chicken into bite-sized strips.

Put all the remaining ingredients, except the garnish, into a large saucepan and bring to the boil. Stir in the chicken strips and reserved stock, cover and simmer for 15 to 20 minutes or until the vegetables are cooked but still crisp.

Meanwhile, make the garnish. Beat the egg yolks and whites separately until they are both well mixed. Lightly oil a heavy-bottomed frying-pan and heat it over moderate heat. Pour in the egg white and spread over the bottom in a thin layer. Cook until the bottom is firm, then turn over and cook until the other side is firm. Slide on to a warmed dish and cook the egg yolks in the same way. Cut the cooked eggs into strips.

Transfer the chicken and vegetables to a warmed serving bowl and scatter over the egg strips before serving.

*Serves 6*

Preparation and cooking time: 2½ hours

# Chicken Teriyaki I

| Metric/Imperial | American |
|---|---|
| 125ml./4fl.oz. sake or dry sherry | ½ cup sake or dry sherry |
| 50ml./2fl.oz. soya sauce | ¼ cup soy sauce |
| 125ml./4fl.oz. dashi | ½ cup dashi |
| 2 tsp. sugar | 2 tsp. sugar |
| 2 tsp. cornflour | 2 tsp. cornstarch |
| 4 chicken breasts, skinned and boned | 4 chicken breasts, skinned and boned |
| 2 celery stalks, sliced lengthways | 2 celery stalks, sliced lengthways |
| 8 spring onions, trimmed | 8 scallions, trimmed |

*The essence of Japanese cooking is well illustrated in this dish of Chicken Teriyaki I – the simplicity of the presentation and the importance attached to the appearance of the dish. If you wish to eat with chopsticks, cut the meat (to the bone) into thin strips.*

Warm the sake or sherry in a small saucepan. Remove from the heat and carefully ignite, allowing the sake to burn until the flames die down. Stir in the soy sauce and dashi. Put 3 tablespoons of the sake mixture into a small bowl and mix in the sugar and cornflour (cornstarch). Set aside. Pour the remaining sauce into a shallow dish.

Preheat the grill (broiler) to moderately high.

Dip the chicken pieces into the sauce to coat thoroughly, then arrange them on the rack in the grill (broiler). Grill (broil) for about 6 minutes, or until one side is golden brown. Remove the chicken from the heat, coat thoroughly in the sauce again and return to the rack. Grill (broil) the other side for 6 minutes, or until it is golden brown. Remove from the heat again and dip into the sauce then return to the grill (broiler). Brush generously with the cornflour (cornstarch) mixture and grill (broil) for a final 6 minutes, turning the chicken occasionally, or until the meat is cooked through.

Arrange the chicken pieces on a warmed serving plate and either serve as is, or cut into slices. Garnish with the celery and spring onions (scallions).

*Serves 4*

Preparation and cooking time: 45 minutes

# Chicken Teriyaki II

| Metric/Imperial | American |
|---|---|
| 2 Tbs. clear honey | 2 Tbs. clear honey |
| 6 small chicken breasts, skinned and boned | 6 small chicken breasts, skinned and boned |
| MARINADE | MARINADE |
| 125ml./4fl. oz. soya sauce | ½ cup soy sauce |
| salt and pepper | salt and pepper |
| 4cm./1½in. piece of fresh root ginger, peeled and chopped | 1½in. piece of fresh green ginger, peeled and chopped |
| 1 garlic clove, crushed | 1 garlic clove, crushed |
| 125ml./4fl. oz. sake or dry white wine | ½ cup sake or dry white wine |

Combine all the marinade ingredients in a large shallow dish and set aside.

Heat the honey in a small saucepan until it liquefies slightly. Remove the pan from the heat and brush the honey mixture generously over the chicken breasts. Arrange the chicken in the marinade and set aside at room temperature to marinate for 2 hours, basting occasionally.

Preheat the oven to moderate 180°C (Gas Mark 4, 350°F).

Line a deep-sided baking pan with foil and arrange the chicken breasts on the foil. Pour over the marinade. Put the pan into the oven and bake, basting frequently, for 30 to 35 minutes, or until the chicken is cooked through and tender. Remove from the oven and, using a slotted spoon, transfer the chicken to a warmed serving dish. Pour the cooking juices into a warmed serving bowl and serve with the chicken.

*Serves 6*
Preparation and cooking time: 2¾ hours

# Chicken Pokkum

(Stir-Fried Chicken)                                           (Korea)

| Metric/Imperial | American |
|---|---|
| 50ml./2fl.oz. sesame oil | ¼ cup sesame oil |
| 2 chicken breasts, skinned, boned and cut into strips | 2 chicken breasts, skinned, boned and cut into strips |
| 2 spring onions, chopped | 2 scallions, chopped |
| 1 garlic clove, crushed | 1 garlic clove, crushed |
| 4cm./1½in. piece of fresh root ginger, peeled and finely chopped | 1½in. piece of fresh green ginger, peeled and finely chopped |
| 50g./2oz. button mushrooms, sliced | ½ cup sliced button mushrooms |
| 3 Tbs. soya sauce | 3 Tbs. soy sauce |
| 2 Tbs. water | 2 Tbs. water |
| 1 Tbs. sugar | 1 Tbs. sugar |
| 1 Tbs. roasted sesame seeds, ground | 1 Tbs. roasted sesame seeds, ground |

Heat the oil in a large frying-pan. When it is hot, add the chicken strips and stir-fry for 3 minutes, or until they are just cooked through. Stir in the spring onions (scallions), garlic and ginger and stir-fry for 1 minute. Add the mushrooms and stir-fry for 2 minutes. Stir in the soy sauce, water, sugar and sesame seeds and bring to the boil. Cook for 1 minute.

Transfer the mixture to a warmed serving dish and serve at once.

*Serves 3–4*
Preparation and cooking time: 15 minutes

# Yaki Tori

(Barbecued Chicken)

| Metric/Imperial | American |
|---|---|
| ½kg./1lb. chicken breast, skinned, boned and cut into bite-sized pieces | 1lb. chicken breast, skinned, boned and cut into bite-sized pieces |
| ½kg./1lb. leeks, cleaned, cut into 1cm./½in. lengths and parboiled | 1lb. leeks, cleaned, cut into ½in. lengths and parboiled |
| SAUCE | SAUCE |
| 175ml./6fl. oz. soya sauce | ¾ cup soy sauce |
| 175ml./6fl. oz. mirin or sweet sherry | ¾ cup mirin or sweet sherry |
| monosodium glutamate (optional) | MSG (optional) |

Thread the chicken pieces on to small skewers. Thread the leek pieces (pierce through the sides) on to separate small skewers. Set aside.

Preheat the grill (broiler) to moderately high.

Meanwhile, to make the sauce, put the soy sauce and mirin into a small saucepan and add monosodium glutamate to taste. Bring to the boil, then cook for a few minutes or until it begins to thicken slightly. Remove from the heat.

Arrange the chicken and leek skewers on the rack of the grill (broiler). (If possible put the leeks further away from the flame to avoid excessive charring.) Grill (broil) for 3 minutes. Remove the skewers from the heat and dip into the sauce mixture, to coat the food thoroughly. Return to the heat, turn the skewers and grill (broil) for a further 3 minutes. Repeat this once more, then cook until the chicken meat is cooked through.

Remove from the heat and dip the skewers once more in the sauce mixture before serving.

*Serves 4*
Preparation and cooking time: 40 minutes
**Note :** Lamb or calf's liver and green pepper pieces can also be cooked in this way.

# Iri Dori

(Chicken Casserole)

*Any vegetables can be used in this dish – variations could include onions, cauliflower and brussels sprouts.*

| Metric/Imperial | American |
|---|---|
| 50ml./2fl.oz. vegetable oil | ¼ cup vegetable oil |
| 2 small chicken breasts, skinned, boned and cut into bite-sized pieces | 2 small chicken breasts, skinned, boned and cut into bite-sized pieces |
| 4 dried mushrooms, soaked in cold water for 30 minutes, drained, stalks removed and caps quartered | 4 dried mushrooms, soaked in cold water for 30 minutes, drained, stalks removed and caps quartered |
| 2 large carrots, diced | 2 large carrots, diced |
| 175g./6oz. tin bamboo shoot, drained and chopped | 6oz. can bamboo shoot, drained and chopped |
| 175ml./6fl.oz. dashi | ¾ cup dashi |
| 4 Tbs. mirin or sweet sherry | 4 Tbs. mirin or sweet sherry |
| 4 Tbs. sugar | 4 Tbs. sugar |
| 4 Tbs. soya sauce | 4 Tbs. soy sauce |
| 3 Tbs. green peas | 3 Tbs. green peas |

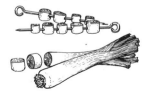

Heat the oil in a large, deep frying-pan. When it is hot, add the chicken pieces, mushrooms, carrots and bamboo shoot and fry, stirring occasionally, for 2 minutes. Add the dashi, mirin or sherry and sugar and cook for a further 10 minutes, stirring occasionally. Reduce the heat to low and stir in the soy sauce. Simmer the mixture until about three-quarters of the liquid has evaporated. Stir in the peas, then remove the pan from the heat.

Transfer the mixture to a warmed serving dish and serve at once.
*Serves 4*
Preparation and cooking time: 1 hour

# Chicken Stew

(Korea)

| Metric/Imperial | American |
|---|---|
| 1 x 2kg./4lb. chicken, cut into 8 serving pieces | 1 x 4lb. chicken, cut into 8 serving pieces |
| MARINADE | MARINADE |
| 4 Tbs. soya sauce | 4 Tbs. soy sauce |
| 125ml./4fl.oz. water | ½ cup water |
| ½ small onion, chopped | ½ small onion, chopped |
| 2 spring onions, chopped | 2 scallions, chopped |
| 1 carrot, chopped | 1 carrot, chopped |
| 1 Tbs. sugar | 1 Tbs. sugar |
| salt and pepper | salt and pepper |
| 5cm./2in. piece of fresh root ginger, peeled and chopped | 2in. piece of fresh green ginger, peeled and chopped |
| 2 garlic cloves, crushed | 2 garlic cloves, crushed |

Put all the marinade ingredients into a saucepan and bring to the boil. Reduce the heat to moderately low and add the chicken pieces, basting thoroughly. Cover the pan and cook the mixture for 30 minutes. Remove from the heat and set aside to cool to room temperature. When the mixture is cool, chill in the refrigerator overnight.

Remove from the refrigerator and set over high heat. Bring to the boil. Reduce the heat to low and simmer the mixture for 20 to 30 minutes, or until the chicken is cooked through and tender.

Serve at once.
*Serves 8*
Preparation and cooking time: 13 hours

# Tori no Sakamushi

(Sake-Steamed Chicken)

| Metric/Imperial | American |
|---|---|
| 4 chicken breasts, skinned, boned and cut into 2½cm./1in. slices | 4 chicken breasts, skinned, boned and cut into 1in. slices |
| 175ml./6fl.oz. sake or dry sherry | ¾ cup sake or dry sherry |
| 1 Tbs. sugar | 1 Tbs. sugar |
| 1 tsp. soya sauce | 1 tsp. soy sauce |
| ¼ tsp. monosodium glutamate (optional) | ¼ tsp. MSG (optional) |

Put the chicken meat slices into a shallow dish and pour over the sake or sherry. Set aside to marinate at room temperature for 1 hour, basting occasionally. Remove the chicken from the marinade and reserve the marinade. Pat the chicken dry with kitchen towels.

Arrange the chicken slices, in one layer, in the top part of a steamer, or on an ovenproof plate. Fill the base of the steamer (or a medium saucepan over which the plate will fit) about two-thirds full of boiling water and fit the top part over. Cover and steam the meat for 10 minutes. Remove the steamer from the heat and set aside.

Preheat the grill (broiler) to high.

Pour the reserved marinade into a small saucepan and stir in the sugar, soy sauce and monosodium glutamate. Bring to the boil, stirring constantly, then remove from the heat.

Arrange the chicken slices on the rack of the grill (broiler), brush with the marinade sauce and grill (broil) for 3 minutes on each side, basting occasionally with the sauce.

To serve, transfer the chicken slices to a warmed serving dish and pour over the remaining sauce.

*Serves 4*
Preparation and cooking time: 1½ hours.

*Tori No Sakamushi (Sake-Steamed Chicken) is first steamed then barbecued to crisp perfection. Serve as either a first course or hors d'oeuvre in the West, or as part of an Oriental meal.*

# FISH

# Shimesaba

(Marinated Mackerel)

| Metric/Imperial | American |
|---|---|
| 1 large fresh mackerel, cleaned, gutted and filleted | 1 large fresh mackerel, cleaned, gutted and filleted |
| 1 tsp. salt | 1 tsp. salt |
| 450ml./15fl.oz. white wine vinegar | 2 cups white wine vinegar |
| 4cm./1½in. piece of fresh root ginger, peeled and grated | 1½in. piece of fresh green ginger, peeled and grated |
| 4 spring onions, finely chopped | 4 scallions, finely chopped |
| 250ml./8fl.oz. soya sauce | 1 cup soy sauce |
| 2 tsp. green horseradish (wasabi), mixed to a paste with 2 tsp. water | 2 tsp. green horseradish (wasabi), mixed to a paste with 2 tsp. water |

Sprinkle the mackerel fillets liberally with salt and put into the refrigerator for 1 hour. Remove from the refrigerator and wash under cold running water. Arrange the fillets in a shallow dish and pour over the vinegar. Soak for 1 hour, turning at least once.

Remove the mackerel from the vinegar and pat dry on kitchen towels. Skin and remove any bones with your fingers. Cut across each fillet at about 2½cm./1in. intervals and arrange the pieces decoratively on a serving dish. Garnish with the grated ginger and spring onions (scallions).

Pour the soy sauce into individual dipping bowls and arrange the horseradish in individual small bowls. To make the dipping sauce, mix the horseradish and soy sauce together to taste and dip in the fish.

*Serves 4*
Preparation and cooking time: 2¼ hours

# Hizakana

(Fish Simmered in Soy Sauce)

*If you prefer, other fish such as mackerel, sole and sardine can be used instead of herrings in this dish.*

| Metric/Imperial | American |
|---|---|
| 4 herrings, gutted and cleaned | 4 herrings, gutted and cleaned |
| 4cm./1½in. piece of fresh root ginger, peeled and sliced | 1½in. piece of fresh green ginger, peeled and sliced |
| SAUCE | SAUCE |
| 250ml./8fl.oz. dashi | 1 cup dashi |
| 250ml./8fl.oz. soya sauce | 1 cup soy sauce |
| 250ml./8fl.oz. sake or dry sherry | 1 cup sake or dry sherry |
| 3 tsp. sugar | 3 tsp. sugar |
| monosodium glutamate (optional) | MAG (optional) |

Put the fish on a chopping board and make two or three cuts through the belly of each one, to allow the sauce to be absorbed while cooking. Set aside.

Put the dashi, soy sauce, sake or sherry, sugar and monosodium glutamate to taste in a saucepan large enough to accommodate the fish. Bring to the boil. Arrange the fish in the bottom of the pan and sprinkle over the ginger slices. Return the dashi mixture to the boil, reduce the heat to low and simmer for 5 minutes. Reduce the heat to very low and continue to simmer for a further 15 minutes.

Transfer the fish to a warmed deep serving dish and pour over some of the cooking liquid. Serve at once.

*Serves 4*

Preparation and cooking time: 30 minutes

# Sansuhn Jim

(Fish with Vegetables)                                                        (Korea)

| Metric/Imperial | American |
|---|---|
| 225g./8oz. braising beef, cut into<br>    thin strips | 8oz. chuck steak, cut into<br>    thin strips |
| 125g./4oz. button mushrooms, sliced | 1 cup sliced button mushrooms, |
| 3 celery stalks, chopped | 3 celery stalks, chopped |
| 1 small turnip or large Japanese<br>    radish, chopped | 1 small turnip or large Japanese<br>    radish, chopped |
| 2 carrots, sliced | 2 carrots, sliced |
| ½kg./1lb. fish fillets, cut into small<br>    bite-sized pieces | 1lb. fish fillets, cut into small<br>    bite-sized pieces |
| 4 spring onions, chopped | 4 scallions, chopped |
| 2 green chillis, finely chopped | 2 green chillis, finely chopped |
| 3 Tbs. soya sauce | 3 Tbs. soy sauce |
| MARINADE | MARINADE |
| 2 tsp. sugar | 2 tsp. sugar |
| 2 Tbs. soya sauce | 2 Tbs. soy sauce |
| 1 garlic clove, crushed | 1 garlic clove, crushed |
| 2 Tbs. sesame oil | 2 Tbs. sesame oil |
| 1 Tbs. roasted sesame seeds, ground | 1 Tbs. roasted sesame seeds, ground |

First, prepare the marinade. Combine all the ingredients in a shallow bowl, beating until they are thoroughly blended. Arrange the beef strips in the marinade, basting and turning to coat them. Set aside at room temperature for 20 minutes, basting and turning the strips from time to time.

Preheat the oven to moderate 180°C (Gas Mark 4, 350°F).

Arrange the beef mixture in the bottom of a medium-sized flameproof casserole. Cover with a layer of mushrooms, then celery, turnip or radish and sliced carrots. Arrange the fish pieces on top and scatter over about three-quarters of the spring onions (scallions) and chillis. Pour just enough water into the casserole to come about half-way up the mixture then add the soy sauce. Bring to the boil on top of the stove, then cover and put into the oven. Cook for 15 to 20 minutes, or until the fish flakes easily.

Remove from the oven and garnish with the remaining spring onions (scallions) and chillis before serving.

*Serves 4–6*

Preparation and cooking time: 1 hour

(See previous page) Yok Kai Chi Sake (Marinated Salmon) is raw, delicate salmon marinated to the succulence of rare beef in a mixture of soy sauce and sake.

# Yok Kai Sake

(Marinated Salmon)

| Metric/Imperial | American |
|---|---|
| ½kg./1lb. fresh salmon, thinly sliced then cut into strips | 1lb. fresh salmon, thinly sliced then cut into strips |
| 2½cm./1in. piece of fresh root ginger, peeled and chopped | 1in. piece of fresh green ginger, peeled and chopped |
| 1 garlic clove, crushed | 1 garlic clove, crushed |
| 2 spring onions, chopped | 2 scallions, chopped |
| 1 tsp. sugar | 1 tsp. sugar |
| 1 tsp. salt | 1 tsp. salt |
| 50ml./2fl.oz. soya sauce | ¼ cup soy sauce |
| 150ml./5fl.oz. sake or dry sherry | ⅔ cup sake or dry sherry |

Arrange the salmon strips in a large shallow serving dish. Combine all of the remaining ingredients in a mixing bowl, beating until they are well blended and the sugar has dissolved. Pour the mixture over the salmon strips and put the dish into the refrigerator for 1 hour.

Remove from the refrigerator and serve at once.

*Serves 4*

Preparation time: 1¼ hours

# Fish in Wine Sauce

| Metric/Imperial | American |
|---|---|
| 4 large herrings, cleaned, gutted and filleted | 4 large herrings, cleaned, gutted and filleted |
| 4 Tbs. sake or dry sherry | 4 Tbs. sake or dry sherry |
| 4 Tbs. mirin or sweet sherry | 4 Tbs. mirin or sweet sherry |
| 125ml./4fl.oz. soya sauce | ½ cup soy sauce |
| 2 Tbs. sugar | 2 Tbs. sugar |
| 1 tsp. black pepper | 1 tsp. black pepper |
| 1 Tbs. chopped parsley | 1 Tbs. chopped parsley |
| 1 tsp. chopped chives | 1 tsp. chopped chives |

Wipe the herrings with damp kitchen towels and place on a chopping board. Cut each one in two lengthways. Make three cuts on the skin side of each fish, taking care not to cut through the flesh completely. Set aside.

Put the sake or sherry and mirin or sherry into a small saucepan and bring to the boil. Remove from the heat and ignite carefully. Leave until the flames have died down, then stir in the soy sauce and sugar. Pour the mixture into a shallow mixing bowl.

Preheat the grill (broiler) to moderate.

Dip the herring into the sauce mixture, then arrange them on the rack of the grill (broiler). Grill (broil) for 5 minutes. Remove the fish from the heat and dip into the sauce again. Return to the heat, turn the fish and grill (broil) for a further 5 minutes.

Transfer the fish to a warmed serving dish and garnish with the pepper, parsley and chives. Pour the basting liquid into a warmed serving bowl and serve with the fish.

*Serves 4*

Preparation and cooking time: 40 minutes

# Misozuke

(Barbecued Mackerel with Miso)

*Although mackerel has been suggested as the fish in the recipe given below, any similar, rather oily fish could be substituted – herrings, fresh large sardines, or even red mullet. This dish can be served either as an hors d'oeuvre (in which case it will serve 8) or as a main course.*

| Metric/Imperial | American |
|---|---|
| 4 mackerel, cleaned, gutted and cut into 5cm./2in. pieces | 4 mackerel, cleaned, gutted and cut into 2in. pieces |
| MARINADE | MARINADE |
| 125g./4oz. miso paste | ½ cup miso paste |
| 50g./2oz. sugar | ¼ cup sugar |
| 2 Tbs. sake or dry sherry | 2 Tbs. sake or dry sherry |
| 2 Tbs. mirin or sweet sherry | 2 Tbs. mirin or sweet sherry |

First, make the marinade. Combine all the ingredients in a large shallow mixing bowl, beating until they are thoroughly blended. Arrange the fish pieces in the marinade, basting to coat them completely. Cover the dish and chill in the refrigerator for at least one day, turning the fish pieces from time to time. Remove the fish pieces from the marinade and pat dry with kitchen towels. Discard the marinade.

Preheat the grill (broiler) to moderate. Arrange the fish pieces on the rack of the grill (broiler) and grill (broil) for 5 minutes. Turn the fish over and grill (broil) for a further 5 to 8 minutes, or until the fish flesh flakes easily.

Transfer the fish pieces to a warmed serving dish and serve at once.
*Serves 4*
Preparation and cooking time: 24½ hours

# Sakana Shioyaki

(Fish Barbecued with Salt)

*This is another very simple yet very popular way of preparing fish in Japan, and is very healthy since the natural flavour of the fish is preserved. The salt is also said to break down the fats under the skin of the fish, and thereby moisten the flesh.*

| Metric/Imperial | American |
|---|---|
| 4 herrings, cleaned and gutted | 4 herrings, cleaned and gutted |
| 3 Tbs. salt | 3 Tbs. salt |

Wash the fish under cold running water, then pat dry with kitchen towels. Cover liberally with salt (use more than suggested if you wish) and set aside at room temperature for at least 30 minutes.

Preheat the grill (broiler) to moderate.

Wipe any excess liquid from the fish and sprinkle with a little more salt, rubbing it well into the tail to prevent burning. Grill (broil) the fish for 15 to 20 minutes, turning occasionally, or until the flesh flakes easily.

Serve at once, with rice, soup and some vegetable side dishes.
*Serves 4*
Preparation and cooking time: 50 minutes

# Washi no Su-Jyoyu Zuke

(Barbecued Sardines)

| Metric/Imperial | American |
| --- | --- |
| 150ml./5fl.oz. soya sauce | $\frac{2}{3}$ cup soy sauce |
| 50ml./2fl.oz. vinegar | $\frac{1}{4}$ cup vinegar |
| 2 Tbs. lemon juice | 2 Tbs. lemon juice |
| 2½cm./1in. piece of fresh root ginger, peeled and chopped | 1in. piece of fresh green ginger, peeled and chopped |
| 2 garlic cloves, crushed | 2 garlic cloves, crushed |
| ½kg./1lb. fresh sardines, cleaned and gutted | 1lb. fresh sardines, cleaned and gutted |
| 2 Tbs. vegetable oil | 2 Tbs. vegetable oil |

Combine the soy sauce, vinegar, lemon juice, ginger and garlic in a small bowl. Arrange the sardines in a large shallow dish and pour over the soy sauce mixture, basting to coat the fish thoroughly. Set aside at room temperature to marinate for 2 hours, basting the fish occasionally.

Preheat the grill (broiler) to high.

Remove the sardines from the marinade and dry them on kichen towels. Discard the marinade. Reduce the grill (broiler) to moderate.

Arrange the sardines on the rack of the grill (broiler) and brush the fish with half the oil. Grill (broil) for 4 minutes, then brush again with the remaining oil. Grill (broil) the other side for 3 minutes, or until the flesh flakes easily.

Remove from the heat and serve at once.

Serves 4

Preparation and cooking time: 2¼ hours

*Washi No Su-Jyoyu Zuke is a delicious dish of sardines marinated first in a mixture of soy sauce, vinegar, lemon juice and ginger, then barbecued.*

# Ika no Tsukeyaki

(Gilled [Broiled] Squid)

| Metric/Imperial | American |
|---|---|
| 4 medium squid, cleaned, spinal bone removed | 4 medium squid, cleaned, spinal bone removed |
| 4 Tbs. grated radish | 4 Tbs. grated radish |
| MARINADE | MARINADE |
| 150ml./5fl.oz. soya sauce | ⅔ cup soy sauce |
| 150ml./5fl.oz. sake or dry sherry | ⅔ cup sake or dry sherry |
| 2 Tbs. sugar | 2 Tbs. sugar |

Remove the tentacles from the squid, then rub away the outer skin. Set side.

Put the soy sauce, sake or sherry and sugar into a small saucepan and bring to the boil. Remove the pan from the heat and pour the mixture into a large shallow dish. Arrange the squid in the dish and set aside at room temperature to marinate for 15 minutes.

Preheat the grill (broiler) to moderate.

Remove the squid from the marinade and pat dry with kitchen towels. Reserve the marinade. Score the surface of the fish and arrange them on the rack of the grill (broiler). Grill (broil) for 8 minutes on each side, basting occasionally with the marinating liquid.

Remove the squid to a chopping board and cut into strips about 2½cm./1in. wide. Arrange decoratively on a serving platter and pour over the remaining marinade. Garnish with grated radish and serve at once.

*Serves 4*
Preparation and cooking time: 30 minutes

# Tarako to Tasai no Niawase

(Cod's Roes and Vegetables Cooked in Soy Sauce)

| Metric/Imperial | American |
|---|---|
| 3 Tbs. vegetable oil | 3 Tbs. vegetable oil |
| 1 large carrot, cut into matchstick strips | 1 large carrot, cut into matchstick strips |
| 50g./2oz. tin shirataki noodles, soaked in hot water for 3 minutes and cut into matchstick strips | 2oz. can shirataki noodles, soaked in hot water for 3 minutes and cut into matchstick strips |
| 1 Tbs. sake or dry sherry | 1 Tbs. sake or dry sherry |
| monosodium glutamate (optional) | MSG (optional) |
| 2 fresh cod's roes, skinned | 2 fresh cod's roes, skinned |
| 250ml./8fl.oz. dashi | 1 cup dashi |
| 2 Tbs. soya sauce | 2 Tbs. soy sauce |
| 1 Tbs. mirin or sweet sherry | 1 Tbs. mirin or sweet sherry |
| 1 leek, cleaned and finely chopped | 1 leek, cleaned and finely chopped |

Heat the oil in a deep frying-pan. When it is hot, add the carrot, shirataki, sake or sherry and monosodium glutamate to taste. Cook, stirring occasionally, for 5 minutes. Add the cod's roes, dashi, soy sauce and mirin and continue to cook until the roes turn white. Stir in the leek and cook for a further 2 minutes.

Transfer the mixture to a warmed serving bowl and serve.

*Serves 4-6*
Preparation and cooking time: 30 minutes

# Sashimi

(Sliced Raw Fish)

*Sashimi is one of the finest and simplest of Japanese fish dishes. Almost any type of fish can be used – dover sole, lemon sole, tuna, squid, abalone, bream or any type of shellfish – but it must be of the very highest quality and be as fresh as possible. To preserve freshness, it is better to buy a whole fish and have the fish merchant clean and fillet it for you, rather than purchase pre-filleted fish.*

| Metric/Imperial | American |
|---|---|
| ½kg./1lb. firm fresh fish (as above) | 1lb. firm fresh fish (as above) |
| 1 Tbs. salt | 1 Tbs. salt |
| SAUCE | SAUCE |
| 2 tsp. green horseradish (wasabi), mixed to a paste with 2 tsp. water | 2 tsp. green horseradish (wasabi), mixed to a paste with 2 tsp. water |
| 125ml./4fl.oz. soya sauce | ½ cup soy sauce |

*Sashimi (Sliced Raw Fish) – the dish that foreigners (rightly) think of as epitomizing Japanese cuisine. Here the fish is as fresh from the sea as possible, and served with a slightly piquant sauce made from horseradish and soy sauce.*

Wash the fillets and sprinkle them lightly with salt. Cover and put into the refrigerator for 30 minutes. (Some people prefer to douse the fish in boiling water, then refresh in cold running water before putting into the refrigerator, to provide protection against surface bacteria.)

Remove the fish from the refrigerator and cut crosswise into bite-sized pieces. Arrange the pieces either on one large serving dish or on individual dishes.

To make the sauce, mix the horseradish into the soy sauce, then pour the mixture into individual dipping bowls. The fish should be dipped in the sauce before eating.

*Serves 2-4*
Preparation time: 40 minutes

# Sushi

(Marinated Fish)

| Metric/Imperial | American |
|---|---|
| ½kg./1lb. mackerel fillets, skinned | 1lb. mackerel fillets, skinned |
| GARNISH | GARNISH |
| 125g./4oz. radish, grated | ⅔ cup grated radish |
| 1 red pepper, pith and seeds removed and chopped | 1 red pepper, pith and seeds removed and chopped |
| 2 Tbs. soya sauce mixed with 2 tsp. lemon juice | 2 Tbs. soy sauce mixed with 2 tsp. lemon juice |
| SAUCE | SAUCE |
| 2 tsp. green horseradish (wasabi), mixed to a paste with 2 tsp. water | 2 tsp. green horseradish (washabi), mixed to a paste with 2 tsp. water |
| 50ml./2fl.oz. soya sauce mixed with 2 Tbs. sake or dry sherry | ¼ cup soy sauce mixed with 2 Tbs. sake or dry sherry |

Put the mackerel fillets in a colander and pour over boiling water. Refresh the fish under cold running-water, then transfer them to a chopping board. Cut the fillets, crosswise, into very thin strips. Arrange the strips on a plate, cover with foil and chill in the refrigerator while you arrange the garnish.

Put the vegetables in a small serving bowl and pour over the soy sauce mixture. Toss gently so that all the vegetable pieces are coated.

Remove the fish from the refrigerator and divide it among six individual serving bowls. Arrange a portion of the garnish beside each bowl.

To make the sauce, stir the horseradish mixture into the soy sauce mixture and pour into individual dipping bowls.

Dip the fish into the sauce mixture before eating and eat at once, with the garnish.

*Serves 6*
Preparation time: 30 minutes


# Kamaboko

(Small Fish Cakes)

*Kamaboko are very popular in Japan as an hors d'oeuvre, but they can also form part of some one-pot meals as well. A canned version is widely used now, but as always, home-made varieties tend to have a much better taste and texture. Almost any type of firm white fish fillet could be used – or a mixture; this is an excellent way to use leftover fillet pieces. They can also be steamed for a more delicate taste.*

| Metric/Imperial | American |
|---|---|
| ½kg./1lb. white fish fillets, skinned and chopped | 1lb. white fish fillets, skinned and chopped |
| 3 Tbs. flour | 3 Tbs. flour |
| 2 egg whites, beaten until frothy | 2 egg whites, beaten until frothy |
| 1 Tbs. mirin or sweet sherry | 1 Tbs. mirin or sweet sherry |
| 1 tsp. sugar | 1 tsp. sugar |
| ½ tsp. monosodium glutamate | ½ tsp. MSG |
| 50g./2oz. cornflour | ½ cup cornstarch |
| 75ml./3fl.oz. vegetable oil | ⅓ cup vegetable oil |

Put the fish pieces into a blender and blend until they form a fairly smooth purée. Transfer the purée to a mixing bowl and stir in the flour, egg whites, mirin or sherry, sugar and monosodium glutamate. Beat briskly until the mixture is thoroughly blended.

Take about 2 tablespoonfuls of the mixture and shape it into a small cake or patty shape with your hands. Dust it lightly with the cornflour (cornstarch) and set aside. Repeat the process until all of the mixture is used up.

Heat the oil in a large frying-pan. When it is hot, add the fish cakes (in batches if necessary) and fry gently for 5 minutes on each side, or until they are golden brown and crisp, and cooked through.

Remove from the pan and drain on kitchen towels. Serve hot.

*Serves 4-6 as an hors d'oeuvre*
Preparation and cooking time: 30 minutes

# Shrimps with Bamboo Shoot

| Metric/Imperial | American |
| --- | --- |
| 50ml./2fl.oz. water | ¼ cup water |
| 50ml./2fl.oz. soya sauce | ¼ cup soy sauce |
| 350g./12oz. shelled prawns | 12oz. shelled shrimp |
| 400g./14oz. tin bamboo shoot, drained and sliced | 14oz. can bamboo shoot, drained and sliced |
| 2 Tbs. sake or dry sherry | 2 Tbs. sake or dry sherry |
| 2 Tbs. mirin or sweet sherry | 2 Tbs. mirin or sweet sherry |

Put the water and soy sauce into a shallow saucepan and bring to the boil. Reduce the heat to moderate and stir in the prawns (shrimp). Cook for 5 minutes. Using a slotted spoon, transfer the prawns (shrimp) to a warmed bowl and keep hot.

Add the bamboo shoot slices to the pan and return to the boil. Stir in the sake or sherry and mirin or sherry and cook for 3 minutes. Return the prawns (shrimp) to the pan and stir until the mixture is blended. Cook for 1 minute.

Transfer the mixture to a warmed serving dish and serve at once.

*Serves 4*
Preparation and cooking time: 15 minutes

# Iri-Tamago

(Eggs with Shrimp and Peas)

| Metric/Imperial | American |
| --- | --- |
| 4 eggs, lightly beaten | 4 eggs, lightly beaten |
| 50ml./2fl.oz. dashi | ¼ cup dashi |
| 1 tsp. sugar | 1 tsp. sugar |
| 2 tsp. soya sauce | 2 tsp. soy sauce |
| 2 tsp. sake or dry sherry | 2 tsp. sake or dry sherry |
| monosodium glutamate (optional) | MSG (optional) |
| 3 Tbs. vegetable oil | 3 Tbs. vegetable oil |
| 125g./4oz. frozen shelled shrimps | 4 oz. frozen shelled shrimp |
| 225g./8oz. frozen green peas | 1 cup frozen green peas |
| 3 dried mushrooms, soaked in cold water for 30 minutes, drained and sliced | 3 dried mushrooms, soaked in cold water for 30 minutes, drained and sliced |

Beat the eggs, dashi, sugar, soy sauce, sake or sherry and monosodium glutamate to taste together until they are thoroughly blended. Set aside.

Heat the oil in a large frying-pan. When it is hot, add the shrimps, peas and mushrooms and stir-fry for 3 to 4 minutes, or until the shrimps and peas are cooked through. Stir in the eggs and reduce the heat to moderately low. Cook the mixture, stirring the eggs from time to time to 'scramble' them, until the egg mixture has just lightly set.

Transfer the mixture to a warmed serving plate and serve at once.

*Serves 2-3*
Preparation and cooking time: 40 minutes

# Mazezushi

(Vegetables and Seafood with Rice)

| Metric/Imperial | American |
|---|---|
| 450g./1lb. short-grain rice | 2⅔ cups short-grain rice |
| 600ml./1 pint water | 2½ cups water |
| VINEGAR SAUCE | VINEGAR SAUCE |
| 50ml./2fl.oz. white wine vinegar | ¼ cup white wine vinegar |
| 1 Tbs. sugar | 1 Tbs. sugar |
| ½ tsp. salt | ½ tsp. salt |
| monosodium glutamate (optional) | MSG (optional) |
| VEGETABLES | VEGETABLES |
| 2 carrots, thinly sliced | 2 carrots, thinly sliced |
| 1 tinned bamboo shoot, drained and thinly sliced | 1 canned bamboo shoot, drained and thinly sliced |
| ¼ small turnip, thinly sliced | ¼ small turnip, thinly sliced |
| 3 Tbs. frozen green peas | 3 Tbs. frozen green peas |
| 175ml./6fl.oz. dashi | ¾ cup dashi |
| 1 Tbs. sake or dry sherry | 1 Tbs. sake or dry sherry |
| 1 Tbs. sugar | 1 Tbs. sugar |
| 1 Tbs. vegetable oil | 1 Tbs. vegetable oil |
| 4 dried mushrooms, soaked in cold water for 30 minutes, drained and sliced | 4 dried mushrooms, soaked in cold water for 30 minutes, drained and sliced |
| 2 Tbs. soya sauce | 2 Tbs. soy sauce |
| OMELET | OMELET |
| 1 Tbs. vegetable oil | 1 Tbs. vegetable oil |
| 3 eggs, lightly beaten | 3 eggs, lightly beaten |
| SEAFOOD | SEAFOOD |
| 125g./4oz. cooked prawns | 4oz. cooked shrimp |
| 125g./4oz. crabmeat, shell and cartilage removed and flaked | 4oz. crabmeat, shell and cartilage removed and flaked |

First make the rice. Cook the rice, following the instructions given in *Gohan*. Transfer the drained rice to a warmed bowl and set aside. To make the vinegar sauce, combine the vinegar, sugar, salt and monosodium glutamate to taste, then pour the mixture over the rice. Stir gently with a wooden spoon and set aside to cool at room temperature.

Meanwhile, prepare the vegetables. Put the carrots, bamboo shoot, turnip and peas into a saucepan and pour over enough water to cover. Bring to the boil and blanch briskly for 2 minutes. Drain the vegetables. Put 125m./4fl. oz. (½ cup) of dashi, the sake or dry sherry and half the sugar in a small saucepan and bring to the boil. Add the drained vegetables and cook for a further 2 minutes. Transfer the vegetables to a bowl and drain and reserve the dashi liquid.

Heat the oil in a small frying-pan. When it is hot, add the mushrooms, the remaining dashi and sugar, and the soy sauce. Cook, stirring constantly, for 3 minutes. Remove from the heat and cool.

To make the omelets, brush the bottom of an omelet pan with some of the oil and pour in about a third of the egg mixture. Tilt the pan so that the mixture covers the bottom of the pan, then leave to cook until the omelet has set. Shake the pan slightly to loosen the omelet, then quickly turn over and cook the other side for 15 seconds. Slide on to a plate and cook the remaining egg mixture in the same way. When all the omelets have been cooked, pile them on top of one another and cut into thin strips.

To assemble, stir the vegetables and reserved cooking liquid gently into the vinegared rice with a wooden spoon. Then stir in the prawns (shrimp) and crabmeat. Arrange the egg strips decoratively over the top and serve at once.
*Serves 6*
Preparation and cooking time: 2 hours

# Hamaguri Shigure-Ni

(Sake and Soy Sauce-Flavoured Clams)

| Metric/Imperial | American |
| --- | --- |
| 50ml./2fl.oz. sake or dry sherry | ¼ cup sake or dry sherry |
| 2 Tbs. sugar | 2 Tbs. sugar |
| 12 clams, removed from their shells | 12 clams, removed from their shells |
| 2 Tbs. soya sauce | 2 Tbs. soy sauce |

In a large, heavy frying-pan combine the sake or sherry, sugar and clams. Stir the mixture thoroughly with a wooden spoon. Bring to the boil and cook for 3 minutes, stirring constantly. Stir in the soy sauce and boil for a further 1 minute, stirring constantly. Using a slotted spoon, transfer the clams to a plate.

Boil the sauce for a further 10 minutes, or until it becomes thick and rather syrupy. Return the clams to the pan and stir them gently into the sauce. Cook the mixture for about 1 minute, or until the clams are thoroughly coated with the sauce.

Remove from the heat and spoon the mixture into a warmed serving dish. Serve at once.
*Serves 4*
Preparation and cooking time: 30 minutes

# Kimini

(Glazed Prawns or Shrimp)

| Metric/Imperial | American |
| --- | --- |
| 12 medium prawns | 12 medium shrimp |
| 50g./2oz. cornflour | ½ cup cornstarch |
| 3½ Tbs. dashi | 3½ Tbs. dashi |
| 2 Tbs. sake or dry sherry | 2 Tbs. sake or dry sherry |
| ½ tsp. sugar | ½ tsp. sugar |
| ¼ tsp. salt | ¼ tsp. salt |
| monosodium glutamate (optional) | MSG (optional) |
| 3 egg yolks, well beaten | 3 egg yolks, well beaten |

Shell the prawns (shrimp), leaving the tails intact. Remove the veins at the head with the tip of a knife, then dip the prawns (shrimp) into the cornflour (cornstarch), shaking off any excess. Drop the prawns (shrimp) into a saucepan of boiling water and cook for about 10 seconds. Remove and rinse under cold running water. Set aside.

Pour the dashi into a small saucepan and stir in the sake or sherry, sugar, salt and monosodium glutamate to taste. Bring to the boil. Arrange the prawns (shrimp) in the pan and return the liquid to the boil, basting the prawns (shrimp). When the liquid boils, pour the beaten egg yolks slowly over the prawns (shrimp). Do not stir, cover the pan and simmer over low heat for 2 minutes. Remove from the heat but leave for a further 2 minutes before serving as a side dish, or as a main dish with vegetables.

*Serves 2-4*
Preparation and cooking time: 20 minutes

*Clams are a popular ingredient in many Japanese dishes. In Hamaguri Shigure-Ni they are cooked in a very special mixture of sake and soy sauce.*

# Kani no Sunomono

(Crab and Cucumber with Vinegar Dressing)

| Metric/Imperial | American |
| --- | --- |
| ½ cucumber | ½ cucumber |
| 225g./8oz. crabmeat, shell and cartilage removed and flaked | 8oz. crabmeat, shell and cartilage removed and flaked |
| VINEGAR DRESSING | VINEGAR DRESSING |
| 2 Tbs. white wine vinegar | 2 Tbs. white wine vinegar |
| 2 Tbs. mirin or sweet sherry | 2 Tbs. mirin or sweet sherry |
| 2 Tbs. dashi | 2 Tbs. dashi |
| 1 Tbs. soya sauce | 1 Tbs. soy sauce |
| 2 tsp. sugar | 2 tsp. sugar |
| monosodium glutamate (optional) | MSG (optional) |

Partially peel the cucumber, leaving some long green strips for colour. Slice as thinly as possible, sprinkle with salt and leave to dégorge in a colander for about 30 minutes. Squeeze out any excess liquid gently with your hands, then dry on kitchen towels. Arrange the cucumber and crabmeat decoratively in a small shallow dish.

To make the vinegar dressing, combine all the ingredients, beating until they are well blended. Pour over the cucumber and crabmeat and toss gently so that they are well coated. Set the dish aside at room temperature to marinate for 30 minutes, tossing gently from time to time. Carefully drain off any excess dressing before serving.

Sunamon ('vinegared things') can accompany main dishes or be served as an hors d'oeuvre.

*Serves 2*
Preparation time: 1¼ hours

# Hamaguri Sakani

(Sake-Flavoured Clams)

| Metric/Imperial | American |
|---|---|
| 50ml./2fl.oz. sake or dry sherry | ¼ cup sake or dry sherry |
| 12 clams, removed from the shells, half the shells scrubbed and reserved | 12 clams, removed from the shells, half the shells scrubbed and reserved |
| GARNISH | GARNISH |
| 12 lemon slices | 12 lemon slices |

Put the sake into a large saucepan and bring to the boil. Add the clams, stirring with a wooden spoon. Cover the pan and reduce the heat to low. Simmer for 5 minutes. Using a slotted spoon, remove the clams and arrange one on each of the reserved shells. Garnish each shell with a lemon slice.

Put the clams on a serving dish and allow them to cool to room temperature.

Chill in the refrigerator for 30 minutes. Remove from the refrigerator and serve as an hors d'oeuvre.

*Serves 4*
Preparation and cooking time: 50 minutes

# Torigai to Wakame no Nuta

(Cockles and Seaweed with Miso)

| Metric/Imperial | American |
|---|---|
| 1 Tbs. wakame or dried seaweed, soaked in water until soft | 1 Tbs. wakame or dried seaweed, soaked in water until soft |
| 8 spring onions, chopped and parboiled | 8 scallions, chopped and parboiled |

| | |
|---|---|
| 225g./8oz. cockles, washed | 8oz. cockles, washed |
| 1 celery stalk, chopped | 1 celery stalk, chopped |
| MISO SAUCE | MISO SAUCE |
| 2½ Tbs. white wine vinegar | 2½ Tbs. white wine vinegar |
| 2½ Tbs. sake or dry sherry | 2½ Tbs. sake or dry sherry |
| 2½ Tbs. sugar | 2½ Tbs. sugar |
| 5 Tbs. miso paste | 5 Tbs. miso paste |

Put the vinegar, sake and sugar into a saucepan and bring to the boil. Remove from the heat and stir in the miso paste until it melts. Pour into individual dipping bowls and set aside.

Chop the wakame into short lengths, then arrange all the remaining ingredients on one large serving platter or individual serving plates. The sauce can either be served separately or, alternatively, it can be mixed into the ingredients and tossed gently before serving.

This dish is usually served as a starter or a side dish.

*Serves 3-4*
Preparation and cooking time: 15 minutes

# Prawns in Batter

(Korea)

| Metric/Imperial | American |
|---|---|
| ½kg./1lb. prawns | 1lb. shrimp |
| vegetable oil for deep-frying | vegetable oil for deep-frying |
| BATTER | BATTER |
| 50g./2oz. rice flour | ½ cup rice flour |
| salt | salt |
| monosodium glutamate (optional) | MSG (optional) |
| 1 egg, lightly beaten | 1 egg, lightly beaten |
| 125ml./4fl.oz. water | ½ cup water |
| DIPPING SAUCE | DIPPING SAUCE |
| 250ml./8fl.oz. soya sauce | 1 cup soy sauce |
| 3 spring onions, chopped | 3 scallions, chopped |

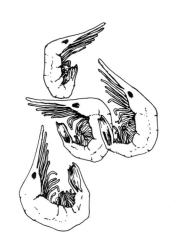

Remove the shells from the prawns (shrimp), leaving the tails intact. Remove the heads and any tentacles.

To make the batter, beat all of the ingredients together in a shallow bowl with a whisk or wooden spoon until they are thoroughly blended.

Set the bowl aside.

Fill a large deep-frying pan one-third full with oil and heat it until it is hot. Dip the prawns (shrimp) first in the batter, coating thoroughly but shaking off any excess, then carefully lower them into the oil, a few at a time. Deep-fry for 2 to 3 minutes, or until the prawns (shrimp) are golden brown. Remove from the oil and drain on kitchen towels. Keep hot while you cook the remaining prawns (shrimp) in the same way.

To make the dipping sauce, combine the soy sauce and spring onions (scallions) and pour into small, individual bowls.

Serve at once, with the prawns (shrimp).

*Serves 4*
Preparation and cooking time: 25 minutes

# ONE-POT

# Shin-Sol-Lo

(Korean Steamboat)

*This exotic soup-like mixture is the 'royal' dish of Korea and, to be absolutely authentic, should be cooked in a special shin-sol-lo cooker as suggested below. They can be obtained from Chinese or other large Oriental stores. If you don't have one, however, a fondue pot or flameproof casserole makes a perfectly adequate substitute. In the latter case, just put all the ingredients into the pot together and bring to the boil before serving. Any vegetable of your choice can be substituted for those suggested below.*

| Metric/Imperial | American |
|---|---|
| FISH | FISH |
| 225g./8oz. firm white fish fillet, skinned and cut into large bite-sized pieces | 8oz. firm white fish fillet, skinned and cut into large bite-sized pieces |
| 50g./2oz. cornflour, mixed to a paste with 125ml./4fl.oz. water | ½ cup cornstarch, mixed to a paste with ½ cup water |
| 4 Tbs. peanut oil | 4 Tbs. peanut oil |
| VEGETABLES | VEGETABLES |
| ¼ small Chinese cabbage, shredded | ¼ small Chinese cabbage, shredded |
| 225g./8oz. leaf spinach, chopped | 1⅓ cups chopped leaf spinach |
| 3 carrots, chopped or sliced | 3 carrots, chopped or sliced |
| salt | salt |
| SHIN-SOL-LO | SHIN-SOL-LO |
| 225g./8oz. cooked meat, such as ox tongue, cut into strips | 8oz. cooked meat, such as ox tongue, cut into strips |
| 1 large red pepper, pith and seeds removed and sliced | 1 large red pepper, pith and seeds removed and sliced |
| 4 large button mushrooms, sliced | 4 large button mushrooms, sliced |
| 2 spring onions, chopped | 2 scallions, chopped |
| 125g./4oz. Chinese fish cake, sliced (optional) | 4oz. Chinese fish cake, sliced (optional) |
| 125g./4oz. frozen peeled prawns | 4oz. frozen peeled shrimp |
| 1.2 l./2 pints boiling beef stock | 5 cups boiling beef stock |
| salt and black pepper | salt and black pepper |

First prepare the fish. Dip the fish pieces in the cornflour (cornstarch) batter and set aside for 5 minutes. Heat the oil in a large frying-pan. When it is hot, add the fish pieces and fry gently for 5 minutes on each side, or until the flesh just flakes. Remove the fish from the heat and drain on kitchen towels. Transfer the pieces to a plate.

Cook the cabbage, spinach and carrots separately in boiling salted water until they are just cooked but still crisp. Remove from the heat, drain and add to the fish pieces.

To prepare the shin-sol-lo, prepare the charcoal so that it is burning. Arrange the fish pieces, vegetables pieces, then meat, red pepper and mushroom slices around the sides of the pot. Scatter over the spring onions (scallions), fish cake and prawns (shrimp), then pour over the stock and season with salt and pepper to taste.

Put the embers from the charcoal into the centre of the pot, then cover with new charcoal, fanning the embers so that the new charcoal will ignite. Cover the pot and steam the shin-sol-lo for 3 to 5 minutes, or until the stock returns to the boil.

Traditionally, the pot is then brought to the table (with the embers still lit) and diners help themselves. Rice is usually served as an accompaniment, in the same bowl as the shin-sol-lo.

*Serves 6–8*
Preparation and cooking time: 45 minutes

# Sukiyaki I

(Quick-Braised Beef and Vegetables)

*Sukiyaki is one of the most popular one-pot dishes in Japan – and is probably the most famous Japanese dish outside the country. To eat it Japanese style, the ingredients for the dish should be arranged decoratively on a serving platter then cooked at the table, fondue-style, with each diner selecting his own food. The cooked food should be dipped in the lightly beaten egg before being eaten.*

| Metric/Imperial | American |
|---|---|
| 1kg./2lb. fillet steak, cut across the grain into thin slices or strips | 2lb. fillet steak, cut across the grain into thin slices or strips |
| 225g./8oz. tin shirataki noodles | 8oz. can shirataki noodles |
| 225g./8oz. small spinach leaves | 2 cups small spinach leaves |
| 450g./1lb. mushrooms, stalks removed and caps halved | 1lb. mushrooms, stalks removed and caps halved |
| 1 large carrot, cut into strips | 1 large carrot, cut into strips |
| 12 spring onions, sliced | 12 scallions, sliced |
| 200g./7oz. tin bamboo shoot, drained and sliced | 7oz. can bamboo shoot, drained and sliced |
| 1 bean curd cake (tofu), cubed | 1 bean curd cake (tofu), cubed |
| 250ml./8fl.oz. dashi | 1 cup dashi |
| 125ml./4fl.oz. sake or dry sherry | ½ cup sake or dry sherry |
| 6 eggs | 6 eggs |
| 2 Tbs. beef suet or lard | 2 Tbs. beef suet or lard |
| 175ml./6fl.oz. soya sauce | ¾ cup soy sauce |
| 2 Tbs. soft brown sugar | 2 Tbs. soft brown sugar |

Arrange the steak pieces, shirataki noodles, spinach leaves, mushrooms, carrot, spring onions (scallions), bamboo shoot and bean curd cubes decoratively on a large serving platter. Set aside. Mix the dashi and sake together until they are well combined. Set aside. Break the eggs into individual serving bowls and beat lightly. Set aside.

Heat a heavy, flameproof casserole over low heat until it is hot. Spear the suet on a fork and rub gently over the bottom of the casserole, or allow the lard to melt. Discard the suet. Put about a sixth of the meat and vegetables into the casserole, adding about a sixth of the dashi mixture, a sixth of the soy sauce and a sixth of the sugar. Cook for 5 to 6 minutes, stirring and turning frequently, until all the ingredients are tender but still crisp. Using a slotted spoon, transfer the mixture to individual serving plates and serve with the beaten egg. Cook the remaining ingredients in the same way. The liquid should always be simmering. If the food begins to stick in the casserole, add 1 teaspoon of cold water to cool it or to reduce the heat to moderately low. The sauce becomes stronger as more liquid and sugar are added at each cooking stage so it may be necessary to reduce these amounts to your taste.

*Serves 6*
Preparation and cooking time: 45 minutes

*(See over) Sukiyaki is what everyone thinks of when they think of Japanese food, and you can see why when you taste this version (Sukiyaki I). It is also one of the most hospitable of dishes – who can stand on ceremony when faced with a communal pot full of rich, cooking food?*

# Sukiyaki II

(Marinated Braised Beef and Vegetables)

| Metric/Imperial | American |
|---|---|
| 1kg./2lb. fillet steak, cut into thin strips | 2lb. fillet steak, cut into thin strips |
| 300ml./10fl.oz. sake or dry sherry | 1¼ cups sake or dry sherry |
| 4 Tbs. soya sauce | 4 Tbs. soy sauce |
| salt and pepper | salt and pepper |
| 8 spring onions, cut into 2½cm./1in. lengths | 8 scallions, cut into 1in. lengths |
| 12 button mushrooms, stalks removed | 12 button mushrooms, stalks removed |
| 2 large green peppers, pith and seeds removed and cut into strips | 2 large green peppers, pith and seeds removed and cut into strips |
| 225g./8oz. small spinach leaves | 1 cup small spinach leaves |
| vegetable oil for deep-frying | vegetable oil for deep-frying |
| SAUCE | SAUCE |
| 1 eating apple, cored and grated | 1 eating apple, cored and grated |
| 1 large leek, cleaned and chopped | 1 large leek, cleaned and chopped |
| 2 garlic cloves, crushed | 2 garlic cloves, crushed |
| ¼ tsp. cayenne pepper | ¼ tsp. cayenne pepper |
| 1 small red pepper, pith and seeds removed and finely chopped | 1 small red pepper, pith and seeds removed and finely chopped |

Put the beef strips into a large shallow dish and pour over the sake or sherry and soy sauce. Sprinkle over salt and pepper to taste. Set aside at room temperature to marinate for at least 4 hours, turning the meat occasionally. Using a slotted spoon, transfer the meat strips to a plate and reserve the marinade.

Arrange the spring onions (scallions), mushrooms, peppers, and spinach decoratively on a serving platter. Set aside.

Pour the reserved marinade into a serving bowl and stir in the grated apple, leek, garlic, cayenne and red pepper.

Fill a large deep-frying pan one-third full with oil and heat it until it is very hot. Either transfer the oil carefully to a fondue pot or Japanese cooking pot or continue cooking in the saucepan. Carefully lower a few pieces of meat and vegetables into the oil and cook for 1 to 2 minutes, or until they are just crisp. Remove from the oil and drain on kitchen towels. Keep hot while you cook the remaining ingredients in the same way.

The cooked food should be dipped into the sauce before eating.

*Serves 6*
Preparation and cooking time: 4½ hours

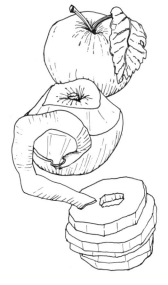

# Chiri Nabe

(Fish and Vegetable Casserole)

| Metric/Imperial | American |
|---|---|
| 1 small Chinese cabbage, trimmed | 1 small Chinese cabbage, trimmed |
| 1 large bream or similar fish, cleaned, gutted and filleted | 1 large bream, or similar fish, cleaned, gutted and filleted |
| 3 leeks, cleaned and cut into 1cm./½in. lengths | 3 leeks, cleaned and cut into ½in. lengths |
| 3 bean curd cakes (tofu), cubed | 3 bean curd cakes (tofu), cubed |

| | |
|---|---|
| 1.21/2 pints dashi | 5 cups dashi |
| 150ml./5fl.oz. soya sauce | ⅔ cup soy sauce |
| 6 spring onions, chopped | 6 scallions, chopped |
| 1 small turnip, grated | 1 small turnip, grated |
| juice of two lemons | juice of two lemons |

Cook the cabbage in boiling water for 5 minutes. Drain, then chop diagonally into 5cm./2in. lengths. Cut the fish into large pieces and arrange the fish, cabbage, leeks and bean curd on a large serving platter.

Pour the dashi into a flameproof casserole or fondue pot and bring to the boil. Add the ingredients to the dashi, a few at a time, and cook for 3 to 5 minutes, or until they are cooked through.

Mix the soy sauce, spring onions (scallions), turnip and lemon juice together and divide among individual dipping bowls. The cooked food should be dipped in the sauce before eating.

*Serves 4-6*
Preparation and cooking time: 45 minutes

# Botan Nabe

(Pork and Vegetables in Stock)

*The name for this dish comes from the Japanese word for peony because the pork pieces are arranged in the shape of this flower before cooking.*

| Metric/Imperial | American |
|---|---|
| ½kg./1lb. carrots, cut into ½cm./¼in. lengths | 1lb. carrots, cut into ¼in. lengths |
| 1 medium white cabbage, separated into leaves | 1 medium white cabbage, separated into leaves |
| 225g./8oz. mushrooms | 2 cups mushrooms |
| 700g./1½lb. lean pork, very thinly sliced | 1½lb. lean pork, very thinly sliced |
| 3 garlic cloves, crushed | 3 garlic cloves, crushed |
| 4cm./1½in. piece of fresh root ginger, peeled and chopped | 1½in. piece of fresh green ginger, peeled and chopped |
| 250ml./8fl.oz. soya sauce | 1 cup soy sauce |
| 6 spring onions, finely chopped | 6 scallions, finely chopped |
| 2 lemons, cut into small wedges | 2 lemons, cut into small wedges |
| 450ml./15fl.oz. dashi | 2 cups dashi |

Lightly cook the carrots and cabbage separately in boiling water for 3 minutes. Drain and roll up the cabbage leaves into rolls. Arrange the carrots, cabbage rolls and mushrooms decoratively on a serving platter.

Arrange the pork slices carefully in the shape of a flower on a serving plate and garnish with the garlic and ginger to make the centre of the flower.

Combine the soy sauce with about a quarter of the spring onions (scallions) and pour into individual dipping bowls. Arrange the lemon wedges and remaining spring onions (scallions) in separate serving bowls.

Pour the dashi into a saucepan or fondue pot and bring to the boil. Add a few pieces of the pork and cook until it is white. Cook the other ingredients in the same way. The cooked food should be dipped in the sauce before eating.

When all the ingredients have been cooked, the stock may be served as a soup.

*Serves 6*
Preparation and cooking time: 50 minutes

# Tempura

(Deep-Fried Food Japanese Style)

*Although tempura is one of the best known Japanese dishes outside Japan, it is not traditionally Japanese – but rather an adaptation of a Portuguese dish. (The name comes from the Latin word for time.) In Japan there are many restaurants devoted exclusively to tempura and in the West it has now become a popular party dish – and it does lend itself extremely well to fondue-style informality.*

*The oil used to fry the tempura is important; in Japan a mixture of cotton seed, sesame seed and groundnut oil is a favourite and we would suggest here that you use groundnut oil and sesame oil in the proportions of 4 to 1.*

| Metric/Imperial | American |
|---|---|
| 12 fresh prawns, heads removed but still in shell | 12 fresh shrimp, with the heads removed but still in shell |
| 4 plaice fillets, skinned and cut into 2½cm./1in. pieces | 4 flounder fillets, skinned and cut into 1in. pieces |
| 1 medium squid, skinned and cut into 2½cm./1in. pieces | 1 medium squid, skinned and cut into 1 in. pieces |
| 225g./8oz. cod fillet, skinned and cut into 2½cm./1in. pieces | 8oz. cod fillet, skinned and cut into 1in. pieces |
| 1 large green pepper, pith and seeds removed and cut into 2½cm./1in. pieces | 1 large green pepper, pith and seeds removed and cut into 1in. pieces |
| 12 small button mushrooms | 12 small button mushrooms |
| 1 tinned bamboo shoot, drained and cut into ½cm./¼in. pieces | 1 canned bamboo shoot, drained and cut into ¼in. pieces |
| 12 cauliflower flowerets | 12 cauliflower flowerets |
| mixed oil for deep-frying | mixed oil for deep-frying |
| BATTER | BATTER |
| 1 egg, plus 1 egg yolk, lightly beaten | 1 egg, plus 1 egg yolk, lightly beaten |
| 175ml./6fl.oz. water | ¾ cup water |
| 125g./4oz. flour | 1 cup flour |
| SAUCE | SAUCE |
| 250ml./8fl.oz. soya sauce | 1 cup soy sauce |
| 250ml./8fl.oz. water | 1 cup water |
| 2 small turnips or large Japanese radishes, grated | 2 small turnips or large Japanese radishes, grated |

Put the prawns (shrimp) on a board and slit them lengthways, leaving the tails intact. Remove and discard the shells and open out the flesh so that they stay flat. Arrange the prawns (shrimp), plaice (flounder) pieces, squid, cod, green pepper, mushrooms, bamboo shoot and cauliflower flowerets on a large serving platter.

To make the batter, combine all the batter ingredients and beat with a fork until it forms a smooth paste.

Fill a large deep-frying pan one-third full with the oil and heat it until it is very hot. Either continue cooking in this pan or transfer the oil to a fondue pot and continue cooking over a spirit burner.

Using Japanese cooking chopsticks or a long-handled two-prong fork, spear a piece of food and dip it into the batter. Then carefully lower it into the oil and cook for 2 to 4 minutes, depending on the food being cooked, or until it is golden brown. Remove from the oil and transfer to kitchen towels to drain. Keep hot while you cook the remaining food in the same way.

To make the dipping sauce, combine all the ingredients and pour into individual dipping bowls. The cooked food should be dipped into the sauce before eating.
*Serves 8*
Preparation and cooking time: 1 hour

# Mizataki

(Chicken and Vegetable One-Pot Dish)

| Metric/Imperial | American |
| --- | --- |
| 1 x 1½kg./3lb. chicken, cut through the bones with a cleaver into bite-sized pieces | 1 x 3lb. chicken, cut through the bones with a cleaver into bite-sized pieces |

| | |
|---|---|
| 1 bean curd cake (tofu), cubed | 1 bean curd cake (tofu), cubed |
| 225g./8oz. mushrooms, stalks removed | 2 cups mushrooms, stalks removed |
| 1 small cabbage, separated into leaves | 1 small cabbage, separated into leaves |
| 4 carrots, thinly sliced | 4 carrots, thinly sliced |
| 1 bunch of watercress | 1 bunch of watercress |
| 2 leeks, cleaned and cut diagonally into 2½cm./1in. lengths | 2 leeks, cleaned and cut diagonally into 1in. lengths |
| 450ml./15fl.oz. dashi | 2 cups dashi |
| 250ml./8fl.oz. soya sauce | 1 cup soy sauce |
| lemon slices | lemon slices |
| grated radish | grated radish |

Put the chicken and bean curd on a serving platter. Chop or shred the vegetables attractively and arrange them on a serving platter.

Pour the dashi into a flameproof casserole or fondue pot and bring to the boil. Keep it over low heat and add some chicken and vegetables. Cook for 3 to 5 minutes, or until the meat is just cooked through. Each guest should help himself individually, replenishing the pot as necessary.

Pour the soy sauce into individual dipping bowls and garnish with lemon slices and radish.

The cooked food should be dipped into the sauce before eating.

*Serves 4*
Preparation and cooking time: 1 hour

# Shabu Shabu

(Beef with Cabbage and Spinach)

*The name of this dish comes from the sound the ingredients make as they are being cooked in the soup.*

| Metric/Imperial | American |
|---|---|
| 1 medium white cabbage, separated into leaves | 1 medium white cabbage, separated into leaves |
| 12 button mushroom caps | 12 button mushroom caps |
| ½kg./1lb. spinach, chopped | 3 cups chopped spinach |
| 1 bean curd cake (tofu), cubed | 1 bean curd cake (tofu), cubed |
| 700g./1½lb. rump steak, cut across the grain into thin strips | 1½lb. rump steak, cut across the grain into thin strips |
| 150ml./5fl.oz. soya sauce | ⅔ cup soy sauce |
| 2 radishes, grated | 2 radishes, grated |
| 4 spring onions, finely chopped | 4 scallions, finely chopped |
| juice of 2 lemons | juice of 2 lemons |
| 1.2l./2 pints dashi | 5 cups dashi |

Cook the cabbage leaves lightly for 3 minutes, then drain and remove from the pan. Roll up the leaves into rolls. Arrange all the vegetables and bean curd cubes decoratively on a serving platter. Arrange the beef slices decoratively on a second, smaller platter. Set aside.

Mix the soy sauce, radishes, spring onions (scallions) and lemon juice together and pour into individual dipping bowls.

Pour the dashi into a saucepan or fondue pot and bring to the boil. Cook the ingredients in the stock, a few at a time, until they are just cooked through.

The cooked food should be dipped into the sauce before eating.

*Serves 4*
Preparation and cooking time: 50 minutes

# Yose Nabe

(Chicken and Oyster Casserole)

*Yosenabe literally means 'a collection of everything', so the ingredients below are just that – suggestions. Almost anything suitable that takes your fancy could be substituted!*

| Metric/Imperial | American |
| --- | --- |
| 900ml./1½ pints dashi | 3¾ cups dashi |
| 2 chicken breasts, skinned, boned and cubed | 2 chicken breasts, skinned, boned and cubed |
| 2 large carrots, sliced | 2 large carrots, sliced |
| 12 radishes, thinly sliced | 12 radishes, thinly sliced |
| 50ml./2fl.oz. soya sauce | ¼ cup soy sauce |
| 150ml/5fl.oz. sake or dry sherry | ⅔ cup sake or dry sherry |
| 225g./8oz. tin shirataki noodles | 8oz. can shirataki noodles |
| 3 sheets of nori (seaweed), cubed | 3 sheets of nori (seaweed), cubed |
| 8 spring onions, cut into small lengths | 8 scallions, cut into small lengths |
| 12 raw prawns, shelled | 12 raw shrimp, shelled |
| 18 oysters or clams, shells removed | 18 oysters or clams, shells removed |
| 225g./8oz. cod fillet, skinned and cubed | 8oz. cod fillet, skinned and cubed |
| 18 button mushroom caps | 18 button mushroom caps |

Pour the dashi into a large saucepan and bring to the boil. Reduce the heat to low, add the chicken cubes and simmer for 10 minutes, or until the cubes are almost tender. Add the carrots and radishes and simmer for a further 5 minutes. Remove the pan from the heat and transfer the chicken and vegetables to a plate. Strain the stock into a large fondue pot or flameproof casserole and stir in the soy sauce and sake or sherry. Bring to the boil.

Arrange all the remaining ingredients on a large serving platter.

Cook the ingredients in the hot stock for 1 to 2 minutes before eating. When all the ingredients have been cooked, the stock may be served as a soup.

*Serves 4*
Preparation and cooking time: 1 hour


# Oden

(Tokyo Hotchpotch)

*Street stalls selling this warming dish – which is supposed to have originated in Tokyo – are a common sight in Japan during winter. It is also an excellent dish for parties since it can be left on very low heat for guests to help themselves as and when they want to eat.*

| Metric/Imperial | American |
| --- | --- |
| 2.5l./4 pints dashi | 2½ quarts dashi |
| 6 Tbs. soya sauce | 6 Tbs. soy sauce |
| 1½ Tbs. sugar | 1½ Tbs. sugar |
| monosodium glutamate (optional) | MSG (optional) |
| 1 large squid, cleaned and cut into rings | 1 large squid, cleaned and cut into rings |
| 2 medium turnips, cut into chunks | 2 medium turnips, cut into chunks |
| 2 large carrots, cut into chunks | 2 large carrots, cut into chunks |
| 4 medium potatoes, cut into chunks | 4 medium potatoes, cut into chunks |
| 2 pieces of konnyaku, cut into largish triangles | 2 pieces of konnyaku, cut into largish triangles |

| Metric/Imperial | American |
|---|---|
| 4 pieces of abura age, cut into largish triangles and parboiled to remove excess oil | 4 pieces of abura age, cut into largish triangles and parboiled to remove excess oil |
| 4 hard-boiled eggs | 4 hard-cooked eggs |
| 1 bean curd cake (tofu), cubed | 1 bean curd cake (tofu), cubed |
| MEATBALLS | MEATBALLS |
| 350g./12oz. minced beef | 12oz. ground beef |
| 2 spring onions, finely chopped | 2 scallions, finely chopped |
| 2½cm./1in. piece of fresh root ginger, peeled and grated | 1in. piece of fresh green ginger, peeled and grated |
| 1½ Tbs. flour | 1½ Tbs. flour |
| 2 tsp. soya sauce | 2 tsp. soy sauce |
| 2 small eggs, beaten | 2 small eggs, beaten |
| monosodium glutamate (optional) | MSG (optional) |
| vegetable oil for deep-frying | vegetable oil for deep-frying |

First prepare the meatballs. Combine the beef, spring onions (scallions), ginger, flour, soy sauce, eggs and monosodium glutamate to taste in a large bowl. Using the palm of your hand, gently shape the mixture into small balls, about 2½cm./1in. in diameter.

Fill a large deep-frying pan about one-third full with oil and heat it until it is very hot. Carefully lower the meatballs, a few at a time, into the oil and fry until they are golden brown. Using a slotted spoon, remove the meatballs from the oil and drain on kitchen towels. Keep hot while you fry the remaining meatballs in the same way. Set aside.

Pour the dashi into a large flameproof casserole and add the soy sauce, sugar and monosodium glutamate to taste. Add all the remaining ingredients, including the meatballs but excepting the bean curd, to the pan and bring to the boil. Reduce the heat to very low and simmer for 2 to 3 hours. Add the bean curd about 30 minutes before you wish to serve the dish.

Oden is usually served with mustard to taste.

*Serves 8*

Preparation and cooking time: 3½ hours

# Tempura Harusame

(Deep-Fried Food coated in Harusame Noodle)

*Harusame is a Japanese noodle somewhat similar in texture to Chinese cellophane noodles – and these latter can be substituted if harusame is difficult to obtain.*

| Metric/Imperial | American |
|---|---|
| 8 large prawns, shelled | 8 large shrimp, shelled |
| 1 cod fillet, skinned and cut into 5cm./2in. pieces | 1 cod fillet, skinned and cut into 2in. pieces |
| 1 large plaice fillet, skinned and cut into 5cm./2in. pieces | 1 large flounder fillet, skinned and cut into 2in. pieces |
| 2 scallops, coral removed and quartered | 2 scallops, coral removed and quartered |
| 8 button mushrooms | 8 button mushrooms |
| 1 tinned bamboo shoot, drained and cut into 5cm./2in. pieces | 1 canned bamboo shoot, drained and cut into 2in. pieces |
| 1 carrot, sliced | 1 carrot, sliced |
| 50g./2oz. flour | ½ cup flour |
| 2 egg whites, well beaten | 2 egg whites, well beaten |

175g./6oz. harusame, cut into small
  pieces
vegetable oil for deep-frying
SAUCE
175ml./6fl.oz. dashi
2 Tbs. soya sauce
2 Tbs. mirin or sweet sherry
1 tsp. grated daikon or turnip

6oz. harusame, cut into small
  pieces
vegetable oil for deep-frying
SAUCE
¾ cup dashi
2 Tbs. soy sauce
2 Tbs. mirin or sweet sherry
1 tsp. grated daikon or turnip

Arrange the prawns (shrimp), cod, plaice (flounder), scallops, mushrooms, bamboo shoot and carrot on a large platter. Dip them, one by one, first in the flour, shaking off any excess, then in the egg whites and finally roll them in the chopped noodles to coat them thoroughly. Set aside.

Fill a large deep-frying pan about one-third full of vegetable oil and heat it until it is very hot. Carefully lower the food pieces, two or three at a time, into the oil and fry until they are golden brown and the noodles have expanded. Remove from the oil and transfer to kitchen towels to drain. Keep hot while you cook the remaining pieces in the same way.

To make the sauce, put the dashi, soy sauce and mirin or sherry into a saucepan. Bring to the boil, then stir in the grated daikon or turnip. Remove from the heat and pour into a dipping bowl.

Serve the tempura pieces while they are still piping hot, with the dipping sauce.
*Serves 6*
Preparation and cooking time: 40 minutes

*The classic tempura batter contains egg, water and flour but sometimes in Japan there is another ingredient – harusame. Harusame are small white noodles which expand gloriously in the oil when frying and provide the most deliciously crunchy coating for the succulent fish and vegetables being cooked.*

# VEGETABLES & PICKLES

# Tamago Dashimaki

(Rolled Omelet)

*Japanese omelet pans (tamago pans) are rectangular in shape, not round as in the West, but a conventional rounded omelet pan can be substituted. If you have a rectangular flameproof griddle, this would be even better.*

| Metric/Imperial | American |
|---|---|
| 4 eggs, beaten | 4 eggs, beaten |
| 125ml./4fl.oz. dashi | ½ cup dashi |
| pinch of salt | pinch of salt |
| 1 tsp. soya sauce | 1 tsp. soy sauce |
| 3 Tbs. vegetable oil | 3 Tbs. vegetable oil |
| DIPPING SAUCE | DIPPING SAUCE |
| 50ml./2fl.oz. soya sauce | ¼ cup soy sauce |
| 1 tsp. grated daikon, radish or turnip | 1 tsp. grated daikon, radish or turnip |

First, prepare the dipping sauce. Combine the ingredients together, beating until they are thoroughly blended. Pour into a small dipping bowl and set aside.

Combine the eggs, dashi, salt and soy sauce in a small bowl.

Using a pastry brush, generously brush the surface of an omelet pan with a little of the oil. When the pan is hot, pour in about a third of the egg mixture, tilting the pan so that the mixture runs over the bottom. Reduce the heat to low and cook until the omelet is set. Using tongs or a spatula, carefully roll up the omelet away from you, then slide on to the far side of the pan. Using the pastry brush, grease the vacant part of the pan with some more of the oil and, when it is hot, pour in half the remaining mixture, gently lifting the rolled omelet so that the mixture covers the entire bottom of the pan. Cook again until the omelet is set, then roll up the second omelet as before, enclosing the first omelet within the second one.

Repeat this process, using the remaining oil and remaining egg mixture and again enclosing the rolled-up omelet in a third roll. Carefully slide the completed omelet on to a flat serving dish and cut into thick slices.

Serve at once, with the dipping sauce.

*Serves 2–3*
Preparation and cooking time: 20 minutes


# Cha Soh Juhn

(Vegetable Croquettes)                                                                  (Korea)

| Metric/Imperial | American |
|---|---|
| 1 large potato, very finely chopped | 1 large potato, very finely chopped |
| 2 carrots, coarsely grated | 2 carrots, coarsely grated |
| 1 large onion, very finely chopped | 1 large onion, very finely chopped |
| 1 garlic clove, crushed | 1 garlic clove, crushed |
| 2 eggs, lightly beaten | 2 eggs, lightly beaten |
| 50ml./2fl.oz. water | ¼ cup water |

| | |
|---|---|
| 1 Tbs. soya sauce | 1 Tbs. soy sauce |
| ½ tsp. salt | ½ tsp. salt |
| 75g./3oz. flour | ¾ cup flour |
| 50ml./2fl.oz. vegetable oil | ¼ cup vegetable oil |
| SAUCE | SAUCE |
| 50ml./2fl.oz. soya sauce | ¼ cup soy sauce |
| 50ml./2fl.oz. wine vinegar | ¼ cup wine vinegar |
| 1 Tbs. sugar | 1 Tbs. sugar |

Put the potato, carrots, onion and garlic into a medium mixing bowl and beat until they are thoroughly blended. In a second bowl, beat the eggs, water, soy sauce and salt together until they are thoroughly blended, then gradually fold in the flour until the mixture forms a smooth batter. Stir in the vegetable mixture until it is well blended.

Heat the oil in a large frying-pan. When it is hot, carefully arrange the mixture in the pan, in heaped tablespoons and fry gently until they are browned on one side. Carefully turn over and fry until the croquettes are golden brown on the other side.

Remove from the oil and drain on kitchen towels.

To make the sauce, combine all the ingredients together in a dipping bowl. Serve the croquettes at once, with the sauce.

*Serves 4*
Preparation and cooking time: 25 minutes

# Ko Chooh Juhn

(Fried Green Peppers)                                                         (Korea)

| Metric/Imperial | American |
|---|---|
| 4 green peppers, halved lengthwise and with pith and seeds removed | 4 green peppers, halved lengthwise and with pith and seeds removed |
| 225g./8oz. minced beef | 8oz. ground beef |
| 1 small onion, very finely chopped | 1 small onion, very finely chopped |
| 1 garlic clove, crushed | 1 garlic clove, crushed |
| 1 Tbs. soya sauce | 1 Tbs. soy sauce |
| ¼ tsp. hot chilli powder | ¼ tsp. hot chilli powder |
| 1 tsp. roasted sesame seeds, ground | 1 tsp. roasted sesame seeds, ground |
| 2 eggs, lightly beaten | 2 eggs, lightly beaten |
| 25g./1oz. flour | ¼ cup flour |
| 50ml./2fl.oz. vegetable oil | ¼ cup vegetable oil |
| DIPPING SAUCE | DIPPING SAUCE |
| 125ml./4fl.oz. soya sauce | ½ cup soy sauce |
| 125ml./4fl.oz. wine vinegar | ½ cup wine vinegar |
| 1 garlic clove, crushed | 1 garlic clove, crushed |

Put the pepper halves into a large saucepan and just cover with water. Bring to the boil and blanch the peppers for 5 minutes. Drain and set them aside while you make the filling.

Put the beef, onion, garlic, soy sauce, chilli powder and sesame seeds into a mixing bowl and beat them until they are thoroughly blended. Spoon the beef mixture into the pepper halves until they are level with the edges. Carefully dip the pepper halves in the beaten eggs, then in the flour, shaking off any excess. Set aside.

To make the dipping sauce, combine all the ingredients in a small bowl,

beating until they are thoroughly blended. Pour into a dipping bowl.

Heat the oil in a large frying-pan. Fry gently for 10 to 15 minutes, turning the peppers occasionally, or until the meat is cooked through.

Remove from the pan and serve at once, accompanied by the dipping sauce.

*Serves 4*

Preparation and cooking time: 30 minutes

# Kong-Na-Mool

(Bean Sprouts)                                                                    (Korea)

| Metric/Imperial | American |
| --- | --- |
| 1kg./2lb. bean sprouts | 4 cups bean sprouts |
| 2 tsp. soya sauce | 2 tsp. soy sauce |
| 1 Tbs. roasted sesame seeds, ground | 1 Tbs. roasted sesame seeds, ground |
| salt | salt |
| 2 spring onions, green part only, finely chopped | 2 scallions, green part only, finely chopped |
| 1 tsp. sesame oil | 1 tsp. sesame oil |

Put the bean sprouts into a saucepan and cover with boiling water. Cook for 5 to 10 minutes, or until they are just tender. Drain and return the bean sprouts to the pan.

Stir in the remaining ingredients, a little at a time, and cook over moderate heat until all are combined.

Serve at once.

*Serves 6*

Preparation and cooking time: 15 minutes

# Umani

(Vegetables Simmered in Soy Sauce)

| Metric/Imperial | American |
| --- | --- |
| 2 carrots, sliced diagonally into short lengths | 2 carrots, sliced diagonally into short lengths |
| 200g./7oz. tin bamboo shoot, drained and cut into 5cm./2in. lengths | 7oz. can bamboo shoot, drained and cut into 2in. lengths |
| 200g./7oz. tin konnyaku, cut into 5cm./2in. cubes | 7 oz. can konnyaku, cut into 2in. cubes |
| 600ml./1 pint dashi | 2½ cups dashi |
| 5 Tbs. soya sauce | 5 Tbs. soy sauce |
| 2 Tbs. sugar | 2 Tbs. sugar |
| 1 Tbs. mirin or sweet sherry | 1 Tbs. mirin or sweet sherry |
| 1 tsp. salt | 1 tsp. salt |
| 6 dried mushrooms, soaked in cold water for 30 minutes, drained, and stalks removed | 6 dried mushrooms, soaked in cold water for 30 minutes, drained and stalks removed |

| | |
|---|---|
| 125g./4oz. French beans, chopped | ⅔ cup chopped green beans |
| MEATBALLS | MEATBALLS |
| ½kg./1lb. minced beef | 1lb. ground beef |
| 1 Tbs. soya sauce | 1 Tbs. soy sauce |
| 1 Tbs. mirin or sweet sherry | 1 Tbs. mirin or sweet sherry |
| 2 Tbs. cornflour | 2 Tbs. cornstarch |
| 3 Tbs. dashi | 3 Tbs. dashi |

First make the meatballs. Combine all the ingredients in a large mixing bowl. Using the palm of your hands, gently shape the mixture into balls about 5cm./2in. in diameter. Set aside.

Put the carrots, bamboo shoot and konnyaku into a saucepan and add the dashi, soy sauce, sugar, mirin or sherry and salt. Bring to the boil, then reduce the heat to low. Add the meatballs to the pan, cover and simmer for 15 minutes. Add the mushroom caps and French (green) beans to the pan and simmer for a further 10 minutes.

Serve as a vegetable side dish, hot or cold.

*Serves 4-6*
Preparation and cooking time: 1¼ hours

# Yasi no Kushiage

(Vegetable Shis-kebab)

| Metric/Imperial | American |
|---|---|
| 3 eggs, lightly beaten | 3 eggs, lightly beaten |
| 50g./2oz. dry breadcrumbs | ⅔ cup dry breadcrumbs |
| flour for coating | flour for coating |
| ½ medium cauliflower, separated into small flowerets | ½ medium cauliflower, separated into small flowerets |
| 125g./4oz. mushroom caps | 1 cup button mushroom caps |
| 2 courgettes, sliced | 2 zucchini, sliced |
| 2 onions, cut downwards into 8 pieces | 2 onions, cut downwards into 8 pieces |
| vegetable oil for deep-frying | vegetable oil for deep-frying |
| SAUCE | SAUCE |
| 1 Tbs. miso paste | 1 Tbs. miso paste |
| 1 tsp. vinegar | 1 tsp. vinegar |
| 150ml./5fl.oz. mayonnaise | ⅔ cup mayonnaise |

First make the sauce. Beat the miso paste and vinegar together until they are well blended, then stir into the mayonnaise. Set aside while you cook the vegetables.

Put the eggs, breadcrumbs and flour into separate, shallow bowls. Dip all of the vegetable pieces first in the eggs, then in the flour and finally in the breadcrumbs, shaking off any excess.

Arrange the pieces on to metal skewers, repeating on different skewers until they are used up. (The skewers will be put into a large saucepan, so make sure the vegetables are arranged in such a way that they can be deep-fried.)

Fill a large deep-frying pan about one-third full with oil and heat it until it is very hot. Carefully lower the skewers into the hot oil and fry until the vegetables are deep golden. Remove the skewers from the oil and drain on kitchen towels.

Arrange the vegetable kebabs on serving platters and either pour over the sauce or serve it as an accompaniment. Serve at once.

*Serves 4*
Preparation and cooking time: 45 minutes

*(See over) Pride of place in this picture is given to Yasi no Kushiage (Vegetable Shis-kebab)– delightfully filling and savoury kebabs which can be a light meal on their own, or be served perhaps with some Sashimi or other light fish dish. Also in the picture are Carrot Salad and Goma Joyu Ae (Green Beans with Sesame Dressing).*

# Niyakko Tofu

(Cold Bean Curd)

| Metric/Imperial | American |
|---|---|
| 4 bean curd cakes (tofu) | 4 bean curd cakes (tofu) |
| GARNISH | GARNISH |
| 2 garlic cloves, crushed | 2 garlic cloves, crushed |
| 2½cm./1in. piece of fresh root ginger, peeled and grated | 1in. piece of fresh green ginger, peeled and grated |
| 4 mint leaves, chopped | 4 mint leaves, chopped |
| ½ leek, cleaned and sliced into thin strips | ½ leek, cleaned and sliced into thin strips |
| DIPPING SAUCE | DIPPING SAUCE |
| 75ml./3fl.oz. soya sauce | 6 Tbs. soy sauce |
| 1½ Tbs. sake or dry sherry | 1½ Tbs. sake or dry sherry |
| monosodium glutamate (optional) | MSG (optional) |

Cut the bean curd into small cubes and divide among individual serving bowls. Add chilled water, so that the bean curd cubes are floating.

Arrange the garlic, ginger, mint and leek decoratively on a small serving dish. Combine all the ingredients for the sauce in a small mixing bowl, then divide among individual small dipping bowls.

To serve, each diner sprinkles the garnish offerings to taste into the dipping sauce, and dips in the bean curd cubes before eating.

*Serves 4*
Preparation time: 10 minutes

# Shirasu Ae

(Vegetables Mixed in White Sesame Sauce)

*This dish originated with Zen monks in Japan and is considered an exercise in skill to prepare – but although it is a little time-consuming, the end result is well worth the effort. The 'secret' of making good Shirasu Ae is to remove as much water from the vegetables as possible.*

| Metric/Imperial | American |
|---|---|
| 175g./6oz. dried broad white beans, soaked overnight | 1 cup dried lima beans, soaked overnight |
| 2 medium aubergines | 2 medium eggplants |
| 5 Tbs. water | 5 Tbs. water |
| 2 Tbs. soya sauce | 2 Tbs. soy sauce |
| 2 tsp. sugar | 2 tsp. sugar |
| 4 dried mushrooms, soaked in cold water for 30 minutes, drained, stalks removed and caps thinly sliced | 4 dried mushrooms, soaked in cold water for 30 minutes, drained, stalks removed and caps thinly sliced |
| SESAME SAUCE | SESAME SAUCE |
| ½ bean curd cake (tofu), boiled for 3 minutes and drained | ½ bean curd cake (tofu), boiled for 3 minutes and drained |
| 4 Tbs. white sesame seeds | 4 Tbs. white sesame seeds |
| 1 Tbs. sugar | 1 Tbs. sugar |

| | |
|---|---|
| 3 Tbs. vinegar | 3 Tbs. vinegar |
| 1 Tbs. mirin or sweet sherry | 1 Tbs. mirin or sweet sherry |
| ½ tsp. salt | ½ tsp. salt |

First prepare the dressing. Put the drained bean curd into a cloth and gently squeeze out as much water as possible (the bean curd should break up). Set aside. Gently fry the sesame seeds in a small frying-pan until they begin to 'jump', taking care not to burn them too much. Remove from the heat and put them into a mortar. Grind with a pestle until the seeds form a paste (this may take some time – so be prepared!). Stir the bean curd into the mortar and continue to pound with the pestle for a further 3 minutes. Stir in the remaining sauce ingredients and continue pounding until the sauce is smooth and sticky and makes a sort of suction noise when the pestle is moved around the mortar. Set aside.

Meanwhile, prepare the vegetables. Put the beans and their soaking liquid into a small saucepan and bring to the boil. Reduce the heat to moderately low and cook for about 1 hour, or until they are tender. Replenish the liquid if necessary during cooking. Cook the aubergines (eggplants) in boiling salted water for 1 hour or until they are tender. Drain and transfer to a chopping board. Cut the aubergines (eggplants) lengthways into thin slices, then halve each round to make a half-moon shape. Set aside.

Put the water, soy sauce and sugar into a small saucepan and bring to the boil, stirring constantly until the sugar dissolves. Add the mushroom slices to the pan, reduce the heat to low and simmer for 10 minutes, so that the mushrooms absorb the flavour of the liquid. Drain the mushrooms and put into a cloth. Gently squeeze as much liquid as possible out of the mushrooms.

To serve, combine all the vegetables together, then pour over the sesame sauce. Stir gently to coat the vegetables in the sauce and serve the dish at room temperature.

*Serves 6*
Preparation and cooking time: 1½ hours

# Carrot Salad

| Metric/Imperial | American |
|---|---|
| 4 carrots, scraped | 4 carrots, scraped |
| 2 Japanese radishes (daikon), peeled | 2 Japanese radishes (daikon), peeled |
| 1 tsp. salt | 1 tsp. salt |
| 150ml./5fl.oz. cider vinegar | 10 Tbs. cider vinegar |
| 2 Tbs. sugar | 2 Tbs. sugar |
| 1 Tbs. soya sauce | 1 Tbs. soy sauce |
| 1cm./½in. piece of fresh root ginger, peeled and chopped | ½in. piece of fresh green ginger, peeled and chopped |
| monosodium glutamate (optional) | MSG (optional) |

Carefully cut the carrots and radishes into long, thin strips. Arrange in a bowl, sprinkle with the salt and set aside for 45 minutes. Drain off any water which appears on the surface of the vegetables and dry on kitchen towels. Transfer the vegetable strips to a shallow serving bowl.

Put all the remaining ingredients into a screw-top jar and shake vigorously to mix. Pour the dressing over the salad and serve at once.

*Serves 4*
Preparation time: 1 hour
**Note:** Turnip can be substituted for the daikon if they are not available.

# Goma Joyu Ae

(French [Green] Beans with Sesame Dressing)

| Metric/Imperial | American |
| --- | --- |
| 350g./12oz. French beans, chopped | 2 cups chopped green beans |
| DRESSING | DRESSING |
| 4 Tbs. sesame seeds | 4 Tbs. sesame seeds |
| 2 Tbs. soya sauce | 2 Tbs. soy sauce |
| 1 Tbs. sugar | 1 Tbs. sugar |
| monosodium glutamate (optional) | MSG (optional) |

Cook the beans in lightly salted boiling water for about 5 minutes, or until they are just tender. Drain, then rinse in cold water. Dry on kitchen towels and set aside.

Roast the sesame seeds gently in a small pan until they begin to 'jump' then pound in a mortar with a pestle to release the oil – this takes some time. When they form a reasonably smooth paste, stir in the soy sauce, sugar and monosodium glutamate to taste.

Arrange the beans in a serving dish and spoon over the dressing. Mix gently, making sure the beans are well coated. Serve at once, as a side dish.
*Serves 4*
Preparation and cooking time: 20 minutes

# Mixed Vegetable Salad

(Korea)

| Metric/Imperial | American |
| --- | --- |
| 1 small turnip | 1 small turnip |
| 1 tsp. salt | 1 tsp. salt |
| 3 Tbs. sesame oil | 3 Tbs. sesame oil |
| 1 small onion, finely chopped | 1 small onion, finely chopped |
| 125g./4oz. mushrooms, sliced | 1 cup sliced mushrooms |
| 2 celery stalks, thinly sliced | 2 celery stalks, thinly sliced |
| 3 spring onions, thinly sliced | 3 scallions, thinly sliced |
| 1 carrot, cut into thin strips | 1 carrot, cut into thin strips |
| DRESSING | DRESSING |
| 3 Tbs. soya sauce | 3 Tbs. soy sauce |
| 1 Tbs. soft brown sugar | 1 Tbs. soft brown sugar |
| 1 Tbs. vinegar | 1 Tbs. vinegar |
| $\frac{1}{2}$ tsp. ground ginger | $\frac{1}{2}$ tsp. ground ginger |
| 1 Tbs. finely chopped pine nuts | 1 Tbs. finely chopped pine nuts |

Cut the turnip into long, thin strips, then sprinkle over the salt. Set aside for 15 minutes.

Heat the oil in a small frying-pan. When it is hot, add the turnip strips and fry for 3 to 4 minutes, turning occasionally, or until they are crisp. Transfer to kitchen towels to drain. Add the onion to the pan and fry until it is golden brown. Transfer to kitchen towels to drain. Add the mushrooms and fry them for 4 minutes, stirring frequently. Transfer to kitchen towels to drain. Finally, fry the celery in the pan for 3 minutes, then transfer to kitchen towels. Put all the vegetables in a bowl and leave until they are cold.

Stir in the spring onions (scallions) and carrot. Combine all the dressing

ingredients, then pour over the mixture. Toss lightly before serving.
*Serves 4*
Preparation and cooking time: 2 hours

# Horeso no Chitashi

(Boiled Spinach)

| Metric/Imperial | American |
|---|---|
| ½kg./1lb. spinach leaves, washed | 1lb. spinach leaves, washed |
| 1 Tbs. katsuobushi or dried tuna | 1 Tbs. katsuobushi or dried tuna |
| 1 Tbs. soya sauce | 1 Tbs. soy sauce |
| Monosodium glutamate (optional) | MSG (optional) |

Put the spinach into a saucepan. Do *not* add water (the water clinging to the leaves will be sufficient). Cook gently for 6 to 8 minutes, or until the spinach is tender, taking care not to overcook. Drain, then arrange the spinach on a chopping board so that all the stalks are facing the same way. Shred the spinach, crosswise, into 2½cm./1in. sections. Section by section, gently squeeze out the water from the spinach.

Arrange the dry spinach on a serving plate and sprinkle over the katsuobushi, soy sauce and monosodium glutamate to taste. Serve cold, as a side dish with meat or fish.
*Serves 4*
Preparation and cooking time: 20 minutes
**Note:** Watercress or cos (romaine) lettuce can be cooked in this way.

*A delicious, filling dish from Korea is Mixed Vegetable Salad. This version contains turnip, carrot, celery, mushrooms and spring onions (scallions), but you can add your favourite vegetables as you wish.*

# Kabu no Tsukemono

(Pickled Turnip)

| Metric/Imperial | American |
| --- | --- |
| 1 large turnip, sliced as thinly as possible | 1 large turnip, sliced as thinly as possible |
| 1 piece of kombu (seaweed), about 2½ x 5cm./1 x 2in. | 1 piece of kombu (seaweed), about 1 x 2in. |
| 4cm./1½in. piece of fresh root ginger, peeled and sliced | 1½in. piece of fresh green ginger, peeled and sliced |
| 2 dry red chillis, chopped | 2 dry red chillis, chopped |
| chopped rind of ½ lemon | chopped rind of ½ lemon |
| ½ carrot, cut into matchstick strips | ½ carrot, cut into matchstick strips |
| 2 tsp. salt | 2 tsp. salt |
| DRESSING | DRESSING |
| 1 Tbs. mirin or sweet sherry | 1 Tbs. mirin or sweet sherry |
| 1 Tbs. soya sauce | 1 Tbs. soy sauce |

Put the turnip, kombu, ginger, red chillis, lemon rind, carrot and salt into a deep plate. Cover and place a heavy object, such as an iron on top to compress the mixture. Leave for at least 12 hours.

To serve, remove the heavy object and uncover. Using your hands, gently squeeze any excess moisture from the pickle. Transfer to a serving bowl and pour over the soy sauce and mirin or sherry. Toss gently to mix and serve at once.
*Serves 4*
Preparation time: 12¼ hours

# Kim Chee I

(Pickled Cabbage)

| Metric/Imperial | American |
| --- | --- |
| 1 large celery or Chinese cabbage, shredded | 1 large celery or Chinese cabbage, shredded |
| 125g./4oz. rock salt | ½ cup rock salt |
| 900ml./1½ pints water | 3¼ cups water |
| 6 spring onions, finely chopped | 6 scallions, finely chopped |
| 2 tsp. sugar | 2 tsp. sugar |
| 5cm./2in. piece of fresh root ginger, peeled and cut into strips | 2in. piece of fresh green ginger peeled and cut into strips |
| 2 chillis, finely chopped | 2 chillis, finely chopped |

Put the shredded cabbage in a large bowl and sprinkle over the salt. Pour over the water, cover and set aside overnight.

Combine the spring onions (scallions), sugar, ginger and chillis.

Drain, then rinse and drain the cabbage again. Put the cabbage in a fresh bowl and stir in the spring onion (scallion) mixture. Pack into sterilized pickling jars, cover and set aside for 4 to 5 days before using.
*Makes about 1.2l./2 pints (5 cups)*
Preparation time: 6 days

# Kim Chee II

(Pickled Cabbage)                                               (Korea)

| Metric/Imperial | American |
| --- | --- |
| 1 Chinese cabbage, quartered | 1 Chinese cabbage, quartered |
| 3 Tbs. salt | 3 Tbs. salt |
| 2 tsp. hot chilli powder | 2 tsp. hot chilli powder |
| 2 garlic cloves, crushed | 2 garlic cloves, crushed |
| 4 spring onions, chopped | 4 scallions, chopped |
| 1 small onion, chopped | 1 small onion, chopped |
| 1 small carrot, chopped | 1 small carrot, chopped |
| 1 Tbs. sugar | 1 Tbs. sugar |
| 1 large ripe pear, peeled, cored and roughly chopped | 1 large ripe pear, peeled, cored and roughly chopped |
| monosodium glutamate (optional) | MSG (optional) |

Put the cabbage into a large shallow bowl and sprinkle over the salt. Leave overnight to dégorge.

Remove the cabbage from the bowl and wash under cold running water. Squeeze all the moisture from the cabbage with your hands, then shred finely.

Put the cabbage, and all the remaining ingredients, into a large jar or deep bowl and cover with a heavy weight. Set aside for 1 to 2 days before serving.

*Serves* 8
Preparation time: 3 days

# Na-Moul

(Spinach Pickle)                                               (Korea)

| Metric/Imperial | American |
| --- | --- |
| 1kg./2lb. leaf spinach | 2lb. leaf spinach |
| 2 garlic cloves, crushed | 2 garlic cloves, crushed |
| 1 Tbs. roasted sesame seeds, ground | 1 Tbs. roasted sesame seeds, ground |
| 1 Tbs. sesame oil | 1 Tbs. sesame oil |
| 2 spring onions, finely chopped | 2 scallions, finely chopped |
| 1 tsp. hot chilli powder | 1 tsp. hot chilli powder |

Wash the spinach thoroughly in cold, running water. Put into a saucepan and bring to the boil (do not add any more water – the water clinging to the leaves will make enough liquid). Reduce the heat to low and cook the spinach for 5 to 8 minutes, or until it is tender. Remove the saucepan from the heat and drain the spinach very thoroughly, squeezing as much moisture from the leaves as possible.

Transfer the drained spinach to a shallow serving dish. Stir in all of the remaining ingredients until the mixture is well blended. Set aside at room temperature for 3 hours before serving.

*Serves* 8
Preparation and cooking time: $3\frac{1}{4}$ hours

# GLOSSARY

**Abure age**
Fried bean curd, usually sold in thin, frozen sheets. Obtainable from Japanese stores. Substitute other types of bean curd, as available – but the taste will be different.

**Agar-agar**
A gelatinous substance obtained from seaweed, widely used in Japanese cooking. Used as a substitute setting gel in vegetarian cooking. Obtainable from oriental and health food stores. If unavailable (and you are not a vegetarian) substitute gelatine (gelatin).

**Aji-no-moto**
The Japanese word for monosodium glutamate (MSG), which is widely used as a catalyst substance in cooking. For ease of reference, it is always referred to by its English name in this book. Obtainable from oriental stores and most supermarkets. It can safely be omitted from recipes if you prefer.

**Bean curd**
Bean curd, called tofu in Japan, is made from soya beans and is an important ingredient in most oriental cuisines. Sold fresh, in shimmering, white 'cakes'. Store fresh bean curd in water in the refrigerator; keeps for two to three days. Also available canned. When canned bean curd is opened, treat as for fresh. For ease of reference, both English and Japanese names are given in this book. Obtainable from Chinese, Japanese and all other oriental stores.

**Daikon**
A mild, long white radish very popular throughout Japan. Used both in cooking and as a garnish, and somewhat resembles the parsnip in appearance, although it is much paler in colour. Sometimes available from Chinese or Japanese stores. If unobtainable, small white turnips may be substituted.

**Dashi**
The basic stock of all Japanese cooking (see recipe). It is now often made from an instant powder in Japan called dashi-no-moto. The powder can be obtained in Japanese supermarkets. If unavailable, chicken stock can be substituted.

**Ginger**
Ginger is used extensively throughout the orient, and usually in its knobbly, root form rather than ground. To use fresh (green) ginger root, remove the brown skin and woody areas and chop the moist flesh. To store, either wrap tightly, unpeeled, in plastic film, or cover with dry sherry. Always keep in the refrigerator. Stored in this way it will keep for about six weeks. *In extremis* ground ginger can be substituted (although the taste is quite definitely not the same) – about ½ teaspoon equals a 4cm./1½in. piece of fresh (green) ginger root. Ginger is available from all oriental stores and some specialty vegetable shops.

**Ginko nuts**
(Also called ginnan in Japan) the kernels of the maidenhair tree. Used both as a flavouring and an ingredient in Japanese cooking. Available canned from Japanese stores. If it is unobtainable, omit from the recipe.

**Ginseng**
Many drinks are made from the root of the ginseng plant. In Korea, the tea made from ginseng is very popular and many miraculous – and aphrodisiac – properties are attributed to it. Several liquors of varying strength are also made from the plant.

**Hichimi togarashi**
A seven-flavour spice used as a garnish in Japanese cooking. It is darkish red in colour. Available from Japanese stores. If unobtainable, substitute paprika.

**Kanpyo**
Dried gourd strips used as an ingredient in Japanese cooking. Available only from Japanese stores. No substitute.

**Katsuobushi**
Katsuobushi are dried bonito (tuna fish) flakes, one of the basic ingredients in a proper dashi stock. Sold in flake form from Japanese general stores. There is no substitute.

**Kombu**
A dried kelp, a sort of seaweed, sold in greyish-black ribbon blocks. Used as a flavouring in dashi and also to flavour vinegared rice (sushi). Available from Japanese or other oriental stores and health food shops.

**Konnyaku**
Small, gelatinous white cakes, sold canned in Japanese or oriental stores. Often added to soups, chopped into bite-sized pieces. There is no substitute.

**Mirin**
A sweet Japanese rice wine used only for cooking. If unobtainable sweet or medium sherry can be substituted. Available from Japanese stores.

**Miso**
Miso is a fermented, dark grey paste made from cooked soya beans. Often added to dashi to make a thicker, more substantial stock for soups and dips. Miso is sold in plastic packs from Japanese stores or health food shops.

| **Noodles** | Noodles of one type or another are very popular in Japanese cooking. There are four main types: *harusame* the equivalent of Chinese cellophane noodles, which are usually either soaked and added to recipes or deep-fried; *soba*, thin, green-brown noodles made from buckwheat flour; *somen*, fine white noodles, used in the same way as vermicelli – if they are unavailable, vermicelli can be used as a substitute; and *udon*, thicker noodles made from white flour – spaghetti makes an acceptable equivalent if they are unavailable. |
|---|---|
| **Nori** | Dried laver, an edible form of seaweed, is one of the most popular garnishes in Japanese cooking. Usually toasted until crisp, then crumbled over ingredients such as rice or noodles. It is available in blackish sheets from Japanese stores and some health food shops. |
| **Sake** | Japan's favourite rice wine, a dryish, greyish liquid that seems milder than it is. Used extensively in cooking, particularly in marinades and dipping sauces. Substitute dry sherry or dry white wine if unobtainable. Available usually from Japanese and other oriental stores and also better liquor stores. |
| **Sesame seed** | Used extensively as a flavouring in both Japanese and Korean cooking. In Japan it is usually toasted then pounded in a mortar until it releases its oil; in Korea it is roasted then ground and sprinkled over practically everything. |
| **Shiitake** | The Japanese form of dried mushrooms, a delicacy popular throughout the Orient. Available from Japanese or other oriental stores. If unavailable substitute Chinese dried mushrooms – and always treat in the same way, that is, soak in cold water for 30 minutes, drain and remove stalks before using. Do not substitute European dried mushrooms – the taste is completely different. |
| **Shirataki** | A type of transparent noodle made not from flour but from the starch of vegetable plants. Usually sold canned in Japanese stores. No substitute. |
| **Soy sauce** | Yet another product of the ubiquitous soya bean plant, and used by almost every cuisine in the Orient. In Japan, a lighter slightly less salty soy sauce (called shoyu) is used and if you are cooking Japanese food this version should be used if possible. Koreans use both the Chinese and Japanese versions, according to the dish being cooked. |
| **Wakame** | A type of dried seaweed. It is sold, dried, in ribbon strands in Japanese stores and some health food shops. |
| **Wasabe** | A green horseradish powder very popular as a garnish and as an ingredient in dipping sauces in Japan. Usually sold in tins and served mixed to a paste with cold water – see specific recipes for proportions. Sold in Japanese stores and some better supermarkets. If unavailable, substitute western horseradish or mustard paste. |

# INTRODUCTION TO SOUTH EAST ASIA
Sharmini Tiruchelvam

It has been said that all South-East Asian cooking is essentially peripheral to the cuisine of China. True – yet not quite true. The influence is certainly there: Singapore, Malaysia and Indonesia contain large immigrant Chinese populations which retain their traditional styles of cooking, undoubtedly influencing the cuisine of these countries, and both Vietnam and Burma became vassal states of China in the reign of the Emperor Chien-lung, with consequent effects on both culture and gastronomy. Despite this, however, the cuisines of Malaysia, Indonesia, Thailand and Burma (which together with those of Singapore, Vietnam, the Philippines and Cambodia are commonly and collectively called South-East Asian) remain more accurately and essentially based on the cuisine of India, on its methods and styles of cooking and types of dishes.

There are the hot spiced gravy dishes called *gulehs* or *kares* or curries, similar to the curries of South India, although usually much less spicy and hot. The custom in Indonesia, Burma and Thailand of having savoury-soupy accompaniments to some of their rice meals again resembles that of South India with its *rasams* and *mulligatawnies*. The *sambals* are very like the Indians' too: piquant hot mixtures, with chilli always present in some form or other, and in South-East Asia invariably combined with prawn or shrimp paste (*blachan*). As with the Indians, sambals are served both as appetizers and as an integral part of the main meal, and in South-East Asia the idea has been further refined to make *sambals goreng* dishes in which sambal sauces are combined with other ingredients (herbs, spices, sugar and thick coconut milk) and fried with meat, fish or vegetables.

The *rendangs* of the Malays are obviously derived from the great 'dry' curries of India although, again, made much less hot and marginally sweeter with the addition of ingredients such as jaggery (raw sugar) or a sweet fruit. The Malays also have a mild, thick-gravied meat dish which they call *korma*, which is patently one form of the Indians' classic range of the same name.

From the Chinese, though, comes one of the most popular forms of cooking: stir-frying in a wok. And, from them, too, the art of tossing together unusual assortments of fresh and dried meats, fresh, preserved and dried seafood, fresh and preserved vegetables, herbs, spices and flavourings, in apparently numberless computations of combi-nations. The mixing of several kinds of meat and seafood within the same dish is so popular here that it is now widely regarded as a typically South-East Asian trait!

When a blander dish is absorbed from another cuisine – especially the Chinese – it is invariably adapted to the local taste by being 'hotted' up either by being combined with a spicy sauce, or by being accompanied by a hot or piquant dip. *Poppia*, that inspired Malaysian snack, is a perfect example: a version of the much simpler Chinese spring roll, it is made of diced ban quan (Chinese turnip), cooked shrimps, shredded crab and chicken, uncooked fresh bean sprouts, tiny cubes of fried bean curd, crisp-fried and cubed pork fat, dried prawns (shrimp), all wrapped up in fresh lettuce leaves, then in wafer-thin white pancakes, or fried crisp within a thin, light pastry. *Poppia* has two important points to it: first, the combination of fresh and dried versions of some of the same ingredients and, second, a smear of hot *blachan* (shrimp paste) within the pancake. This seems not only to give the whole dish a 'kick' but also to combine all the other mouth-watering flavours more successfully.

There are certain herbs, grasses, leaves, roots, fruits, seeds, nuts and dried preparations which are an essential part of the cooking and flavours of the region: lemon grass, daun pandan, laos, blachan, celery, cumin, coriander and coriander leaf (Chinese parsley), cloves, cardamoms, green ginger, fennel, curry leaves, sesame seed, sesame oil, limes and lemons, mustard seeds (whole or bruised but not powdered), whole nutmeg (grated freshly just before use), bean sprouts, black bean sauce, soy beans, soy sauce, bean curd, lotus seeds, water chestnuts, Chinese mushrooms, spring onion (scallions), tamarind, turmeric, peppers – green and red, dried squid, dried scallop cakes, dried prawns and shrimps, the list is exotic – and endless. Yet you can manage with only a few really indispensable ones, plus some inspired substitution! Which is how, in fact, many of the cuisines of the area were created.

All the lands of South-East Asia have access to the sea; all have therefore a great range of seafood at their disposal – the cooking of which they are all expert. Great attention is paid to what fish is in 'season'. What will cook best in what manner – What is best sautéed? . . . What steams or stir-fries

best? . . . What is best curried or devilled? – are all important questions. Mackerel does not steam well whereas it will sauté beautifully, sea bass and turbot are delicious steamed; pike poaches well; bream and red mullet both sauté and fry well. All are recognized and the most of them made. Fish-based soups and bouillons are popular especially in Burma, Thailand and Indonesia.

Like the Chinese, the South-East Asian cook pays very great attention to the quality and intrinsic properties of the ingredients; knowing what will combine most successfully with what is considered to be of paramount importance. Which leads to another very important aspect of South-East Asian cooking: it is not only the knowledge of these qualities but having the skill to choose the best raw materials that is important. It is, in fact, the starting point for much of the cooking. Many rules, handed down for generations by word of mouth within families, exist side by side with regional folklore.

Some foods are considered more healthy and 'cooling', others rich and/or 'heaty'. Like the Yin and Yang of the Chinese: 'heaty' and 'cooling' balancing opposites. One must learn how to combine them within a meal. Crabs, lobsters and oysters, for example, are heaty foods, as is garlic: they inflame the body and the passions, they say. White marrow (squash), lettuce, cucumber and milk are cooling. Pineapples and mangoes are heaty whereas limes and lemons are cooling. Yams and potatoes are heaty. Durian inflames; mangosteens

cool. It is always wise to follow a meal of the former group with a balancing amount of the latter. Many of the injunctions turn out to be surprisingly accurate. Drink milk or water out of the shell of the durian whose flesh you have eaten and you will not have any durian breath – a social disaster far worse than garlic breath. It is true! And . . . never buy crabs which have been caught in the waning season of the moon. The flesh is full and firm only when the moon is waxing, they say. Astonishingly, again, this too turns out to be true. The shells are a quarter or more filled with liquid and the flesh rather soft. But once the rules for the selection of the raw materials and the combination of the ingredients have been observed, along with the basic rules of health and hygiene, the rest is wide open to invention and innovation. In short, they are culinarily adventurous.

Derived then from the two great cuisines of the East – Indian and Chinese – influenced early by the trader Arabs and the Polynesians, linked together later still by invading foreigners from the West – the Portuguese, Dutch and English – South-East Asian cooking is not so much a great cuisine as it is a no-holds-barred amalgam of many cuisines.

There is no doubt that there is a strong regional similarity, especially between countries like Malaysia and Indonesia, Burma and Thailand. Indeed there is a great regional link, based on similar geography and climate – with access to the same food-rich terrain, oceans, seas and rivers. Common historical and ethnic bonds further bind them.

Despite all that, however, the cooking of each of the different countries is today quite distinct. Gourmets and experts on the cooking of the region can easily differentiate between the same dish cooked in the styles of two different countries: they can say, for example, if it is an Indonesian or Malaysian *rendang* merely by smelling it . . . So they say!

## Malaysia and Singapore

There are four main groups of people in Malaysia and Singapore: the indigenous Malays, the immigrant Chinese, the once itinerant trader Indians and Sri Lankans, the former invader Europeans . . . . What is most important about the various groups is the fact that they all still keep to their own traditional styles of cooking, adding greatly to the local repertoire, even as they have adapted their own palates – religious taboos allowing in some instances – to appreciate a wide variety of other ethnic foods.

**The Malays:** Malaysian cooking is like that of their close relatives, the Indonesians, and has evolved most directly from the availability of foodstuffs locally, combined with the outside influence of the trader Arabs bringing in the spices of the Indians. Finally when the Indians themselves settled in their midst they were greatly influenced by that cuisine and from the names of their dishes alone one can trace the links (many of them shared with the Indonesians): *rendangs, gulehs, ajars, sambals, sambals goreng.*

Sate (or satay in Malaysia) is a good example of the development of the Malaysian (and Indonesian) cuisine. Undoubtedly it is descended from the trader Arabs' kebab, yet it has been developed into such a unique culinary item as to merit being classified as a classic dish in its own right. The Malaysian and Indonesian sate is made from sliver-thin pieces of beef, veal, lamb, poultry of any kind, livers, tripe (or even pork – this usually being cooked by the Chinese, pork being taboo to the Muslim Malay). These are first marinated in a sauce before being skewered and barbecued. Cooked correctly, sate should melt in the mouth. It is served straight off the fire on the skewers on which it was cooked, together with pieces of raw onions and cucumber cubes (thereby correctly balancing the overall dish) and a hot, cooked sate sauce, with a base of chillis and ground roasted peanuts (or peanut butter). It makes a marvellous first course to a meal.

**The Chinese:** In many of the South-East Asian cities, and especially in Singapore and Malaysia, there are whole streets of restaurants and mobile kitchens (stalls) which specialize in the cooking of any one of the separate regions or schools of Chinese cooking such as Peking (Shantung), Honan, Hunan, Fukien, Schezwan, Yang Chow, Hokien and, of course, Canton. In the final analysis, however, there are really three main types of Chinese cooking in South-East Asia: the *haute cuisine* of China as practised by the chefs in the restaurants; the provincial and regional home-cooking of China as made every day in the homes of the Chinese, and the Malaysian-Chinese cooking which has been evolving over the past century since the arrival of the immigrant Chinese coolie population within the Malay Archipelago.

All Malaysian-Chinese dishes have been adapted from the Chinese with a couple of exceptions such as pork or tripe sate taken from the Malays and dishes like *curry mee* taken from the Indians. Very popular dishes in this range too, are *mah mi, quay thiau* and *mi hoon* – which are made *goreng, rubus* or *soto* – i.e. fried, boiled or soupy.

*Quay Thiau Goreng*, for example, is a sort of *tagliatelle al vongole*, made with clams, eggs, flat noodles, bean sprouts, a soupçon of chilli powder, garlic, onion (optional), salt and soy sauce stir-fried in a wok. In a very grand version of this one you could use oysters! Perak, in North-Central Malaysia is supposed to make the best *quay thiau*. And one little man with a mobile stall, in Ipoh, called 'the Spider' makes it so well, with clams, that gourmets from all over the East, from princes to poor men, come to eat nightly at his stall.

*Poppia* has already been described. *Lobak* is a sort of *tempura*: soft-shelled baby crabs, crayfish, baby lobsters, giant prawns (shrimps) in their shell, squid, peppers and certain yams and a marvellous Chinese sausage are all dipped into the lightest of batters and crisp-fried, so that it is possible to eat the whole crab or prawn without having to spit out the shell. *Yong thou foo* is another delicacy, made with peppers, seeded red chillis, aubergines (eggplants), marrows (squash), bitter gourds and bean curd cakes all stuffed with quenelles of pounded fresh fish or pork with onions, garlic and herbs and cooked for a very few minutes in simmering, delicate fish broth.

These Malaysian-Chinese dishes are made particularly well by the stall and mobile kitchen cooks. Throughout the whole of South-East Asia there is the phenomenon of the nocturnal cities and towns. Hundreds of thousands of mobile kitchens and stalls (each usually specializing in one or two dishes) mushroom even in the residential districts around the towns after sundown, and keep going until about midnight. Their expertise is hard to equal.

In Malaysia, especially in Malacca and Penang where the races intermarried more than on the mainland, there developed yet another strain of cooking primarily derived from the Chinese, but clearly and equally mixed with Indian and Malay cooking. Nowadays, it is called Straits Chinese or *nonya* cooking and there is great interest in it, especially in Singapore. The cuisine evolved when many of the Chinese men who came to these areas, well-off and ambitious traders who did not bring their own women, married the local Indian and Malay women (called *nonya* – hence the name of the cuisine). These men lived like princes and ate even better ... for their foreign wives, wanting to please them, learned how to prepare their native dishes but invariably adapted them to their own tastes and local availability.

**The Indians and Sri Lankans:** As with the Chinese, there are as many different sects and groups of Indians and Sri Lankans here as there are to be found on their mainland – Punjabis, Bengalis, Gujeratis, Sindhis, Telugus, Nepalese, Pathans, Kashmiris, Goans, Tamils, Singhalese – and each continues to practise its own regional and classic cooking. But undoubtedly the greatest influence has been that of the South Indians, most specifically the Indian Tamils.

Indonesia
The cuisine of Indonesia is very similar to that of Malaysia, having basic ethnic, geographical, cultural, historical and religious links, and also having been influenced in turn by the Arabs, the Indians and the Chinese – each bringing their own culinary customs and religious taboos. More particularly, however, Indonesia's cuisine must be described as having been formed out of the cuisine of what was once Java and Sumatra.

**The Javanese and Sumatrans:** Javanese cuisine is based on the availability of local produce, the fruit of a fertile land tended by a fairly well populated and highly agricultural community. Everything is used very fresh and according to season, and the

dishes, although sometimes quite sophisticated, contain fewer Indian spices than Sumatra, which was more exposed to the Arab and Indian trader traffic. Instead, the Javanese use more sugar (which grows there), and much trasi (dried shrimp paste).

The Sumatrans, early exposed to Islamic traders, soon adapted their cuisine to the use of the imported spices: fennel, cumin, coriander, chilli, ginger, cardamoms, cinnamon, so that it was recognizably different from that of Java with its sweeter, trasi-flavoured dishes. They also use more chillis and ginger than the Javanese. In central Sumatra, where a very orthodox form of Islam is practised, meat and fish are prepared in a very austere way; in contrast to Central Java where there is a great light-heartedness – much more truly South-East Asian!

**The Dutch:** There is some confusion, especially in Western minds, about the influence of the Dutch on Indonesian cooking. It is believed that they *invented* Rijsttafel. Certainly the word is Dutch, (it means, literally translated, rice table). But it is not a dish but the description of a table set at once with about 30–40 dishes ranging from complex meat, fish and vegetable curries, sates, rendangs, soups, sambals, ajars, gado-gados and other accompaniments. In short it is a table holding practically all the various famous Indonesian and Indian dishes of that area, in quantities to enable everyone to have a bit of everything. The Dutch loved eating it! The basis is usually a great dish of exquisite, plain white boiled rice, although a saffron or turmeric flavoured rice is sometimes served. The average Indonesian meal consists of the classic combination of chicken, meat, fish, vegetable and egg dishes together with a savoury soup, various sambals, ajars, etc. There are usually about eight accompanying dishes to the basic rice of the meal.

Thailand
Although geographically closer to Malaysia, by some curious quirk Thai food is remarkably similar to that of Java! Like most Indonesians and unlike most Malays, they invariably serve a soup with their rice meals. And like the Javanese they use chillis, sugar, garlic, blachan and laos powder. Like the Indonesians, too, they decorate their food wonderously.

Thailand is a particularly excellent example of the dual heritage from India and China. For an average Thai meal will have, if rice based, a savoury soup eaten with the rice as the Southern Indians do, a curry or two and one or two obviously Chinese dishes only slightly modified to the South-East Asian taste.

The herb for which they have a passion is coriander leaf, and it is sprinkled liberally over almost every dish in the cuisine. They also use a great deal of crushed garlic and coriander root –

which is very much an acquired taste. *Nam pla* is a pungent fish sauce which is used greatly as a base in their cooking and *nam prik* is a hot fish sauce which is found on every Thai table – like soy sauce at a Chinese meal! It is used with everything except the sweet . . . .

*Lahp Isan* is a sort of Northern Thai spiced and savoury steak tartare. Java has Gado-Gado and Malaysia Rojak and so, too, in Thailand are *Yam Chomphu* a tart fruit salad, flavoured with fish sauce, tamarind or lemon-water, and sugar, *Yam Taong* and *Som Tom* the former with cooked shrimps, pork, crabmeat and dried shrimp with vegetables, the latter with mixed vegetables only. In Thailand, fish sauce replaces the Indonesian blachan-peanut-chilli sauce.

### Burma

Once again the two parent cuisines are recognizable, but combined here in a typically Burmese way. In their daily life the Burmese have dishes which, like the Thais, clearly shows them to have a cuisine which is an amalgam of both the Indian and Chinese cuisines seafood and fish gravies dominate. Soups like *Hincho* with a fish gravy base, courgettes (zucchini) and cabbage and *Nga Hin*, again with a fish gravy base, fish, oil, sugar, tomatoes, onions and garlic are much loved. Each person usually has a bowl of soup with the rice-based meal. Mutton, especially, and beef are cooked with more spices than fish or poultry. Pork dishes are usually cooked Chinese-style. Shrimps fried with onions, garlic, ginger, chillis and a dash of sugar summarizes the South-East Asian cooking story here.

### Vietnam and Cambodia

Vietnam and Cambodia have a cuisine which has been chiefly derived from the Chinese but greatly influenced by the presence of the French in their midst. Both have 'hot' dishes, which they call curries, but which owe more to Burma than to India, and which are served with noodles as often as with rice. Both have a passion for fish sauce – the Vietnamese version is heavier and saltier than anywhere else and is used not only in cooking but, diluted (called *nuoc cham*), as a garnish over almost everything!

### The Philippines

The islands of the Philippines are rather an anomaly in South-East Asia, for here the influence is as much Spanish and American as Indian and Chinese, and both living and eating styles reflect this. The most popular stew, made with pork, or pork and chicken, is called *adobo*, and there is a version of that perennial Spanish favourite *arroz con pollo*. But the Chinese and Malay-Chinese influence *is* there, in a national snack called *lumpia* (a sort of spring roll), in

*pancit molo* (a sort of wonton soup) and a fondness for cooking in coconut milk.

Garnishes

South-East Asians have great grace and talent in garnishing their food, even the simplest daily meal. They use their natural materials – especially their fruit and vegetables – with considerable awareness of colour and texture. It is an art at which they all seem to be naturally adept: making lotuses out of onions, wild lilies out of carrots and chillis, crysanthemums out of papayas, roses from tomatoes, sea-anemones out of mangoes and melons, radish carnations, and Birds of Paradise out of pineapples and assortments of other fruits and vegetables, with an apparent ease as to make a sculptor swoon with envy.

There is one more quality common to all the countries of South-East Asia: a marvellous regional spirit. It pervades everything, not least their food. The ritual and enjoyable aspects of eating and serving food is very much to the taste and nature of the South-East Asian, the 'ritual' being of a Polynesian hedonistic sort rather than that of the courtly sophistication or religious traditions of the Chinese and Indians.

The very breaking open of crabs, lobsters or crayfish at the table; the breaking open and assessing of the first fruit of the seasons; the informality of using one's fingers; the creative delight of 'orchestrating' one's meal, dipping in at will, into the several flavours of the accompanying sauces and dips; the generous ceremonies of sharing and eating together, invariably informally and very relaxed, has a marvellous sensual sense of the sheer daily celebration of life . . . .

*Since time immemorial the junk has plied the seas of the Orient, transporting everything from food to people. Even in modern times its popularity remains undiminished – the picture left shows a present day version entering Singapore harbour, its cargo of fish destined for the markets there.*

111

# SOUPS

## SINIGANG

(Fish Soup)                                                          (Philippines)

| Metric/Imperial | American |
| --- | --- |
| 400g./14oz. tin tomatoes | 14oz. can tomatoes |
| 2 onions, finely chopped | 2 onions, finely chopped |
| 1 large sweet potato, peeled and cut into cubes | 1 large sweet potato, peeled and cut into cubes |
| 225g./8oz. spinach, chopped | 1⅓ cups chopped spinach |
| 1 Tbs. tamarind pulp (optional) | 1 Tbs. tamarind pulp (optional) |
| 1.2l./2 pints water | 5 cups water |
| salt and pepper | salt and pepper |
| ½kg./1lb. firm white fish fillets, chopped | 1lb. firm white fish fillets, chopped |

Put the tomatoes and liquid, onions, vegetables and tamarind into a large saucepan. Pour over the water and seasoning to taste and bring to the boil. Reduce the heat to low and simmer for 15 minutes. Stir in the fish fillets and simmer for a further 15 to 20 minutes, or until the fish flakes easily. Serve at once.
*Serves 6*
Preparation and cooking time: 45 minutes

## TOM YAM KUNG

(Shrimp and Lemon Soup)                                               (Thailand)

| Metric/Imperial | American |
| --- | --- |
| 1kg./2lb. prawn in the shell | 2lb. shrimp in the shell |
| 1.75l./3 pints water | 1½ quarts water |
| 2 tsp. chopped lemon grass or grated lemon rind | 2 tsp. chopped lemon grass or grated lemon rind |
| ¼ tsp. ground ginger | ¼ tsp. ground ginger |
| 3 lemon, lime or other citrus leaves (optional) | 3 lemon, lime or other citrus leaves (optional) |
| 2 dried whole chillis | 2 dried whole chillis |
| 1 Tbs. fish sauce | 1 Tbs. fish sauce |
| 2 Tbs. lemon juice | 2 Tbs. lemon juice |
| 1 red chilli, finely chopped | 1 red chilli, finely chopped |
| 3 spring onions, chopped | 3 scallions, chopped |
| 2 Tbs. chopped coriander leaves | 2 Tbs. chopped coriander leaves |

Shell and devein the prawns (shrimp) setting aside the meat. Put the shells and heads into a large saucepan and pour over the water. Stir in the lemon grass or rind, ginger, lemon or other leaves and whole chillis and bring to the boil. Reduce the heat to low and simmer the mixture for 10 minutes. Remove from the heat, strain the stock and set it aside.

Pour the stock into a second saucepan and return to the boil. Stir in the fish sauce and lemon juice, then stir in the prawns (shrimp). Cook over moderate heat for 5 minutes, or until they are cooked through. Stir in the chopped chilli, spring onions (scallions) and coriander leaves and remove from the heat.

Transfer the mixture to a warmed tureen and serve at once.

*Serves 6-8*

Preparation and cooking time: 40 minutes

# KAENG CHUD SAKU

(Tapioca Soup)                                                          (Thailand)

| Metric/Imperial | American |
| --- | --- |
| 1.2l./2 pints chicken stock | 5 cups chicken stock |
| 225g./8oz. minced pork | 8oz. ground pork |
| ½ tsp. salt | ½ tsp. salt |
| 125g./4oz. tapioca | ⅔ cup tapioca |
| 225g./8oz. crabmeat, shell and cartilage removed | 8oz. crabmeat, shell and cartilage removed |
| 1 small Chinese cabbage, shredded | 1 small Chinese cabbage, shredded |
| 1 Tbs. soya sauce | 1 Tbs. soy sauce |

Bring the chicken stock to the boil in a large saucepan. Add the pork and salt, stirring constantly to separate the meat. Reduce the heat to low and stir in the tapioca. Simmer for 20 minutes, or until the pork is cooked.

Flake the crabmeat and stir into the soup with the cabbage. Cover and simmer for 2 to 4 minutes, or until the crabmeat is heated through.

Stir in the soy sauce before serving.

*Serves 6-8*

Preparation and cooking time: 35 minutes

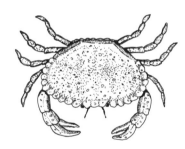

# HINCHO

(Mixed Vegetable Soup)                                                   (Burma)

*The selection of vegetables given below is optional; any green vegetable, such as cauliflower, okra or cucumber could be added.*

| Metric/Imperial | American |
| --- | --- |
| 1.2l./2 pints stock | 5 cups stock |
| 2 garlic cloves, crushed | 2 garlic cloves, crushed |
| 1 large onion, finely chopped | 1 large onion, finely chopped |
| 2 Tbs. dried prawns or 3 shelled fresh prawns | 2 Tbs. dried shrimp or 3 shelled fresh shrimp |
| 2 tsp. blachan (dried shrimp paste) | 2 tsp. blachan (dried shrimp paste) |
| ½ small Chinese cabbage, shredded | ½ small Chinese cabbage, shredded |
| 2 courgettes, thinly sliced | 2 zucchini, thinly sliced |
| 225g./8oz. pumpkin flesh, cubed | 1⅓ cups cubed pumpkin flesh |
| pepper and salt | pepper and salt |

Put the stock, garlic, onion, dried prawns or shrimp and blachan into a saucepan and bring to the boil. Add the remaining vegetables, adding those which take longest to cook first, and simmer until all are cooked through (about 5 minutes in all). Adjust seasoning and serve at once.

*Serves 6-8*

Preparation and cooking time: 20 minutes

*Two traditional South-East Asian favourites, Top: Mah Mi (Singapore Soup Noodles), a fabulous and filling main dish soup; and Below: Soto Ayam from Indonesia, a spicy curried chicken soup with exotic garnishes.*

# MAH MI

(Singapore Soup Noodles)

| Metric/Imperial | American |
|---|---|
| ½kg./1lb. prawns, shelled and with the shells and heads reserved | 1lb. shrimp, shelled and with the shells and heads reserved |
| salt and pepper | salt and pepper |
| 3 Tbs. peanut oil | 3 Tbs. peanut oil |
| 3 garlic cloves, crushed | 3 garlic cloves, crushed |
| 4cm./1½in. piece of fresh root ginger, peeled and chopped | 1½in. piece of fresh green ginger, peeled and chopped |
| 225g./8oz. cooked pork, cut into strips | 8oz. cooked pork, cut into strips |
| 225g./8oz. bean sprouts | 1 cup bean sprouts |
| 125g./4oz. fine noodles or vermicelli | 4oz. fine noodles or vermicelli |
| GARNISH | GARNISH |
| 125g./4oz. tin crabmeat, shell and cartilage removed | 4oz. can crabmeat, shell and cartilage removed |
| ¼ cucumber, peeled and diced | ¼ cucumber, peeled and diced |
| 6 spring onions, chopped | 6 scallions, chopped |

First make the stock. Put the prawn or shrimp shells and heads into a saucepan and pour over about 1.2l./2 pints (5 cups) of water. Add salt and pepper to taste and bring to the boil. Reduce the heat to low and simmer the mixture for 30 minutes. Remove from the heat and strain the stock, reserving about 900ml./1½ pints (3½ cups). Set aside.

Heat the oil in a large saucepan. When it is very hot, add the garlic and ginger and stir-fry for 1 minute. Add the pork, prawns or shrimp and bean sprouts and stir-fry for 3 minutes. Pour over the reserved stock and bring to the boil. Stir in the noodles and cook the mixture for 5 minutes.

Transfer the mixture to a large serving bowl and garnish with the flaked crabmeat, cucumber and spring onions (scallions) before serving.
*Serves 4-6*
Preparation and cooking time: 1 hour

# SOTO AYAM

(Chicken Soup)                                                    (Indonesia)

| Metric/Imperial | American |
|---|---|
| 1 x 1½kg./3lb. chicken | 1 x 3lb. chicken |
| 1.75l./3 pints water | 7½ cups water |
| salt and pepper | salt and pepper |
| 2 medium onions, sliced | 2 medium onions, sliced |
| 3 Tbs. peanut oil | 3 Tbs. peanut oil |
| 2 garlic cloves, crushed | 2 garlic cloves, crushed |
| 4cm./1½in. piece of fresh root ginger, peeled and chopped | 1½in. piece of fresh green ginger, peeled and chopped |
| 2 red chillis, crumbled | 2 red chillis, crumbled |
| 1 tsp. blachan (dried shrimp paste) | 1 tsp. blachan (dried shrimp paste) |
| 1 tsp. turmeric | 1 tsp. turmeric |
| 2 tsp. ground coriander | 2 tsp. ground coriander |
| ½ tsp. grated nutmeg | ½ tsp. grated nutmeg |

GARNISH
125g./4oz. cooked vermicelli
4 Tbs. chopped spring onions
2 hard-boiled eggs, sliced

GARNISH
1 cup cooked vermicelli
4 Tbs. chopped scallions
2 hard-cooked eggs, sliced

Put the chicken into a large saucepan and pour over the water. Add salt and pepper to taste and one onion, and bring to the boil. Cover, reduce the heat to low and simmer the chicken for 1 hour, or until the chicken is cooked through. Remove from the heat. Transfer the chicken to a plate to cool and reserve the stock.

When the chicken is cool enough to handle, remove the skin and cut the meat into bite-sized pieces. Set aside.

Heat the oil in a large saucepan. When it is hot, add the remaining onion, the garlic, ginger, chillis and blachan and fry, stirring occasionally, until the onion is soft. Stir in the spices and fry for 1 minute. Pour over the stock and bring to the boil. Reduce the heat to low and simmer the soup for 15 minutes, skimming the surface occasionally.

Put the chicken meat and cooked vermicelli into a large tureen and pour over the stock. Add the spring onions (scallions) and egg slices before serving. Sometimes, dry fried chillis and sambal ulek are passed around in separate bowls to eat with the soup.

*Serves 6-8*
*Preparation and cooking time: 1½ hours*

# MOHINGHA

(Fish Soup with Noodles)                                                      (Burma)

*Mohingha has often been described as the Burmese national dish – cooked and served on every conceivable occasion from family celebrations to roadside stalls. It is a meal in itself.*

| Metric/Imperial | American |
| --- | --- |
| ½kg./1lb. whole fish, such as whiting, mackerel or herring | 1lb. whole fish, such as whiting, mackerel or herring |
| 600ml./1 pint water | 2½ cups water |
| grated rind of 1 large lemon | grated rind of 1 large lemon |
| 4 large onions, 2 finely chopped and 2 sliced | 4 large onions, 2 finely chopped and 2 sliced |
| 4 garlic cloves, crushed | 4 garlic cloves, crushed |
| 4cm./1½in. piece of fresh root ginger, peeled and chopped | 1½in. piece of fresh green ginger, peeled and chopped |
| 1 tsp. turmeric | 1 tsp. turmeric |
| 50ml./2fl.oz. sesame oil | ¼ cup sesame oil |
| ½ tsp. blachan (dried shrimp paste) | ½ tsp. blachan (dried shrimp paste) |
| 1 Tbs. fish sauce | 1 Tbs. fish sauce |
| 2 tsp. chick-pea flour | 2 tsp. chick-pea flour |
| 600ml./1 pint coconut milk | 2½ cups coconut milk |
| ¼ Chinese cabbage, shredded | ¼ Chinese cabbage, shredded |
| 350g./12oz. rice vermicelli | 12oz. rice vermicelli |
| 2 hard-boiled eggs, sliced | 2 hard-cooked eggs, sliced |
| GARNISH | GARNISH |
| 3 spring onions, chopped | 3 scallions, chopped |
| 2 Tbs. chopped coriander leaves | 2 Tbs. chopped coriander leaves |
| 1 lemon, cut into wedges | 1 lemon, cut into wedges |

Fillet the fish and put the heads, tails, skin and bones into a saucepan. Add the water and lemon rind and bring to the boil. Reduce the heat to low, cover the pan and simmer the stock for 15 minutes. Strain the liquid and set aside.

Meanwhile, put the chopped onions, garlic, ginger and turmeric into a blender and blend to a purée. Transfer to a small bowl. Heat the oil in a large saucepan. When it is hot, add the onion mixture and fry gently for 2 minutes, stirring constantly. Add the fish pieces and fry on both sides until they are lightly browned. Pour over the fish stock and bring to the boil.

Beat the blachan into the fish sauce, then stir in the flour. Stir the mixture into the mixture in the saucepan until it is thoroughly blended. Pour over the coconut milk and bring to the boil. Add the remaining onions and cabbage and reduce the heat to low. Cover the pan and simmer the soup for 15 minutes.

Meanwhile soak the rice vermicelli in warm water for 10 minutes or until it is cooked through. Drain and transfer to a warmed serving bowl.

Stir the egg slices into the fish soup, then transfer the mixture to a large, warmed tureen. Arrange the garnish ingredients in small, separate bowls.

To serve, spoon the vermicelli into individual serving bowls then pour over the fish soup. Garnish with spring onions (scallions), coriander leaves and lemon wedges to taste.

*Serves 4*
Preparation and cooking time: 2 hours

# KAENG CHUD KAI HED

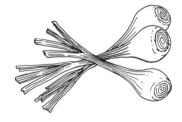

(Chicken and Mushroom Soup)                                    (Thailand)

| Metric/Imperial | American |
|---|---|
| 1 x 2kg./4lb. chicken | 1 x 4lb. chicken |
| 1.2l./2 pints chicken stock | 5 cups chicken stock |
| 1 tsp. salt | 1 tsp. salt |
| 6 spring onions, finely chopped | 6 scallions, finely chopped |
| 2 Tbs. vegetable oil | 2 Tbs. vegetable oil |
| 2 garlic cloves, crushed | 2 garlic cloves, crushed |
| 2 Tbs. chopped coriander leaves | 2 Tbs. chopped coriander leaves |
| 125g./4oz. bean sprouts | ½ cup bean sprouts |
| 1 Tbs. fish sauce | 1 Tbs. fish sauce |
| 4 dried mushrooms, soaked in cold water for 30 minutes, drained and finely chopped | 4 dried mushrooms, soaked in cold water for 30 minutes, drained and finely chopped |
| 1 small cucumber, peeled (skin reserved) and flesh chopped | 1 small cucumber, peeled (skin reserved) and flesh chopped |

Put the chicken in a large saucepan and pour over the stock. Add the salt and spring onions (scallions), cover and bring to the boil. Reduce the heat to low and simmer for 1¼ hours, or until the chicken is cooked through. Remove from the heat. Transfer the chicken to a plate and reserve the stock.

When the chicken is cool enough to handle, tear it into shreds with your fingers. Set aside.

Heat the oil in a large saucepan. When it is hot, add the garlic, coriander and bean sprouts and stir-fry for 2 minutes. Add the chicken pieces, fish sauce and mushrooms and stir-fry for 3 minutes. Add the reserved stock and bring to the boil. Reduce the heat to low and simmer for 3 minutes.

Transfer to a warmed tureen and float curls of cucumber skin on the surface. Serve with the chopped cucumber flesh.

*Serves 4-6*
Preparation and cooking time: 2½ hours

*(See over) Thailand is the home of Kaeng Chud Kai Hed, a filling chicken and mushroom soup.*

# NOODLES & RICE

## RICE NOODLES WITH SPICY BEEF

(Thailand)

| Metric/Imperial | American |
|---|---|
| ½kg./1lb. rice noodles | 1lb. rice noodles |
| 3 Tbs. peanut oil | 3 Tbs. peanut oil |
| 1 onion, thinly sliced | 1 onion, thinly sliced |
| 4cm./1½in. piece of fresh root ginger, peeled and chopped | 1½in. piece of fresh green ginger, peeled and chopped |
| 1 green chilli, chopped | 1 green chilli, chopped |
| 700g./1½lb. rump steak, cut into strips | 1½lb. rump steak, cut into strips |
| 1 Tbs. fish sauce | 1 Tbs. fish sauce |
| 125g./4oz. roasted peanuts, crushed | 1 cup roasted peanuts, crushed |

Cook the noodles in boiling salted water for 5 minutes. Drain and pour over cold water. Drain again. Transfer to a warmed serving dish and keep hot.

Heat the oil in a large frying-pan. When the oil is hot, add the onion, ginger, chilli and beef and stir-fry for 5 minutes. Add the fish sauce and remove the pan from the heat.

Spoon the mixture over the noodles and sprinkle over the peanuts before serving.

*Serves 4-6*
Preparation and cooking time: 15 minutes

## PANCIT

(Fried Noodles)                                                    (Philippines)

*Pancit in Filipino means simply noodles – usually egg – which are served in a whole variety of delicious ways. The recipe given below is a fairly basic version and can be added to or subtracted from at will – for instance, cooked pork or fish fillets can be blended in pancit, and bean sprouts could be substituted for the cabbage suggested here.*

| MetricI/mperial | American |
|---|---|
| 450g./1lb. egg noodles | 1lb. egg noodles |
| ½kg./1lb. shrimps, in the shell | 1lb. shrimp, in the shell |
| 300ml./10fl.oz. water | 1¼ cups water |
| 50g./2oz. lard | 4 Tbs. lard |
| 1 large onion, chopped | 1 large onion, chopped |
| 2 garlic cloves, crushed | 2 garlic cloves, crushed |
| 1 cooked chicken breast, skinned, boned and cut into strips | 1 cooked chicken breast, skinned, boned and cut into strips |
| 225g./8oz. cooked ham, cut into strips | 8oz. cooked ham, cut into strips |
| 5 leaves Chinese cabbage, shredded | 5 leaves Chinese cabbage, shredded |
| ¼ cucumber, chopped or sliced | ¼ cucumber, chopped or sliced |
| 2 Tbs. soya sauce | 2 Tbs. soy sauce |

| | |
|---|---|
| Salt and pepper | Salt and pepper |
| 3 spring onions, chopped | 3 scallions, chopped |

Cook the egg noodles in boiling, salted water for 5 minutes, or until they are just tender. Drain under cold running water and set aside.

Put the shrimps and water into a large saucepan and bring to the boil. Reduce the heat to low and simmer for 10 minutes. Remove from the heat and strain and reserve about 250ml./8fl.oz. (1 cup) of the cooking liquid. Shell and devein the shrimps and set them aside.

Melt half the lard in a large, deep frying-pan. Add the noodles and stir-fry for 3 minutes, or until they are evenly browned (cook them in batches if necessary). Using tongs or a slotted spoon, transfer the noodles to a plate and keep warm while you cook the meat and vegetables.

Melt the remaining lard in the frying-pan. Add the onion and garlic and fry, stirring occasionally, until the onion is soft. Add the chicken, ham, cabbage and cucumber and stir-fry for 3 minutes. Stir in the shrimps, the reserved cooking liquid, soy sauce and salt and pepper to taste. Bring the liquid to the boil. Return the noodles to the pan and stir-fry for a further 2 minutes, or until they are heated through.

Transfer the mixture to a warmed serving bowl and garnish with the spring onions (scallions) before serving.

*Serves 6*

Preparation and cooking time: 50 minutes

# RICE NOODLES WITH PORK & PRAWNS OR SHRIMPS

(Thailand)

| Metric/Imperial | American |
|---|---|
| ½kg./1lb. rice noodles | 1lb. rice noodles |
| 4 Tbs. peanut oil | 4 Tbs. peanut oil |
| 350g./12oz. pork fillet, cut into strips | 12oz. pork tenderloin, cut into strips |
| 225g./8oz. prawns, shelled | 8oz. shrimp, shelled |
| 6 spring onions, chopped | 6 scallions, chopped |
| 1 garlic clove, crushed | 1 garlic clove, crushed |
| 6 dried mushrooms, soaked in cold water for 30 minutes, drained and sliced | 6 dried mushrooms, soaked in cold water for 30 minutes, drained and sliced |
| ½ tsp. sugar | ½ tsp. sugar |
| 2 Tbs. fish sauce | 2 Tbs. fish sauce |
| 1 Tbs. chopped coriander leaves | 1 Tbs. chopped coriander leaves |

Cook the noodles in boiling salted water for 5 minutes. Drain and pour over cold water. Drain again. Transfer to a warmed serving dish and keep hot.

Heat the oil in a large frying-pan. When it is hot, add the pork strips and stir-fry for 3 minutes. Add the prawns or shrimp and stir-fry for 3 minutes. Add the spring onions (scallions), garlic and mushrooms and stir-fry for 2 minutes. Stir in the remaining ingredients and remove the pan from the heat.

Spoon the mixture over the noodles and garnish with coriander leaves before serving.

*Serves 4-6*

Preparation and cooking time: 20 minutes

*(See over) Rice noodles form the basis of many Oriental dishes and none is more delicious than this Thai version, Rice Noodles with Pork and Prawns or Shrimps.*

121

# BAHMI GORENG

(Indonesian Fried Noodles) (Indonesia)

| Metric/Imperial | American |
|---|---|
| 225g./8oz. fine egg noodles (vermicelli) | 8oz. fine egg noodles (vermicelli) |
| 4 Tbs. peanut oil | 4 Tbs. peanut oil |
| 1 onion, finely chopped | 1 onion, finely chopped |
| 2 garlic cloves, crushed | 2 garlic cloves, crushed |
| 2½cm./1in. piece of fresh root ginger, peeled and finely chopped | 1in. piece of fresh green ginger, peeled and finely chopped |
| ½ tsp. blachan (dried shrimp paste) | ½ tsp. blachan (dried shrimp paste) |
| 1 tsp. dried chillis or sambal ulek | 1 tsp. dried chillis or sambal ulek |
| 1 chicken breast, boned and cut into thin strips | 1 chicken breast, skinned, boned and cut into thin strips |
| 50g./2oz. frozen prawns, thawed | ¼ cup frozen shrimp, thawed |
| 1 large celery stalk, sliced | 1 large celery stalk, sliced |
| 2 Chinese or white cabbage leaves, shredded | 2 Chinese or white cabbage leaves, shredded |
| 2 Tbs. soya sauce | 2 Tbs. soy sauce |
| GARNISH | GARNISH |
| 1 Tbs. chopped peanuts | 1 Tbs. chopped peanuts |
| 2 spring onions, chopped | 2 scallions, chopped |

Cook the noodles in boiling salted water for 3 to 5 minutes, or until they are just tender. Drain and rinse under cold running water, then set aside.

Heat the oil in a large deep frying-pan. When it is hot, add the onion, garlic, ginger, blachan and sambal ulek and stir-fry for 3 minutes. Stir in the chicken and prawns (shrimp) and cook for a further 2 minutes. Add the celery and cabbage and stir-fry for 2 minutes. Stir in the noodles and cook for a further 2 to 3 minutes, or until they are heated through. Stir in the soy sauce.

Transfer the mixture to a large, warmed serving bowl and garnish with the chopped peanuts and spring onions (scallions) before serving.
*Serves 3-4*
Preparation and cooking time : 30 minutes


# MIKROB

(Fried Crisp Noodles) (Thailand)

| Metric/Imperial | American |
|---|---|
| vegetable oil for deep frying | vegetable oil for deep frying |
| ½kg./1lb. rice vermicelli | 1lb. rice vermicelli |
| 50ml./2fl.oz. peanut oil | ¼ cup peanut oil |
| 4 spring onions, chopped | 4 scallions, chopped |
| 3 garlic cloves, crushed | 3 garlic cloves, crushed |
| 175g./6oz. pork fillet, cut into strips | 6oz. pork tenderloin, cut into strips |
| 1 chicken breast, skinned, boned and cut into strips | 1 chicken breast, skinned, boned and cut into strips |
| 125g./4oz. shelled prawns, chopped | 4oz. shelled shrimp, chopped |
| 1 bean curd cake, chopped | 1 bean curd cake, chopped |
| 225g./8oz. bean sprouts | 1 cup bean sprouts |
| 2 Tbs. sugar | 2 Tbs. sugar |
| 4 Tbs. vinegar | 4 Tbs. vinegar |

| 4 Tbs. fish sauce | 4 Tbs. fish sauce |
| 1 Tbs. lemon juice | 1 Tbs. lemon juice |
| 1 Tbs. grated orange rind | 1 Tbs. grated orange rind |
| 5 eggs, lightly beaten | 5 eggs, lightly beaten |
| GARNISH | GARNISH |
| chopped coriander leaves | chopped coriander leaves |
| 1 dried red chilli, crumbled | 1 dried red chilli, crumbled |

Fill a large deep-frying pan one-third full with the oil and heat it until it is hot. Carefully lower the vermicelli (straight from the packet, in batches), into the hot oil and fry until it is golden brown. Using a slotted spoon, remove from the oil and drain on kitchen towels. Keep hot while you cook the remaining vermicelli in the same way.

Heat the peanut oil in a deep frying-pan. When it is very hot, add the spring onions (scallions) and garlic and fry, stirring occasionally, until the spring onions (scallions) are soft. Add the meat, prawns (shrimp), bean curd and bean sprouts and stir-fry for 5 minutes. Add the sugar, vinegar, fish sauce, lemon juice and orange rind and mix well. Stir in the eggs and cook, stirring occasionally, until they have set.

Arrange the vermicelli in a warmed serving bowl. Pour over the meat mixture and garnish with the coriander leaves and chilli before serving.

*Serves 6-8*
Preparation and cooking time: 45 minutes

# PHAT WUN SEN

(Fried Vermicelli)                                                      (Thailand)

| Metric/Imperial | American |
| --- | --- |
| 350g./12oz. rice vermicelli | 12oz. rice vermicelli |
| 50ml./2fl.oz. peanut oil | ¼ cup peanut oil |
| 2 garlic cloves, crushed | 2 garlic cloves, crushed |
| 1 red chilli, chopped | 1 red chilli, chopped |
| 4 spring onions, chopped | 4 scallions, chopped |
| 1 pork chop, boned and cut into strips | 1 pork chop, boned and cut into strips |
| 125g./4oz. frozen prawns, thawed | 4oz. frozen shrimp, thawed |
| 8 dried mushrooms, soaked in cold water for 30 minutes, drained and sliced | 8 dried mushrooms, soaked in cold water for 30 minutes, drained and sliced |
| 2 carrots, thinly sliced | 2 carrots, thinly sliced |
| 1½ Tbs. fish sauce | 1½ Tbs. fish sauce |
| 1 Tbs. malt vinegar | 1 Tbs. cider vinegar |
| 1½ tsp. sugar | 1½ tsp. sugar |
| salt and pepper | salt and pepper |
| 2 Tbs. chopped coriander leaves | 2 Tbs. chopped coriander leaves |

Put the rice vermicelli into a large bowl and just cover with boiling water. Set aside to soak for 10 minutes, then drain thoroughly and set aside.

Meanwhile, heat the oil in a large saucepan. When it is hot, add the garlic, chilli and spring onions (scallions) and stir-fry for 2 minutes. Add the pork and stir-fry for a further 2 minutes. Add the prawns (shrimp), mushrooms and carrots and stir-fry for 1 minute. Add the fish sauce, vinegar, sugar and salt and pepper to taste and bring to the boil. Stir in the vermicelli and continue to stir-fry for a further 2 minutes, or until the mixture is throughly blended and the vermicelli heated through.

Transfer the mixture to a warmed serving dish and garnish with the coriander leaves before serving.

*Serves 4-6*

Preparation and cooking time: 1 hour

# FRIED RICE

(Malaysia)

| Metric/Imperial | American |
|---|---|
| 350g./12oz. long-grain rice, soaked in cold water for 30 minutes and drained | 2 cups long-grain rice, soaked in cold water for 30 minutes and drained |
| 2 tsp. salt | 2 tsp. salt |
| 650ml./22fl.oz. water | 2¾ cups water |
| 50ml./2fl.oz. vegetable oil | ¼ cup vegetable oil |
| 2 medium onions, chopped | 2 medium onions, chopped |
| 2 red chillis, chopped | 2 red chillis, chopped |
| ½ tsp. blachan (dried shrimp paste) | ½ tsp. blachan (dried shrimp paste) |
| 1 garlic clove, crushed | 1 garlic clove, crushed |
| 2 tsp. ground coriander | 2 tsp. ground coriander |
| 175g./6oz. cooked shrimps, shelled | 6oz. cooked shrimp, shelled |
| 175g./6oz. cooked lamb or beef, sliced | 6oz. cooked lamb or beef, sliced |
| 2 tsp. soft brown sugar mixed with 1 Tbs. treacle and 2 Tbs. soya sauce | 2 tsp. soft brown sugar, mixed with 1 Tbs. molasses and 2 Tbs. soy sauce |
| GARNISH | GARNISH |
| 1 Tbs. butter | 1 Tbs butter |
| 2 eggs, lightly beaten | 2 eggs, lightly beaten |
| ¼ tsp. salt | ¼ tsp. salt |
| 2 Tbs. vegetable oil | 2 Tbs. vegetable oil |
| 2 red chillis, sliced | 2 red chillis, sliced |
| 2 onions, thinly sliced | 2 onions, thinly sliced |
| ½ cucumber, peeled and diced | ½ cucumber, peeled and diced |
| 6 spring onions, sliced | 6 scallions, sliced |

Put the rice, 1 teaspoon of salt and the water into a saucepan and bring to the boil. Reduce the heat to low, cover the pan and simmer for 15 to 20 minutes, or until the rice is tender and the water is absorbed.

Heat the oil in a large saucepan. When it is hot, add the onions and fry, stirring occasionally, until they are golden brown. Add the chillis, blachan, garlic and coriander and fry for 5 minutes, stirring constantly.

Stir in the shrimps and meat and fry for 1 to 2 minutes, or until they are well mixed with the spices. Stir in the rice, the soy sauce mixture and remaining salt. Reduce the heat to low and cook for 10 minutes, stirring occasionally.

Meanwhile, prepare the garnishes. Melt the butter in a small frying-pan. Add the eggs and salt and cook until the bottom is set and lightly browned. Turn the omelet over and fry for another 2 minutes. Remove from the heat and slide the omelet on to a plate. Cut into strips and set aside.

Wipe out the pan and heat the oil in it over moderately high heat. When it is hot, add the chillis and fry for 2 minutes, stirring constantly. Add the onions and fry, stirring occasionally, until they are golden brown. Remove from the heat and set aside.

When the rice mixture is ready, turn it out on to a warmed serving platter. Scatter the cucumber, spring onions (scallions), fried onions, chillis and the shredded omelet on top. Serve at once.

*Serves 6*

Preparation and cooking time: 1½ hours

# NASI GORENG

(Indonesian Rice)                                    (Indonesia)

| Metric/Imperial | American |
| --- | --- |
| 350g./12oz. long-grain rice, soaked in cold water for 30 minutes and drained | 2 cups long-grain rice, soaked in cold water for 30 minutes and drained |
| 725ml./1¼ pints water | 3 cups water |
| 1 tsp. salt | 1 tsp. salt |
| 2 Tbs. vegetable oil | 2 Tbs. vegetable oil |
| 3 eggs, lightly beaten | 3 eggs, lightly beaten |
| 1 medium onion, finely chopped | 1 medium onion, finely chopped |
| 2 green chillis, finely chopped | 2 green chillis, finely chopped |
| 1 garlic clove, crushed | 1 garlic clove, crushed |
| ½kg./1lb. cooked chicken meat, cut into thin slices | 1lb. cooked chicken meat, cut into thin slices |
| 225g./8oz. prawns, shelled and chopped | 8oz. shrimp, shelled and chopped |
| 2 celery stalks, finely chopped | 2 celery stalks, finely chopped |
| 2 Tbs. soya sauce | 2 Tbs. soy sauce |

Put the rice into a large saucepan. Pour over the water and salt and bring to the boil. Reduce the heat to low, cover and simmer for 15 to 20 minutes, or until the rice is tender and the liquid absorbed. Set aside.

Heat half the oil in a small frying-pan. When it is hot, add the eggs and fry for 3 minutes on each side, or until they form an omelet. Slide the omelet on to a plate and cut into thin strips. Set aside.

Heat the remaining oil in a large frying-pan. When the oil is hot, add the onion, chillis and garlic and fry, stirring occasionally, until the onion is soft. Add the chicken, prawns or shrimp and celery and cook, stirring occasionally, until they are well mixed. Stir in the cooked rice, soy sauce and the omelet strips and cook for 3 to 5 minutes, or until all the ingredients are warmed through and well blended.

Transfer the mixture to a warmed serving bowl and serve at once.

*Serves 6-7*
Preparation and cooking time: 45 minutes


# KAO PAD

(Thai Fried Rice)                                    (Thailand)

| Metric/Imperial | American |
| --- | --- |
| 4 Tbs. peanut oil | 4 Tbs. peanut oil |
| 1 large onion, chopped | 1 large onion, chopped |
| 1 red chilli, chopped | 1 red chilli, chopped |
| 225g./8oz. pork fillet, cut into strips | 8oz. pork tenderloin, cut into strips |
| 225g./8oz. frozen prawns | 8oz. frozen shrimp |
| 125g./4oz. crabmeat, shell and cartilage removed | 4oz. crabmeat, shell and cartilage removed |
| 3 eggs, lightly beaten | 3 eggs, lightly beaten |
| 2 Tbs. fish sauce | 2 Tbs. fish sauce |
| 350g./12oz. cooked long-grain rice | 4 cups cooked long-grain rice |
| 3 Tbs. tomato purée | 3 Tbs. tomato paste |
| 6 spring onions, chopped | 6 scallions, chopped |
| 2 Tbs. chopped coriander leaves | 2 Tbs. chopped coriander leaves |

Heat the oil in a large saucepan. When it is hot, add the onion and chilli and fry, stirring occasionally, until the onion is soft. Add the pork strips and stir-fry for 3 minutes. Add the prawns (shrimp) and crabmeat to the mixture and stir-fry for 2 minutes.

Break the eggs into the centre of the mixture and quickly stir until they are thoroughly combined. Stir in the fish sauce, cooked rice and tomato purèe (paste) and stir-fry for 5 minutes or until the rice is completely heated through and the mixture is blended.

Transfer the mixture to a large warmed serving bowl and garnish with the spring onions (scallions) and chopped coriander leaves.

Serve at once.

*Serves 4-6*

Preparation and cooking time: 50 minutes

*Indonesian Liver and Rice is a satisfying one-dish meal, adapted from the traditional Indonesian Nasi Goreng.*

# INDONESIAN LIVER & RICE

| Metric/Imperial | American |
| --- | --- |
| 450g./1lb. long-grain rice, soaked in cold water for 30 minutes and drained | 2⅔ cups long-grain rice, soaked in cold water for 30 minutes and drained |
| 1.2l./2 pints water | 5 cups water |
| 1 tsp. salt | 1 tsp. salt |
| 3 Tbs. peanut oil | 3 Tbs. peanut oil |
| 3 eggs, lightly beaten | 3 eggs, lightly beaten |
| 4 spring onions, chopped | 4 scallions, chopped |
| 75g./3oz. mushrooms, sliced | ¾ cup sliced mushrooms |
| 1 tinned pimiento, drained and finely chopped | 1 canned pimiento, drained and finely chopped |
| 1 red chilli, chopped | 1 red chilli, chopped |
| 2 garlic cloves, crushed | 2 garlic cloves, crushed |
| 5cm./2in. piece of fresh root ginger, peeled and finely chopped | 2in. piece of fresh green ginger, peeled and finely chopped |
| 2 Tbs. soya sauce | 2 Tbs. soy sauce |
| LIVER | LIVER |
| 4 Tbs. soya sauce | 4 Tbs. soy sauce |
| 4 Tbs. beef stock | 4 Tbs. beef stock |
| 1 Tbs. wine vinegar | 1 Tbs. wine vinegar |
| 2 Tbs. water | 2 Tbs. water |
| salt and pepper | salt and pepper |
| 1 garlic clove, crushed | 1 garlic clove, crushed |
| 10cm./4in. piece of fresh root ginger, peeled and chopped | 4in. piece of fresh green ginger, peeled and chopped |
| 2 tsp. cornflour | 2 tsp. cornstarch |
| 1½kg./3lb. lambs liver, thinly sliced | 3lb. lambs liver, thinly sliced |
| 50ml./2fl.oz. peanut oil | ¼ cup peanut oil |
| 2 celery stalks, chopped | 2 celery stalks, chopped |
| 350g./12oz. bean sprouts | 1½ cups bean sprouts |

First prepare the liver. Combine the soy sauce, stock, vinegar, water, seasoning, garlic, half the ginger and cornflour (cornstarch) in a shallow bowl. Add the liver slices and set aside to marinate for 45 minutes, basting frequently.

Meanwhile, prepare the rice. Put the rice, water and salt into a large saucepan and bring to the boil. Cover, reduce the heat to low and simmer for 15 to 20 minutes, or until the rice is tender and the liquid absorbed. Remove from the heat and set aside.

Heat 1 tablespoon of the oil in a small frying-pan. When it is hot, add the eggs and fry on each side until they are set in a thin omelet. Slide the omelet on to a plate and cut into thin strips. Set aside.

Preheat the oven to very cool 130°C (Gas Mark ½, 250°F).

Heat the remaining oil in a large frying-pan. When it is hot, add the spring onions (scallions), mushrooms, pimiento, chilli, garlic and ginger and fry until the spring onions (scallions) are soft. Stir in the rice, soy sauce and omelet strips and fry for 3 minutes, stirring occasionally. Transfer to an ovenproof dish and keep hot in the oven while you cook the liver.

Heat the oil in a large frying-pan. When it is hot, add the remaining ginger and fry for 2 minutes. Increase the heat to moderately high and add the liver and marinade to the pan. Fry, stirring and turning occasionally, for 6 minutes. Stir in the remaining ingredients and fry for 3 minutes, or until the liver slices are cooked through.

Remove the dish from the oven and arrange the liver slices over the rice. Spoon over the sauce and vegetables and serve at once.

*Serves 8*
Preparation and cooking time: 1 hour

# YELLOW RICE

(Indonesia)

| Metric/Imperial | American |
|---|---|
| 3 Tbs. vegetable oil | 3 Tbs. vegetable oil |
| 1 large onion, finely chopped | 1 large onion, finely chopped |
| 2 garlic cloves, crushed | 2 garlic cloves, crushed |
| 1 Tbs. turmeric | 1 Tbs. turmeric |
| salt and pepper | salt and pepper |
| 1 tsp. finely chopped lemon grass or grated lemon rind | 1 tsp. finely chopped lemon grass or grated lemon rind |
| 450g./1lb. long-grain rice, soaked in cold water for 30 minutes and drained | 2⅔ cups long-grain rice, soaked in cold water for 30 minutes and drained |
| 600ml./1 pint water | 2½ cups water |
| 300ml./10fl.oz. coconut milk | 1¼ cups coconut milk |
| 2 bay leaves | 2 bay leaves |
| GARNISH | GARNISH |
| 3 hard-boiled eggs, quartered | 3 hard-cooked eggs, quartered |
| 125g./4oz. roasted peanuts | ⅔ cup roasted peanuts |
| 2 bananas, sliced | 2 bananas, sliced |
| coriander sprigs | coriander sprigs |

Heat the oil in a large saucepan. When it is hot, add the onion and garlic and fry, stirring occasionally, until the onion is soft. Stir in the turmeric, seasoning to taste, lemon grass or rind and rice and fry for 3 minutes, stirring constantly. Pour over the water and coconut milk and bring to the boil. Reduce the heat to low, add the bay leaves and cover the pan. Simmer for 15 to 20 minutes, or until the rice is tender and the liquid absorbed. Discard the bay leaves.

Transfer the rice to a warmed serving dish, shaping it into a dome. Garnish with the eggs, peanuts, bananas and coriander and serve at once.
*Serves 6*
Preparation and cooking time: 35 minutes

# INDONESIAN SPICED RICE

| Metric/Imperial | American |
|---|---|
| 50g./2oz. tamarind | ¼ cup tamarind |
| 250ml./8fl.oz. boiling water | 1 cup boiling water |
| 350g./12oz. long-grain rice, soaked in cold water for 30 minutes and drained | 2 cups long-grain rice, soaked in cold water for 30 minutes and drained |
| 1 tsp. salt | 1 tsp. salt |
| 2 Tbs. dark treacle | 2 Tbs. molasses |
| 1 tsp. ground cumin | 1 tsp. ground cumin |
| 1 Tbs. soya sauce | 1 Tbs. soy sauce |
| 1 Tbs. ground coriander | 1 Tbs. ground coriander |
| 1 tsp. hot chilli powder | 1 tsp. hot chilli powder |
| ½ medium coconut, grated | ½ medium coconut, grated |
| 4 Tbs. vegetable oil | 4 Tbs. vegetable oil |
| 1 medium onion, thinly sliced | 1 medium onion, thinly sliced |
| 125g./4oz. chopped peanuts | ⅔ cup chopped peanuts |
| 450ml./15fl.oz. boiling chicken stock | 2 cups boiling chicken stock |

Put the tamarind pulp into a bowl and pour over the water. Set aside to cool. Pour the contents of the bowl through a strainer into a saucepan, pressing as much pulp through as possible.

Half fill a large saucepan with water and bring to the boil. Add the rice and salt and boil briskly for 2 minutes. Drain, discard the cooking liquid and set the rice aside.

Stir the treacle (molasses), cumin, soy sauce, coriander and chilli powder into the tamarind liquid. Bring to the boil, then cook for 5 to 10 minutes, stirring occasionally, or until the mixture thickens slightly. Stir in the rice and grated coconut, remove from the heat and keep hot.

Heat the oil in a large saucepan. When it is hot, add the onion and fry, stirring occasionally, for 3 minutes. Add the peanuts and fry for 5 minutes, or until both they and the onions are browned. Stir in the rice mixture and cook for a further 2 minutes. Pour over the stock, cover and reduce the heat to low. Simmer for 10 to 15 minutes, or until the rice is tender and the liquid absorbed.

Transfer to a warmed serving bowl and serve at once.

*Serves 4-6*
Preparation and cooking time: 1¼ hours

# FRIED RICE WITH MEATS

*In Vietnam, the rice for this dish is traditionally 'roasted' in an earthenware pot. However, the method suggested below is somewhat easier for less experienced rice cooks to follow and produces authentic – and excellent – results.*

| Metric/Imperial | American |
| --- | --- |
| 75ml./3fl. oz. peanut oil | 6 Tbs. peanut oil |
| 350g./12oz. long- or medium-grain rice soaked in cold water for 30 minutes and drained | 2 cups long- or medium-grain rice, soaked in cold water for 30 minutes and drained |
| 600ml./1 pint boiling water | 2½ cups boiling water |
| 4cm./1½in. piece of fresh root ginger, peeled and chopped | 1½in. piece of fresh green ginger, peeled and chopped |
| 1 garlic clove, crushed | 1 garlic clove, crushed |
| 4 spring onions, chopped | 4 scallions, chopped |
| 1 chicken breast, skinned, boned and cut into thin strips | 1 chicken breast, skinned, boned and cut into thin strips |
| 125g./4oz. lean pork meat, cut into thin strips | 4 oz. lean pork meat, cut into thin strips |
| 8 dried mushrooms, soaked in cold water for 30 minutes, drained and chopped | 8 dried mushrooms, soaked in cold water for 30 minutes, drained and chopped |
| 1 Tbs. fish sauce | 1 Tbs. fish sauce |
| 2 eggs | 2 eggs |
| 1 Tbs. chopped coriander leaves | 1 Tbs. chopped coriander leaves |

Heat half the oil in a large saucepan. When it is hot, add the rice and stir-fry for 2 minutes, or until it becomes opaque. Reduce the heat to very low and simmer the rice gently for a further 10 minutes, stirring occasionally. Pour over the water and return to the boil. Reduce the heat to low, cover the pan and simmer the rice for 10 to 15 minutes, or until it is tender and the liquid absorbed.

Meanwhile, heat the remaining oil in a large, deep frying-pan. When it is hot, add the ginger, garlic and about three-quarters of the spring onions (scallions) and stir-fry for 2 minutes. Add the chicken and pork meat and continue to stir-fry for 4 minutes, or until the meat is cooked through. Add the mushrooms and fish sauce and stir-fry for 2 minutes. Remove the pan from the heat.

When all the liquid has been absorbed from the rice, make a well in the centre and carefully pour in the chicken and pork mixture. Break the eggs into the centre of the chicken and pork mixture and stir-fry briskly into the meat, then the rice until the eggs are 'cooked'.

Transfer the mixture to a warmed serving bowl or platter and garnish with the remaining spring onion (scallion) and chopped coriander leaves before serving.

*Serves 4*

Preparation and cooking time: 1 hour 10 minutes

# NASI KUNING LENGKAP

(Festive Rice) (Indonesia)

| Metric/Imperial | American |
|---|---|
| 2 Tbs. peanut oil | 2 Tbs. peanut oil |
| 1 large onion, chopped | 1 large onion, chopped |
| 2 garlic cloves, crushed | 2 garlic cloves, crushed |
| 1 tsp. chopped lemon grass or grated lemon rind | 1 tsp. chopped lemon grass or grated lemon rind |
| 1 tsp. turmeric | 1 tsp. turmeric |
| ½ tsp. laos powder | ½ tsp. laos powder |
| 3 curry or bay leaves | 3 curry or bay leaves |
| 1 tsp. salt | 1 tsp. salt |
| 450g./1lb. long-grain rice, soaked in cold water for 30 minutes and drained | 2⅔ cups long-grain rice, soaked in cold water for 30 minutes and drained |
| 1.2l./2 pints coconut milk | 5 cups coconut milk |
| GARNISH | GARNISH |
| 1 Tbs. vegetable oil | 1 Tbs. vegetable oil |
| 2 small eggs, beaten | 2 small eggs, beaten |
| 4 spring onions, chopped | 4 scallions, chopped |
| 2 red chillis, quartered | 2 red chillis, quartered |
| 2 green chillis, quartered | 2 green chillis, quartered |
| 2 hard-boiled eggs, sliced | 2 hard-cooked eggs, sliced |
| ⅓ cucumber, sliced or cut into 2½cm./ 1in. lengths | ⅓ cucumber, sliced or cut into 1in. lengths |

Heat the peanut oil in a large saucepan. When it is hot, add the onion and garlic and fry, stirring occasionally, until the onion is soft. Stir in the lemon grass or rind, turmeric, laos powder, curry or bay leaves and salt. Add the rice and stir-fry for 2 to 3 minutes, or until it becomes opaque. Pour over the coconut milk and bring to the boil. Reduce the heat to low, cover the pan and simmer the mixture for 20 to 25 minutes, or until the rice is cooked and tender and the liquid absorbed.

Meanwhile, make the garnish. Heat the vegetable oil in a small frying-pan. When it is hot, add the eggs and cook until the bottom is set and lightly browned. Turn the omelet over and cook for another 2 minutes. Remove from the heat and slide the omelet onto a plate. Cut into strips and set aside.

When the rice is cooked, transfer to a large serving dish. Using greaseproof or waxed paper, carefully pat the rice into a conical shape (if you have a cone-shaped strainer, you can put the rice into this, then carefully unmould it on to the dish). Put the chillis in rows up and down the shaped rice and scatter the omelet strips over the top. Arrange the hard-boiled (hard-cooked) egg slices and cucumbers (plus any of the other garnishes suggested) around the base of the rice.

Serve at once.

*Serves 6*

Preparation and cooking time: 1¼ hours

# BEEF

## STIR-FRIED BEEF

(Malaysia)

| Metric/Imperial | American |
|---|---|
| 3 Tbs. dark soya sauce | 3 Tbs. dark soy sauce |
| 2 garlic cloves, crushed | 2 garlic cloves, crushed |
| 2 tsp. cornflour | 2 tsp. cornstarch |
| 1 tsp. sugar | 1 tsp. sugar |
| 700g./1½lb. rump steak, cut into strips | 1½lb. rump steak, cut into strips |
| 4 Tbs. vegetable oil | 4 Tbs. vegetable oil |
| 7½cm./3in. piece of fresh root ginger, peeled and chopped | 3in. piece of fresh green ginger, peeled and chopped |
| 225g./8oz. bean sprouts | 1 cup bean sprouts |

Combine the soy sauce, garlic, cornflour (cornstarch) and sugar in a shallow bowl. Add the beef strips and mix well. Cover and set aside for 30 minutes, stirring occasionally.

Heat the oil in a large frying-pan. When it is hot, add the ginger and stir-fry for 3 minutes. Add the beef mixture and stir-fry for 5 minutes. Stir in the bean sprouts and stir-fry for a further 4 minutes.

Spoon into a warmed bowl and serve at once.

*Serves 4-6*
*Preparation and cooking time: 50 minutes*

## MORCON

(Beef Roll with Tomato Sauce)                                      (Philippines)

| Metric/Imperial | American |
|---|---|
| 1½kg./3lb. beef skirt, cut crosswise into 2 or 3 pieces and flattened by beating to ½cm./¼in. thick | 3lb. beef flank, cut crosswise into 2 or 3 pieces and flattened by beating to ¼in. thick |
| ½ tsp. salt | ½ tsp. salt |
| ¼ tsp. pepper | ¼ tsp. pepper |
| 1 Tbs. lemon juice | 1 Tbs. lemon juice |
| 1 garlic clove, crushed | 1 garlic clove, crushed |
| 4 cooked ham slices | 4 cooked ham slices |
| 4 hard-boiled eggs, sliced | 4 hard-cooked eggs, sliced |
| 125g./4oz. Cheddar cheese, thinly sliced | 4oz. Cheddar cheese, thinly sliced |
| 225g./8oz. green olives, stoned and chopped | 2 cups green olives, pitted and chopped |
| 75ml./3fl.oz. vegetable oil | ⅓ cup vegetable oil |
| 25g./1oz. butter | 2 Tbs. butter |
| ½kg./1lb. tomatoes, blanched, peeled and chopped | 1lb. tomatoes, blanched, peeled and chopped |
| 1 Tbs. soya sauce | 1 Tbs. soy sauce |
| 125ml./4fl.oz. water | ½ cup water |
| 25g./1oz. beurre manié | 2 Tbs. beurre manié |

133

Put the beef pieces on a flat surface, overlapping to make a large oblong. Pound the overlapping edges together to seal. Sprinkle over the salt, pepper, lemon juice and garlic.

Arrange the ham slices over the beef, then the egg slices, in lines. Top with the cheese. Sprinkle over the olives and a third of the oil. Roll up Swiss (jelly) roll fashion and secure with string at intervals to keep the shape.

Melt the butter with the remaining oil in a large saucepan. Add the meat roll and brown, turning from time to time, for 10 minutes. Reduce the heat to low and add the tomatoes, soy sauce and water and bring to the boil. Cover and simmer for 45 minutes to 1 hour, or until the meat is cooked through.

Remove the roll to a carving board and discard the string. Cut into 2½cm./1in. slices and arrange on a heated serving dish. Keep warm.

Bring the pan juices to the boil and add the beurre manié, stirring constantly until it has dissolved. Cook for 3 to 5 minutes, or until the sauce has thickened. Pour over the meat before serving.

*Serves 6*
Preparation and cooking time: 1¾ hours

# RENDANG

(Spicy Beef)                                                          (Malaysia)

| Metric/Imperial | American |
| --- | --- |
| 1kg./2lb. topside of beef, cut into cubes | 2lb. top round of beef, cut into cubes |
| 2 garlic cloves, crushed | 2 garlic cloves, crushed |
| 2½cm./1in. piece of fresh root ginger, peeled and chopped | 1in. piece of fresh green ginger, peeled and chopped |
| 1 green chilli, chopped | 1 green chilli, chopped |
| 1 tsp. salt | 1 tsp. salt |
| 2 tsp. hot chilli powder | 2 tsp. hot chilli powder |
| 1 Tbs. ground coriander | 1 Tbs. ground coriander |
| 1 tsp. ground cumin | 1 tsp. ground cumin |
| 1 tsp. turmeric | 1 tsp. turmeric |
| 1 tsp. sugar | 1 tsp. sugar |
| 2 medium onions, chopped | 2 medium onions, chopped |
| 1 stalk lemon grass or 1 x 5cm./2in. piece finely pared lemon rind | 1 stalk lemon grass or 1 x 2in. piece of finely pared lemon rind |
| juice of ½ lemon | juice of ½ lemon |
| 600ml./1 pint thick coconut milk | 2½ cups thick coconut milk |

Put the beef cubes in a large bowl. Mix the garlic, ginger, chilli and salt together and rub the mixture into the cubes. Set aside for 30 minutes.

Combine the chilli powder, coriander, cumin, turmeric, sugar, onions, lemon grass or rind, lemon juice and coconut milk in a saucepan and bring to the boil. Add the beef cubes and bring to the boil again, stirring constantly. Reduce the heat to moderately low and cook uncovered, for 1 to 1¼ hours, or until the beef is cooked through and tender. Reduce the heat to low and cook, stirring constantly, until the meat is golden brown and all the liquid has evaporated.

Remove from the heat and transfer the meat to a warmed serving dish. Serve at once.

*Serves 4-6*
Preparation and cooking time: 2¼ hours.
**Note:** great care must be taken during the last stage of cooking. The heat must be carefully adjusted and the ingredients stirred constantly or else the meat will burn and the dish will be ruined.

*Bun Bo could be described as the Vietnamese national dish – a platter of vermicelli, one of succulent meat garnished with crushed peanuts, and a third containing refreshing salad. And, of course, always on the Vietnamese table is Nuoc Cham, a dipping sauce made from fish sauce. It is used as a condiment in much the same way as ketchup is used in the West.*

# BUN BO

(Stir-fried Beef with Noodles)           (Vietnam)

| Metric/Imperial | American |
|---|---|
| ½kg./1lb. rice vermicelli | 1lb. rice vermicelli |
| 50ml./2fl.oz. peanut oil | ¼ cup peanut oil |
| 1kg./2lb. rump steak, cut into strips | 2lb. rump steak, cut into strips |
| 2 onions, chopped | 2 onions, chopped |
| 1 Tbs. fish sauce | 1 Tbs. fish sauce |
| 125g./4oz. roasted peanuts, crushed | ⅔ cup roasted peanuts, crushed |
| GARNISH | GARNISH |
| 1 small crisp lettuce, shredded | 1 small crisp lettuce, shredded |
| ½ small cucumber, chopped | ½ small cucumber, chopped |
| 3 spring onions (green part only), chopped | 3 scallions (green part only), chopped |
| 1 serving nuoc cham (page 412 ) | 1 serving nuoc cham (page 412 ) |

Cook the vermicelli in boiling salted water for 5 minutes. Drain, refresh under cold water, then keep hot while you cook the meat.

Heat the oil in a large frying-pan. When it is hot, add the meat and onions and stir-fry for 5 minutes. Stir in the fish sauce and stir-fry for a further 1 minute.

To serve, assemble the salad ingredients on one platter, the vermicelli on another and the meat on a third. Sprinkle the meat mixture with the crushed peanuts and serve the dish with the fish sauce.

*Serves 6-8*
Preparation and cooking time: 35 minutes

# JAVANESE CURRY

| Metric/Imperial | American |
|---|---|
| 1 tsp. cumin seeds | 1 tsp. cumin seeds |
| 1 Tbs. coriander seeds | 1 Tbs. coriander seeds |
| 2 Tbs. blanched almonds | 2 Tbs. blanched almonds |
| 2 onions, coarsely chopped | 2 onions, coarsely chopped |
| 3 red or green chillis | 3 red or green chillis |
| 4cm./1½in. piece of fresh root ginger, peeled | 1½in. piece of fresh green ginger, peeled |
| 3 garlic cloves | 3 garlic cloves |
| ½ tsp. blachan (dried shrimp paste) | ½ tsp. blachan (dried shrimp paste) |
| 50ml./2fl.oz. vegetable oil | ¼ cup vegetable oil |
| 1kg./2lb. stewing steak, cubed | 2lb. chuck steak, cubed |
| 300ml./10fl.oz. water | 1¼ cups water |
| 1 tsp. salt | 1 tsp. salt |
| ½ tsp. laos powder (optional) | ½ tsp. laos powder (optional) |
| 1 tsp. chopped lemon grass or grated lemon rind | 1 tsp. chopped lemon grass or grated lemon rind |
| 25g./1oz. tamarind | 2 Tbs. tamarind |
| 125ml./4fl.oz. boiling water | ½ cup boiling water |
| 225g./8oz. green cabbage, shredded | 8oz. green cabbage, shredded |
| 8 spring onions, cut into lengths | 8 scallions, cut into lengths |
| 175ml./6fl.oz. thick coconut milk | ¾ cup thick coconut milk |

Put the cumin, coriander and almonds in a blender with the onions, chillis, ginger,

garlic and blachan. Blend to a paste, adding enough water to prevent the blades from sticking.

Heat the oil in a large saucepan. When it is hot, add the spice paste and fry for 5 minutes, or until it comes away from the sides of the pan. Add the beef cubes and fry until they are evenly browned. Pour in the water and stir in the salt, laos, and lemon grass and bring to the boil. Reduce the heat to low, cover and simmer for 2 to 2½ hours, or until the beef is cooked through and tender.

Meanwhile, put the tamarind into a bowl and pour over the water. Set aside until it is cool. Pour the contents of the bowl through a strainer into a bowl, pressing as much of the pulp through as possible.

Add the shredded cabbage, spring onions (scallions), coconut milk and tamarind liquid to the curry and bring to the boil again. Stir and allow to boil for 2 minutes.

Remove from the heat and transfer to a warmed serving dish. Serve at once.
*Serves 4-6*
Preparation and cooking time: 2½ hours

*Javanese Curry is hot and very spicy. Serve with cooling raitas and sambals and plain rice for the best effect.*

# BEEF SATE

(Indonesia)

| Metric/Imperial | American |
|---|---|
| 1 Tbs. coriander seeds | 1 Tbs. coriander seeds |
| 2 garlic cloves | 2 garlic cloves |
| 2 green chillis | 2 green chillis |
| 1 tsp. turmeric | 1 tsp. turmeric |
| 2½cm./1in. piece of fresh root ginger, peeled | 1in. piece of fresh green ginger, peeled |
| 2 medium onions, chopped | 2 medium onions, chopped |
| 2 Tbs. lemon juice | 2 Tbs. lemon juice |
| 1 Tbs. soya sauce | 1 Tbs. soy sauce |
| 4 Tbs. peanut oil | 4 Tbs. peanut oil |
| 700g./1½lb. rump steak, cubed | 1½lb. rump steak, cubed |
| 250ml./8fl.oz. thick coconut milk | 1 cup thick coconut milk |
| 125ml./4fl.oz. water | ½ cup water |
| 1 curry or bay leaf | 1 curry or bay leaf |

Put the coriander, garlic, chillis, turmeric, ginger, onions, lemon juice and soy sauce into a blender and blend to a smooth purée. Alternatively, pound the ingredients in a mortar with a pestle until they are smooth.

Heat the oil in a large saucepan. When it is hot, add the spice paste and fry for 5 minutes, stirring constantly. Add the meat cubes, and remaining ingredients and bring to the boil. Reduce the heat to low and simmer for 40 to 45 minutes, or until the meat is cooked through and the sauce is very thick. Set aside until the meat is cool enough to handle, then transfer the meat to a plate. Remove the curry or bay leaf and keep the sauce warm.

Preheat the grill (broiler) to high. Thread the cubes on to skewers and arrange on the rack of the grill (broiler). Grill (broil) the meat for 5 minutes on each side, or until it is golden brown, basting frequently with the sauce.

Pile the skewers on to a warmed serving platter and serve with the remaining sauce.

*Serves 6*
Preparation and cooking time: 1¼ hours

# SATE MANIS

(Sweet Sate)                                                                     (Indonesia)

| Metric/Imperial | American |
|---|---|
| 1½ Tbs. jaggery or soft brown sugar | 1½ Tbs. jaggery or soft brown sugar |
| 3 Tbs. soya sauce | 3 Tbs. soy sauce |
| 3 Tbs. water | 3 Tbs. water |
| 2 tsp. lemon juice | 2 tsp. lemon juice |
| 2 garlic cloves, crushed | 2 garlic cloves, crushed |
| 2 red or green chillis, seeded and chopped | 2 red or green chillis, seeded and chopped |
| salt and pepper | salt and pepper |
| 700g./1½lb. rump steak, cut into 2½cm./1in. cubes | 1½lb. rump steak, cut into 1in. cubes |
| 1 Tbs. peanut oil | 1 Tbs. peanut oil |

SAUCE

1 Tbs. peanut oil
2 garlic cloves, crushed
1½ tsp. dried chillis or sambal ulek
1 tsp. blachan (dried shrimp paste)
¼ tsp. laos powder (optional)
½ tsp. jaggery or soft brown sugar
5 Tbs. peanut butter
350ml./12fl. oz. coconut milk or water
2 Tbs. lemon juice

SAUCE

1 Tbs. peanut oil
2 garlic cloves, crushed
1½ tsp. dried chillis or sambal ulek
1 tsp. blachan (dried shrimp paste)
¼ tsp. laos powder (optional)
½ tsp. jaggery or soft brown sugar
5 Tbs. peanut butter
1½ cups coconut milk or water
2 Tbs. lemon juice

Put the jaggery or brown sugar, soy sauce, water and lemon juice into a large shallow dish. Stir in the garlic and chilli and add salt and pepper to taste. Arrange the beef cubes in the mixture and baste well. Set aside at room temperature for 4 hours, basting occasionally. Remove the cubes from the marinade mixture and pat dry with kitchen towels. Discard the marinade.

Preheat the grill (broiler) to moderately high. Thread the beef cubes on to skewers and arrange the skewers on the rack of the grill (broiler) and grill (broil) for 15 to 20 minutes, turning and basting occasionally with the tablespoon of peanut oil, or until the beef is cooked through and tender.

Meanwhile, to make the sauce, heat the oil in a frying-pan. When it is hot, add the garlic and sambal ulek and stir-fry for 1 minute. Stir in the blachan, laos powder and jaggery or brown sugar, until the sugar has dissolved. Add the peanut butter and stir until it becomes smooth. Gradually add the coconut milk or water, stirring constantly and bring to the boil. Remove the pan from the heat. (The sauce should be of a thick pouring consistency so thin down if necessary with more coconut milk or water).

To serve, arrange the beef, on skewers, across a serving dish and spoon a little of the sauce on top. Pour the remaining sauce into a warmed sauceboat and serve it with the sate.

*Serves 4-6*
Preparation and cooking time: 4½ hours

# REMPAH

(Beef and Coconut Patties) (Indonesia)

*Rempah are a sort of Eastern hamburger and are just as delicious to eat and as easy to make as their Western equivalent! They are usually eaten as a snack or hors d'oeuvre and the servings below reflect this. However, they would make an excellent main dish served with a rice or noodle dish and some vegetables – but in this case make double quantities to serve 6-8.*

| Metric/Imperial | American |
| --- | --- |
| 125g./4oz. desiccated coconut | 1 cup shredded coconut |
| 225g./8oz. minced beef | 8oz. ground beef |
| 1 garlic clove, crushed | 1 garlic clove, crushed |
| ¼ tsp. blachan (dried shrimp paste) (optional) | ¼ tsp. blachan (dried shrimp paste) (optional) |
| 1 tsp. ground coriander | 1 tsp. ground coriander |
| ½ tsp. ground cumin | ½ tsp. ground cumin |
| ¼ tsp. laos powder or ground ginger | ¼ tsp. laos powder or ground ginger |
| 1 egg, lightly beaten | 1 egg, lightly beaten |
| 50g./2oz. cornflour | ½ cup cornstarch |
| 125ml./4fl.oz. peanut oil | ½ cup peanut oil |

Put the coconut into a bowl and moisten with about 4 tablespoons of boiling water. Then stir in all the remaining ingredients, except the cornflour (cornstarch) and oil and beat until they are smooth and well blended.

Using your hands, shape the mixture into about 12 small patty shapes. Dip each shape into the cornflour (cornstarch), shaking off any excess.

Heat about half the oil in a large frying-pan. When it is very hot, add half the patties and fry for about 5 minutes on each side, or until they are cooked through and golden. Remove from the heat and drain on kitchen towels. Keep the rempah hot while you cook the remaining batch of patties in the same way.

*Serves 6-8*
Preparation and cooking time: 40 minutes

# KAENG MASAMAN

(Mussulman Curry)                                                        (Thailand)

| Metric/Imperial | American |
|---|---|
| 1kg./2lb. braising steak, cubed | 2lb. chuck steak, cubed |
| 900ml./1½ pints thick coconut milk | 3¾ cups thick coconut milk |
| 125g./4oz. roasted peanuts | ⅔ cup roasted peanuts |
| 1 Tbs. fish sauce (optional) | 1 Tbs. fish sauce (optional) |
| 25g./1oz. tamarind | 2 Tbs. tamarind |
| 50ml./2fl.oz. boiling water | ¼ cup boiling water |
| 2 Tbs. lime or lemon juice | 2 Tbs. lime or lemon juice |
| 2 tsp. soft brown sugar | 2 tsp. soft brown sugar |
| CURRY PASTE | CURRY PASTE |
| 1 Tbs. hot chilli powder | 1 Tbs. hot chilli powder |
| 2 Tbs. ground coriander | 2 Tbs. ground coriander |
| 2 tsp. ground cumin | 2 tsp. ground cumin |
| ½ tsp. ground fennel | ½ tsp. ground fennel |
| 1 tsp. laos powder | 1 tsp. laos powder |
| 1 tsp. ground ginger | 1 tsp. ground ginger |
| ½ tsp. ground cardamom | ½ tsp. ground cardamom |
| ½ tsp. ground cinnamon | ½ tsp. ground cinnamon |
| ½ tsp. ground cloves | ½ tsp. ground cloves |
| 2 tsp. chopped lemon grass or grated lemon rind | 2 tsp. chopped lemon grass or grated lemon rind |
| 3 Tbs. peanut oil | 3 Tbs. peanut oil |
| 4 garlic cloves, crushed | 4 garlic cloves, crushed |
| 1 large onion, chopped | 1 large onion, chopped |
| ½ tsp. blachan (dried shrimp paste) | ½ tsp. blachan (dried shrimp paste) |

To make the curry paste, combine the chilli powder, coriander, cumin, fennel, laos, ginger, cardamom, cinnamon and cloves. Stir in the lemon grass or rind. Heat the oil in a small frying-pan. When it is hot, add the garlic, onion and blachan and fry, stirring occasionally, until the onion is soft. Remove from the heat and set aside to cool. When the mixture has cooled a little, put it into a blender and blend to a purée. Stir the purée into the ground spice mixture until all the ingredients are well blended.

Put the beef and coconut milk into a saucepan and bring to the boil. Add the peanuts and fish sauce and reduce the heat to low. Simmer the mixture, uncovered, for 2 hours, or until the beef is cooked through and tender. Using a slotted spoon, transfer the meat to a plate.

Set the pan with the cooking liquid over high heat and bring to the boil. Continue to boil rapidly until the gravy has reduced by about one-third.

A mini-Rijsttafel with a
marvellous taste! Left:
Semur Banka, a superb
Malay-Chinese beef stew
in soy sauce; Centre:
Chicken Sate with its spicy
peanut sauce (almost the
Indonesian national dish);
and Right: Baked
Bananas, one of the very
best of the rijsttafel
accompaniments.

Meanwhile, put the tamarind into a bowl and pour over the water. Set aside until it is cool. Pour the contents of the bowl through a strainer into a bowl, pressing as much of the pulp through as possible. Set aside.

Stir the curry paste into the pan containing the gravy, then return the beef cubes to the pan. Simmer for 5 minutes, basting the beef thoroughly in the liquid. Stir in the tamarind water, lime or lemon juice and brown sugar and heat until just below boiling.

Serve at once.

*Serves 4-6*

Preparation and cooking time: 2½ hours

# SEMUR BANKA

(Beef in Soy Sauce)      (Indonesia)

| Metric/Imperial | American |
| --- | --- |
| 25g./1oz. tamarind | 2 Tbs. tamarind |
| 125ml./4fl.oz. boiling water | ½ cup boiling water |
| 50ml/2fl.oz. groundnut oil | ¼ cup groundnut oil |
| 2 medium onions, thinly sliced | 2 medium onions, thinly sliced |
| 3 garlic cloves, crushed | 3 garlic cloves, crushed |
| 4cm./1½in. piece of fresh root ginger, peeled and finely chopped | 1½in. piece of fresh green ginger, peeled and finely chopped |
| 3 cloves, crushed | 3 cloves, crushed |
| ¼ tsp. grated nutmeg or garam masala | ¼ tsp. grated nutmeg or garam masala |
| ¼ tsp. black pepper | ¼ tsp. black pepper |
| 1kg./2lb. stewing or braising steak, cut into 4cm./1½in. pieces | 2lb. chuck steak, cut into 1½in. pieces |
| 1 tsp. salt | 1 tsp. salt |
| 2 tsp. soft brown sugar mixed with 1 Tbs. treacle and 2 Tbs. dark soy sauce | 2 tsp. soft brown sugar mixed with 1 Tbs. molasses and 2 Tbs. dark soy sauce |
| 150ml./5fl.oz. water | ⅔ cup water |

Put the tamarind into a bowl and pour over the water. Set aside until it is cool. Pour the contents of the bowl through a strainer into a bowl, pressing as much of the pulp through as possible. Set aside the liquid.

Heat the oil in a large deep frying-pan. When it is hot, add the onions and fry, stirring occasionally, until they are soft. Add the garlic, ginger, spices and pepper and fry for 3 minutes, stirring frequently. Add the meat and increase the heat to moderately high. Cook the meat, turning from time to time, until it is deeply and evenly browned.

Stir in the remaining ingredients, including the reserved tamarind, and bring to the boil. Reduce the heat to low, cover the pan and simmer for 2 to 2½ hours, or until the meat is cooked through and tender and the sauce is thick and rather rich in texture.

Remove from the heat, transfer the mixture to a large, warmed serving platter and serve at once.

*Serves 6*

Preparation and cooking time: 3 hours

# CURRY PUFFS

(Malaysia)

| Metric/Imperial | American |
|---|---|
| 350g./12oz. puff pastry | 2 cups puff pastry |
| FILLING | FILLING |
| 2 Tbs. vegetable oil | 2 Tbs. vegetable oil |
| 1 onion, finely chopped | 1 onion, finely chopped |
| 1cm./½in. piece of fresh root ginger, peeled and chopped | 2in. piece of fresh green ginger, peeled and chopped |
| 1 garlic clove, crushed | 1 garlic clove, crushed |
| 2 red or green chillis, finely chopped | 2 red or green chillis, finely chopped |
| 1 tsp. hot chilli powder | 1 tsp. hot chilli powder |
| ½ tsp. turmeric | ½ tsp. turmeric |
| ½ tsp. ground coriander | ½ tsp. ground coriander |
| ½ tsp. salt | ½ tsp. salt |
| 225g./8oz. minced beef | 8oz. ground beef |
| 1 tomato, blanched, peeled and chopped | 1 tomato, blanched, peeled and chopped |
| 3 Tbs. frozen cooked peas | 3 Tbs. frozen cooked peas |
| 2 Tbs. lime or lemon juice | 2 Tbs. lime or lemon juice |

Heat the oil in a frying-pan. When it is hot, add the onion, ginger, garlic and chillis and fry, stirring occasionally, until the onion is soft. Stir in the spices and salt and fry for 3 minutes, stirring constantly. Add the beef and fry for 5 minutes, or until it loses its pinkness. Add the remaining filling ingredients and cook for 5 minutes. Set aside. Preheat the oven to fairly hot 190°C (Gas Mark 5, 375°F).

Roll the dough out to a circle about ¼cm./⅛in. thick. Using a 10cm./4in. pastry cutter, cut it into circles.

Place about 2 teaspoonfuls of the filling mixture slightly to the side of each circle and dampen the edges with water. Fold over one-half of the circle to make a semi-circle and press the edges to seal.

Put the semi-circles on a baking sheet and bake for 30 to 35 minutes, or until they are golden brown. Serve warm.
*Makes 20 puffs*
Preparation and cooking time: 1 hour

# BO XAO MANG

(Beef with Bamboo Shoot)                                                    (Vietnam)

| Metric/Imperial | American |
|---|---|
| 50ml./2fl.oz. peanut oil | ¼ cup peanut oil |
| ½kg./1lb. rump steak, cut into thin strips | 1lb. rump steak, cut into thin strips |
| 400g./14oz. tin bamboo shoot, drained and cut into strips about the same size as the meat | 14oz. can bamboo shoot, drained and cut into strips about the same size as the meat |
| 4 spring onions, chopped | 4 scallions, chopped |
| 1 garlic clove, crushed | 1 garlic clove, crushed |
| 1 Tbs. fish sauce | 1 Tbs. fish sauce |
| salt and pepper | salt and pepper |
| 2 Tbs. roasted sesame seeds, crushed | 2 Tbs. roasted sesame seeds, crushed |

*Two Malaysian dishes: Top: Curry Puffs, succulent semi-circles of pastry enclosing a spicy meat filling; and Below: Stir-Fried Beef, a Malay-Chinese dish starring rump steak and bean sprouts.*

Heat half the oil in a large, deep frying-pan. When it is very hot, add the beef strips and stir-fry for 2 minutes, or until they just lose their pinkness. Using a slotted spoon, transfer them to a plate and keep warm.

Add the remaining oil to the frying-pan. When it is hot, add the bamboo shoot, spring onions (scallions) and garlic to the pan and stir-fry for 3 minutes. Add the fish sauce and salt and pepper to taste, stirring until they are well blended.

Return the beef to the pan and stir in the sesame seeds. Continue to stir-fry for a further 1 minute, or until they are heated through.

Transfer the mixture to a warmed serving dish and serve at once.

*Serves 4*
Preparation and cooking time: 30 minutes

# RENDANG DAGING

(Fried Beef Curry)                                                        (Indonesia)

| Metric/Imperial | American |
|---|---|
| 1 large onion, chopped | 1 large onion, chopped |
| 3 garlic cloves, crushed | 3 garlic cloves, crushed |
| 4cm./1½in. piece of fresh root ginger, peeled and chopped | 1½in. piece of fresh green ginger, peeled and chopped |
| 450ml./15fl. oz. thick coconut milk | 2 cups thick coconut milk |
| 1½ tsp. hot chilli powder | 1½ tsp. hot chilli powder |
| 1 tsp. turmeric | 1 tsp. turmeric |
| 2 tsp. ground coriander | 2 tsp. ground coriander |
| 1 tsp. ground cumin | 1 tsp. ground cumin |
| ½ tsp. laos powder | ½ tsp. laos powder |
| 50ml./2fl. oz. vegetable oil | ¼ cup vegetable oil |
| 1kg./2lb. braising steak, cut into strips or small cubes | 2lb. chuck steak, cut into strips or small cubes |
| 2 Tbs. desiccated coconut, roasted | 2 Tbs. shredded coconut, roasted |
| ½ tsp. chopped lemon grass or grated lemon rind | ½ tsp. chopped lemon grass or grated lemon rind |
| 25g./1oz. tamarind | 2 Tbs. tamarind |
| 125ml./4fl. oz. boiling water | ½ cup boiling water |
| 1 tsp. soft brown sugar | 1 tsp. soft brown sugar |

Put the onion, garlic and ginger into a blender with about 50ml./2fl.oz. (¼ cup) of coconut milk and blend to a smooth, thick paste. Stir in the ground chilli powder, turmeric, coriander, cumin and laos powder until the mixture is thoroughly blended. Set aside.

Heat the oil in a large saucepan. When it is hot, add the beef pieces and fry, stirring occasionally, until they are browned. Add the coconut mixture and fry for 3 minutes, stirring constantly. Add a spoonful or two of water if the mixture becomes too dry. Stir in the desiccated (shredded) coconut and lemon grass or rind then pour over the remaining coconut milk. Bring to the boil. Reduce the heat to low, cover the pan and simmer the mixture for 1½ hours, stirring occasionally.

Meanwhile, put the tamarind into a bowl and pour over the boiling water. Set aside until it is cool. Put the contents of the bowl through a strainer into the saucepan, pressing as much of the pulp through as possible.

Stir the tamarind liquid and brown sugar into the meat mixture until it is well blended. Re-cover and continue to simmer for a further 30 minutes, or until the meat is cooked through and tender.

Transfer the mixture to a warmed serving bowl and serve at once.

*Serves 4-6*
Preparation and cooking time: 2¾ hours

# LAMB

## SAMBAI GORENG ATI

(Spiced Liver) (Indonesia)

*The best type of liver to use in this recipe is probably calf's liver but lamb's liver or chicken livers could be substituted with very little loss of taste. Don't use pig or ox liver, however; they are rather tough and require longer, slower cooking.*

| Metric/Imperial | American |
|---|---|
| 1 onion, chopped | 1 onion, chopped |
| 1 garlic clove, crushed | 1 garlic clove, crushed |
| 2 tsp. chopped dried chillis or sambal ulek | 2 tsp. chopped dried chillis or sambal ulek |
| ½ tsp. blachan (dried shrimp paste) | ½ tsp. blachan (dried shrimp paste) |
| 1 tsp. laos powder | 1 tsp. laos powder |
| 1 tsp. chopped lemon grass or grated lemon rind | 1 tsp. chopped lemon grass or grated lemon rind |
| 3 Tbs. peanut oil | 3 Tbs. peanut oil |
| ½kg./1lb. liver, cut into strips | 1lb. liver, cut into strips |
| 2 tsp. soft brown sugar | 2 tsp. soft brown sugar |
| 175ml./6fl.oz. thick coconut milk | ¾ cup thick coconut milk |

Put the onion, garlic, chillis or sambal ulek and blachan into a blender and blend to a smooth purée. Stir the laos powder and lemon grass or rind into the mixture.

Heat the oil in a large frying-pan. When it is hot, add the spice mixture and stir-fry for 3 minutes. Add the liver strips and stir-fry for 3 minutes, or until they lose their pinkness. Stir in the sugar and coconut milk and bring to the boil. Reduce the heat to low and simmer the mixture for 5 minutes, or until the liver is cooked through and tender and the liquid has thickened slightly.

Transfer the mixture to a warmed serving dish and serve at once.
*Serves 4*
Preparation and cooking time: 30 minutes

## GULEH KAMBLING

(Lamb Curry) (Indonesia)

| Metric/Imperial | American |
|---|---|
| 5cm./2in. piece of fresh root ginger, peeled and chopped | 2in. piece of fresh green ginger, peeled and chopped |
| 2 garlic cloves, crushed | 2 garlic cloves, crushed |
| 5 green chillis, chopped | 5 green chillis, chopped |
| 1 tsp. ground lemon grass or finely grated lemon rind | 1 tsp. ground lemon grass or finely grated lemon rind |
| ½ tsp. laos powder | ½ tsp. laos powder |
| 2 tsp. turmeric | 2 tsp. turmeric |
| 2 tsp. salt | 2 tsp. salt |
| 50g./2oz. ground almonds | ⅓ cup ground almonds |

| 7 Tbs. vegetable oil | 7 Tbs. vegetable oil |
| 2 medium onions, chopped | 2 medium onions, chopped |
| 1¼kg./2½lb. boned leg of lamb, cubed | 2½lb. boned leg of lamb, cubed |
| 225g./8oz. tomatoes, blanched, peeled and chopped | 8oz. tomatoes, blanched, peeled and chopped |
| 300ml./10fl.oz. coconut milk | 1¼ cups coconut milk |
| 1 small onion, sliced | 1 small onion, sliced |
| 6 cloves, lightly crushed | 6 cloves, lightly crushed |
| 1 Tbs. crushed coriander seeds | 1 Tbs. crushed coriander seeds |
| 1 tsp. crushed cumin seeds | 1 tsp. crushed cumin seeds |

*Another delicious lamb curry from Indonesia, Guleh Kambling is also sometimes served as part of a rijsttafel. However, it also makes an excellent Western-style meal served with rice, salad and chutneys.*

Combine the ginger, garlic, chillis, lemon grass or rind, laos, turmeric, salt and ground almonds with 1 tablespoon of oil and 1 tablespoon of water to make a paste. Add more water if necessary. Set aside.

Heat 50ml./2fl.oz. (¼ cup) of the oil in a large saucepan. When it is hot, add the chopped onions and fry, stirring occasionally, until they are golden brown. Add the spice paste and fry for 5 minutes, stirring frequently. Add the lamb cubes and fry for 15 to 20 minutes, or until they have completely lost their pinkness and are thoroughly coated with the spice mixture.

Stir in the tomatoes and cook for 1 minute. Add the milk and bring to the boil. Reduce the heat to low, cover and simmer the curry for 1 hour, or until the meat is cooked through and tender and the gravy is thick.

Meanwhile, heat the remaining oil in a small frying-pan. When it is hot, add the sliced onion and spices and fry, stirring frequently, until the onion is golden brown. Ten minutes before the end of the cooking time, stir the onion and spice mixture into the lamb.

Transfer the mixture to a warmed serving dish and serve at once.
*Serves 8*
Preparation and cooking time: 2 hours

# MURTABA

(Savoury Lamb Crêpes)                                                    (Singapore)

| Metric/Imperial | American |
| --- | --- |
| 350g./12oz. wholewheat flour | 3 cups wholewheat flour |
| ½ tsp. salt | ½ tsp. salt |
| 250ml./8fl.oz. lukewarm water | 1 cup lukewarm water |
| 50g./2oz. ghee or clarified butter | 4 Tbs. ghee or clarified butter |
| FILLING | FILLING |
| 3 Tbs. vegetable oil | 3 Tbs. vegetable oil |
| 1 onion, finely chopped | 1 onion, finely chopped |
| 1 garlic clove, crushed | 1 garlic clove, crushed |
| 2 green chillis, chopped | 2 green chillis, chopped |
| 350g./12oz. minced lamb | 12oz. ground lamb |
| 1 tomato, blanched, peeled and chopped | 1 tomato, blanched, peeled and chopped |
| 3 Tbs. cooked green peas | 3 Tbs. cooked green peas |
| salt and pepper | salt and pepper |
| 1 tsp. garam masala | 1 tsp. garam masala |
| 1 egg, beaten | 1 egg, beaten |

First make the dough. Put the flour and salt into a bowl and make a well in the centre. Pour in the water and beat briskly until a stiff dough is formed. Cover the bowl and set the dough aside for 1 hour.

Meanwhile, make the filling. Heat the oil in a medium frying-pan. When it is hot, add the onion, garlic and chillis and fry until the onion is soft, stirring occasionally. Stir in the lamb and continue to fry the mixture until the meat loses its pinkness. Stir in the tomato, peas and salt and pepper to taste and cook for a further 3 minutes. Reduce the heat to low and simmer the mixture for 10 minutes. Sprinkle over the garam masala, remove from the heat and keep warm.

Remove the dough from the bowl and knead the dough gently. On a slightly oiled board, divide the mixture into balls, then gently press each ball out into a very thin crêpe (as thin as possible without tearing the dough – it should resemble strudel pastry).

Melt a little ghee in a frying-pan or griddle and gently ease in one of the crêpes. Carefully brush a little beaten egg over the exposed side of the crêpe and spoon over some filling. Fold over the sides of the crêpe so that the filling is completely enclosed and fry for 1 minute. Carefully turn over the crêpe and cook for a further 1 minute, then remove from the pan. Cook the other crêpes in the same way, then serve hot.

Serves 6-8 (as a snack or hors d'oeuvre)
Preparation and cooking time: 1¾ hours

# LAMB SATE

(Indonesia)

| Metric/Imperial | American |
|---|---|
| 3 garlic cloves, crushed | 3 garlic cloves, crushed |
| 4 Tbs. soya sauce | 4 Tbs. soy sauce |
| 1 Tbs. soft brown sugar | 1 Tbs. soft brown sugar |
| 1 small onion, grated | 1 small onion, grated |
| 1 Tbs. lemon juice | 1 Tbs. lemon juice |
| ½ tsp. salt | ½ tsp. salt |
| 1kg./2lb./boned lean lamb, cubed | 2lb. boned lean lamb, cubed |
| SAUCE | SAUCE |
| 150ml./5fl.oz. soya sauce | ⅔ cup soy sauce |
| 1 tsp. ground coriander | 1 tsp. ground coriander |
| 1 garlic clove, crushed | 1 garlic clove, crushed |
| 1 green or red chilli, crumbled | 1 green or red chilli, crumbled |
| 3 Tbs. soft brown sugar | 3 Tbs. soft brown sugar |
| 2 Tbs. dark treacle | 2 Tbs. molasses |
| 1 Tbs. lemon juice | 1 Tbs. lemon juice |

*Sates come in all shapes and forms in Indonesia and can be made from almost any ingredient. While Lamb Sate is more unusual than pork, chicken or beef, it is equally delicious. And in this case the accompanying sauce has a soy sauce base instead of peanuts. Sates are perfect for summer barbecues.*

Mix the garlic, soy sauce, sugar, onion, lemon juice and salt in a small bowl. Add the meat cubes and set aside to marinate for 1 hour, basting occasionally.

Meanwhile, combine all the sauce ingredients in a medium saucepan. Set over moderate heat and bring to the boil, stirring constantly. Reduce the heat to low and simmer for 5 minutes. Remove from the heat and keep warm while you cook the sate.

Preheat the grill (broiler) to high. Thread the cubes on to skewers and arrange on the rack of the grill (broiler). Grill (broil) for 8 minutes, turn and grill (broil) for a further 6 minutes or until the meat is cooked through.

Pile the skewers on to a warmed serving platter. Pour the sauce into a small bowl and serve at once, with the kebabs.
Serves 8
Preparation and cooking time: 1½ hours

# PORK

## THIT KHO

(Pork Stew)                                                                                (Vietnam)

*This is a northern Vietnamese dish, often served during the New Year festival. Belly or bacon of pork is probably the cut the Vietnamese would use but if you prefer leaner meat use blade or even leg.*

| Metric/Imperial | American |
|---|---|
| 3 Tbs. peanut oil | 3 Tbs. peanut oil |
| 2 Tbs. sugar | 2 Tbs. sugar |
| 1kg./2lb. pork meat (with fat), cut into cubes | 2lb. pork meat (with fat), cut into cubes |
| 3 Tbs. fish sauce | 3 Tbs. fish sauce |
| 1 Tbs. soya sauce | 1 Tbs. soy sauce |
| 6 spring onions, chopped | 6 scallions, chopped |
| 3 hard-boiled eggs | 3 hard-cooked eggs |

Heat the oil in a large saucepan. When it is hot, stir in the sugar and cook until it browns slightly. Add the pork cubes and cook, basting with the sugar mixture, until they are browned. Add the fish sauce and soy sauce, and stir-fry for 1 minute. Pour over enough cold water just to cover and bring to the boil. Reduce the heat to low and simmer, uncovered, for 2 to 2½ hours, or until the liquid has reduced by about half, and the meat is very tender.

Add the spring onions (scallions) and sliced eggs and simmer for 5 minutes before serving.
*Serves 6*
Preparation and cooking time: 2¼ hours

## VIETNAMESE PORK LOAF

| Metric/Imperial | American |
|---|---|
| ½kg./1lb. minced pork | 1lb. ground pork |
| 8 dried mushrooms, soaked in cold water for 30 minutes, drained, stalks removed and chopped | 8 dried mushrooms, soaked in cold water for 30 minutes, drained, stalks removed and chopped |
| 4 spring onions, chopped | 4 scallions, chopped |
| 3 eggs, beaten | 3 eggs, beaten |
| 2 tsp. fish sauce | 2 tsp. fish sauce |
| salt and black pepper | salt and black pepper |

Put all the ingredients into a bowl and mix well. Arrange the mixture in a small, greased loaf pan and cover with a double thickness of foil. Place in the top of a steamer or in a large pan one-third full of boiling water. Steam for 1 hour.

Remove the pan from the heat and unwrap the loaf. Leave the loaf in the pan for 10 minutes, then transfer to a chopping board. Cut into thin slices and serve with salad.
*Serves 4*
Preparation and cooking time: 1½ hours

# MAH HO

(Galloping Horses) (Thailand)

*This exotically named dish is a typically Thai mixture of the sweet and savoury – savoury minced (ground) pork served on slices or rounds of sweet fruit. Pineapple is the fruit suggested here but more exotic oriental fruit such as rambutans could also be used. Mah ho is usually served as an hors d'oeuvre.*

| Metric/Imperial | American |
|---|---|
| 2 Tbs. peanut oil | 2 Tbs. peanut oil |
| 1 garlic clove, crushed | 1 garlic clove, crushed |
| 1 small onion, finely chopped | 1 small onion, finely chopped |
| 350g./12oz. minced pork | 12oz. ground pork |
| 3 Tbs. roasted peanuts, ground | 3 Tbs. roasted peanuts, ground |
| 3 Tbs. jaggery or brown sugar | 3 Tbs. jaggery or brown sugar |
| salt and pepper | salt and pepper |
| 1 fresh pineapple, peeled, cored and cut into rounds | 1 fresh pineapple, peeled, cored and cut into rounds |
| 1 dried red chilli, crumbled | 1 dried red chilli, crumbled |
| 2 Tbs. chopped coriander leaves | 2 Tbs. chopped coriander leaves |

Heat the oil in a large frying-pan. When it is hot, add the garlic and onion and fry, stirring occasionally, until the onion is soft. Stir in the minced (ground) pork and fry until it loses its pinkness. Add the roasted peanuts, jaggery or sugar and seasoning to taste. Reduce the heat to low and simmer the mixture for 10 to 15 minutes, or until the pork is cooked through and the mixture is thick and dryish. Remove from the heat.

Arrange the pineapple rounds on a large serving platter. Carefully spoon the mixture over the rounds, doming it up slightly in the middle. Garnish with crumbled red chilli and the coriander leaves. Serve at once.

*Serves 8-10*
Preparation and cooking time: 35 minutes

# PO CHERO

(Mixed Meat and Chick-Pea Ragout) (Philippines)

| Metric/Imperial | American |
|---|---|
| 4 chicken pieces, cut into large bite-sized pieces | 4 chicken pieces, cut into large bite-sized pieces |
| ½kg./1lb. pork fillet, cut into large cubes | 1lb. pork tenderloin, cut into large cubes |
| 3 hot sausages, halved | 3 hot sausages, halved |
| 2 medium onions, sliced | 2 medium onions, sliced |
| salt and pepper | salt and pepper |
| 50ml./2fl.oz. vegetable oil | ¼ cup vegetable oil |
| 3 spring onions, chopped | 3 scallions, chopped |
| 3 garlic cloves, crushed | 3 garlic cloves, crushed |
| 2 sweet potatoes, cubed | 2 sweet potatoes, cubed |
| ½ white cabbage, shredded | ½ white cabbage, shredded |
| 400g./14oz. tin chick-peas, drained | 14oz. can chick-peas, drained |
| 1 Tbs. sugar | 1 Tbs. sugar |
| 2 Tbs. tomato purée | 2 Tbs. tomato paste |

Put the chicken pieces, pork, sausages, onions and salt and pepper to taste in a large saucepan. Just cover with water and bring to the boil. Cover the pan, reduce the heat to low and simmer for 50 minutes to 1¼ hours, or until the meat is cooked through. Remove from the heat, transfer the meat to a plate and strain and reserve 300ml./10fl.oz. (1¼ cups) of the cooking liquid.

Heat the oil in a large, deep frying-pan. When it is hot, add the spring onions (scallions) and garlic and fry for 3 minutes. Pour over the strained liquid and bring to the boil. Add the sweet potato cubes, reduce the heat to low and simmer for 30 minutes. Stir in the meat pieces, cabbage, chick-peas, sugar and tomato purée (paste), and bring to the boil. Reduce the heat to low, cover and simmer for 10 minutes, or until the cabbage is just cooked through and all the meats are tender.

Adjust the seasoning and serve at once.
*Serves 8*
Preparation and cooking time: 2¼ hours

# SWEET & SOUR SPARERIBS

(Singapore)

| Metric/Imperial | American |
|---|---|
| 1½kg./3lb. American-style spareribs, cut into 2in. pieces | 3lb. spareribs, cut into 2-rib serving pieces |
| 2 garlic cloves, crushed | 2 garlic cloves, crushed |
| 3 Tbs. peanut oil | 3 Tbs. peanut oil |
| 5cm./2in. piece of fresh root ginger, peeled and chopped | 2in. piece of fresh green ginger, peeled and chopped |
| 1 large green pepper, pith and seeds removed and sliced | 1 large green pepper, pith and seeds removed and sliced |
| 1 large red pepper, pith and seeds removed and sliced | 1 large red pepper, pith and seeds removed and sliced |
| 175g./6oz. tin pineapple chunks, juice reserved | 6oz. can pineapple chunks, juice reserved |
| 1½ Tbs. wine vinegar | 1½ Tbs. wine vinegar |
| 1½ Tbs. soya sauce | 1½ Tbs. soy sauce |
| 1 Tbs. soft brown sugar | 1 Tbs. soft brown sugar |
| 1 Tbs. cornflour, mixed to a paste with 2 Tbs. water | 1 Tbs. cornstarch, mixed to a paste with 2 Tbs. water |

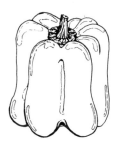

Preheat the oven to hot 220°C (Gas Mark 7, 425°F). Rub the spareribs with half the garlic and arrange them in a roasting pan. Roast for 30 minutes.

Meanwhile, heat the oil in a large frying-pan. When it is hot, add the remaining garlic and ginger and cook for 1 minute. Add the peppers and fry for 5 minutes, stirring occasionally. Stir in the pineapple chunks and fry for 3 minutes. Add the reserved pineapple juice, vinegar, soy sauce and sugar and bring to the boil.

Reduce the oven temperature to moderate 180°C (Gas Mark 4, 350°F).

Remove the ribs from the oven and pour off the fat. Stir in the pineapple mixture, basting the ribs thoroughly, and return the pan to the oven. Cook for 1 hour, basting occasionally, or until the ribs are golden brown and crisp. Remove from the oven and transfer the ribs to a serving plate.

Put the roasting pan over low heat and stir in the cornflour (cornstarch) mixture. Bring to the boil, stirring constantly, then cook until the sauce has thickened slightly and become translucent.

Pour the sauce over the ribs and serve at once.
*Serves 6-8*
Preparation and cooking time: 1¾ hours

# PORK ADOBO

(The Philippines)

| Metric/Imperial | American |
| --- | --- |
| 1½kg./3lb. pork chops or fillet, cut into large cubes | 3lb. pork chops or tenderloin, cut into large cubes |
| 8 garlic cloves, crushed | 8 garlic cloves, crushed |
| 250ml./8fl.oz. wine vinegar | 1 cup wine vinegar |
| 350ml./12fl.oz. water | 1½ cups water |
| 2 tsp. soya sauce | 2 tsp. soy sauce |
| black pepper | black pepper |
| 4 Tbs. vegetable oil | 4 Tbs. vegetable oil |

Put all the ingredients except the oil into a large saucepan and bring to the boil. Cover, reduce the heat to low and simmer gently for 1¼ to 1½ hours, or until the pork is tender. Remove the pork from the pan and set aside. Boil the liquid rapidly until it has reduced by half. Remove from the heat and keep hot.

Meanwhile, heat the oil in a large frying-pan. When it is very hot, add the pork pieces and fry them until they are evenly browned. Transfer them to a serving bowl. Strain over the cooking liquid and serve at once.

*Serves 6*
Preparation and cooking time: 2 hours

# BARBECUED SPARERIBS

(Singapore)

| Metric/Imperial | American |
| --- | --- |
| 1½kg./3lb. American-style spareribs, cut into 2in. pieces | 3lb. spareribs, cut into 2-rib serving pieces |
| salt and pepper | salt and pepper |
| 3 Tbs. soya sauce | 3 Tbs. soy sauce |
| 2 Tbs. clear honey | 2 Tbs. clear honey |
| 2 tsp. brown sugar | 2 tsp. brown sugar |
| 3 Tbs. hoi sin sauce | 3 Tbs. hoi sin sauce |
| 2 Tbs. wine vinegar | 2 Tbs. wine vinegar |
| 1 Tbs. dry sherry | 1 Tbs. dry sherry |
| 1 small onion, chopped | 1 small onion, chopped |
| 3 Tbs. chicken stock | 3 Tbs. chicken stock |
| ½ tsp. 5-spice powder | ½ tsp. 5-spice powder |
| 400g./14oz. tin Chinese plum sauce | 14oz. can Chinese plum sauce |

Rub the spareribs all over with salt and pepper and arrange them in a shallow dish. Mix all the remaining ingredients, except the plum sauce, together, and pour over the spareribs, basting them well. Set aside to marinate at room temperature for 1 hour, basting occasionally.

Preheat the oven to hot 220°C (Gas Mark 7, 425°F). Remove the spareribs from the liquid and pat dry on kitchen towels. Reserve the marinating liquid. Arrange the ribs in a roasting pan and put into the oven for 30 minutes. Remove from the oven and pour off the fat. Stir in the marinating liquid, basting the ribs thoroughly and return the pan to the oven. Reduce the oven temperature to moderate 180°C (Gas Mark 4, 350°F) and roast the ribs for 1 hour, basting occasionally, or until

they are golden brown and crisp. Remove from the oven, and transfer to a serving plate. Strain the cooking liquid and warm it with the plum sauce gently over low heat, stirring occasionally. Pour over the ribs and baste gently until they are thoroughly mixed. Serve at once.
*Serves 6-8*
Preparation and cooking time: 2½ hours

# WETHA HIN LAY

(Pork Curry with Mango)                                                    (Burma)

| Metric/Imperial | American |
| --- | --- |
| 2 medium onions, chopped | 2 medium onions, chopped |
| 3 garlic cloves, crushed | 3 garlic cloves, crushed |
| 4cm./1½in. piece of fresh root ginger, peeled and chopped | 1½in. piece of fresh green ginger, peeled and chopped |
| 1 tsp. ground chilli powder | 1 tsp. ground chilli powder |
| 1 tsp. turmeric | 1 tsp. turmeric |
| 50ml./2fl. oz. sesame oil | ¼ cup sesame oil |
| 1kg./2lb. lean pork, cubed | 2 lb. lean pork, cubed |
| 1 Tbs. tamarind | 1 Tbs. tamarind |
| 50ml./2fl. oz. boiling water | ¼ cup boiling water |
| 1 Tbs. lemon juice | 1 Tbs. lemon juice |
| 2 Tbs. mango pickle | 2 Tbs. mango pickle |
| GARNISH | GARNISH |
| 1 fresh mango, stoned and sliced | 1 fresh mango, pitted and sliced |
| 2 Tbs. chopped coriander leaves | 2 Tbs. chopped coriander leaves |

Put the onions, garlic and ginger into a blender and blend to a smooth purée. Stir the chilli powder and turmeric into the spice mixture.

Heat the oil in a large saucepan. When it is hot, add the spice mixture and stir-fry over low heat for 5 minutes. Add the pork cubes and continue to fry until they are evenly browned. Reduce the heat to low and cover the pan. Simmer the pork for 30 minutes.

Meanwhile, put the tamarind into a bowl and pour over the boiling water. Set aside until it is cool. Put the contents of the bowl through a strainer into a second bowl, pressing as much of the pulp through as possible.

Stir the tamarind liquid, lemon juice and mango pickle into the saucepan, re-cover and continue to simmer the mixture for a further 1 hour, or until the pork is cooked through and tender.

Transfer the mixture to a warmed serving dish and garnish with the mango slices and coriander leaves before serving.
*Serves 6*
Preparation and cooking time: 1¾ hours

# WETHANI

(Golden Pork)                                                              (Burma)
*The amounts of garlic and ginger are not a mistake – they reflect Burmese taste and are also supposed to 'preserve' the pork!*

| Metric/Imperial | American |
|---|---|
| 3 onions, finely chopped | 3 onions, finely chopped |
| 12 garlic cloves, crushed | 12 garlic cloves, crushed |
| 175g./6oz. fresh root ginger, peeled and chopped | 1 cup fresh green ginger, peeled and chopped |
| 1½kg./3lb. lean pork, cubed | 3lb. lean pork, cubed |
| salt | salt |
| 2 Tbs. vinegar | 2 Tbs. vinegar |
| 50ml./2fl.oz. vegetable oil | ¼ cup vegetable oil |
| 1 tsp. hot chilli powder | 1 tsp. hot chilli powder |

Put the onions, garlic and ginger into a blender and blend to a paste. Put the paste into a strainer or cheesecloth and squeeze gently over a bowl to extract as much juice as possible.

Put the liquid into a large saucepan with the pork, salt, vinegar, oil and chilli powder and bring to the boil. Cover, reduce the heat to low and simmer the pork for 2 hours, or until it is very tender. (You may have to add a tablespoon or two of water during the cooking period if the mixture becomes too dry.) The dish should be 'golden' at the end of cooking, as the translation of its name suggests.

*Serves 8*
Preparation and cooking time: 2¼ hours

# PORK SATE

(Indonesia)

| Metric/Imperial | American |
|---|---|
| ½kg./1lb. pork fillet, cut into small cubes | 1lb. pork tenderloin, cut into small cubes |
| MARINADE | MARINADE |
| 3 Tbs. dark soya sauce | 3 Tbs. dark soy sauce |
| 2 dried red chillis, crumbled or 1 tsp. sambal ulek | 2 dried red chillis, crumbled or 1 tsp. sambal ulek |
| 2 garlic cloves, crushed | 2 garlic cloves, crushed |
| 1 Tbs. water | 1 Tbs. water |
| ½ tsp. laos powder | ½ tsp. laos powder |
| SAUCE | SAUCE |
| 1 small onion, chopped | 1 small onion, chopped |
| 2 garlic cloves, crushed | 2 garlic cloves, crushed |
| 2 dried red chillis, crumbled or 1 tsp. sambal ulek | 2 dried red chillis, crumbled or 1 tsp. sambal ulek |
| 1 tsp. blachan (dried shrimp paste) | 1 tsp. blachan (dried shrimp paste) |
| 1 tsp. chopped lemon grass or grated lemon rind | 1 tsp. chopped lemon grass or grated lemon rind |
| 2 tsp. soft brown sugar | 2 tsp. soft brown sugar |
| 3 Tbs. peanut oil | 3 Tbs. peanut oil |
| 1 Tbs. soya sauce | 1 Tbs. soy sauce |
| 2 tsp. lemon juice | 2 tsp. lemon juice |
| 4 Tbs. peanut butter | 4 Tbs. peanut butter |
| 250ml./8fl.oz. coconut milk | 1 cup coconut milk |

Combine all the marinade ingredients in a shallow bowl. Add the pork pieces and marinate for 30 minutes, basting occasionally. Thread the pork on to skewers and reserve the marinade.

Preheat the grill (broiler) to moderately high. Arrange the skewers on the rack of

157

the grill (broiler) and grill (broil) for 20 minutes, turning and basting occasionally with the marinade, or until the pork is cooked through.

To make the sauce, combine the onion, garlic, chillis, blachan, lemon grass and sugar in a blender. Heat the oil in a saucepan. When it is hot, add the spice paste and fry for 2 minutes, stirring constantly. Add all the remaining ingredients and combine thoroughly. Bring to the boil. Remove from the heat.

To serve, pour the sauce into a shallow serving bowl and arrange the skewers across.

*Serves 4*

Preparation and cooking time: 1 hour

# MARINATED PORK CHOPS

(Malaysia)

| Metric/Imperial | American |
|---|---|
| 2 garlic cloves, crushed | 2 garlic cloves, crushed |
| 1 Tbs. crushed coriander seeds | 1 Tbs. crushed coriander seeds |
| 8 crushed peppercorns | 8 crushed peppercorns |
| 3 Tbs. soya sauce | 3 Tbs. soy sauce |
| 1 tsp. soft brown sugar | 1 tsp. soft brown sugar |
| 4 loin pork chops | 4 loin pork chops |

Mix all the ingredients except the chops together in a shallow dish. Put in the chops and coat well. Cover and set aside for 30 minutes, basting the chops occasionally.

Preheat the grill (broiler) to moderately high. Transfer the chops to the rack of the grill (broiler) and reserve the marinade. Grill (broil) the chops for 2 minutes. Reduce the heat to moderate and grill (broil) for 8 to 10 minutes on each side, basting occasionally with the marinating liquid.

Serve at once.

*Serves 4*

Preparation and cooking time: 1 hour

*Easy to make – and even easier to eat – are Marinated Pork Chops, a satisfying dish from Malaysia. Serve with bean sprouts or perhaps mashed potatoes for a filling meal.*

# CHICKEN

## HOT & SOUR CHICKEN, PENANG STYLE

(Malaysia)

| Metric/Imperial | American |
| --- | --- |
| 4 Tbs. vegetable oil | 4 Tbs. vegetable oil |
| 3 medium onions, finely chopped | 3 medium onions, finely chopped |
| 2 garlic cloves, crushed | 2 garlic cloves, crushed |
| 2 red or green chillis, finely chopped | 2 red or green chillis, finely chopped |
| 1 Tbs. soft brown sugar | 1 Tbs. soft brown sugar |
| 8 chicken pieces | 8 chicken pieces |
| 3 Tbs. dark soya sauce | 3 Tbs. dark soy sauce |
| 3 Tbs. wine vinegar | 3 Tbs. wine vinegar |
| 2 Tbs. water | 2 Tbs. water |
| $\frac{1}{2}$ tsp. salt | $\frac{1}{2}$ tsp. salt |

Heat the oil in a deep frying-pan. When it is hot, add the onions, garlic and chillis and fry for 5 minutes, stirring occasionally. Stir in the sugar and fry until the onions are golden brown.

Add the chicken pieces and fry for 8 minutes, turning frequently, or until they are deeply browned. Stir in the remaining ingredients and bring to the boil. Cover, reduce the heat to low and simmer for 15 minutes. Uncover the pan, increase the heat to moderate and cook the chicken for 25 to 30 minutes, or until it is cooked through.

Serve at once.
*Serves 8*
Preparation and cooking time: 1 hour

## SOY SAUCE CHICKEN

(Indonesia)

| Metric/Imperial | American |
| --- | --- |
| 1 tsp. salt | 1 tsp. salt |
| 3 Tbs. wine vinegar | 3 Tbs. wine vinegar |
| 1 Tbs. soft brown sugar | 1 Tbs. soft brown sugar |
| 1 x 1$\frac{1}{2}$kg./3lb. chicken, cut into 12 serving pieces | 1 x 3lb. chicken, cut into 12 serving pieces |
| 2 Tbs. peanut or coconut oil | 2 Tbs. peanut or coconut oil |
| SAUCE | SAUCE |
| 1 onion, finely chopped | 1 onion, finely chopped |
| 1 green chilli, seeded and finely chopped | 1 green chilli, seeded and finely chopped |
| 2 garlic cloves | 2 garlic cloves |
| 250ml./8fl.oz. water | 1 cup water |
| 1 Tbs. wine vinegar | 1 Tbs. wine vinegar |
| 2 Tbs. soya sauce | 2 Tbs. soy sauce |
| 1 Tbs. sugar | 1 Tbs. sugar |
| 4 medium tomatoes, blanched, peeled, seeded and chopped | 4 medium tomatoes, blanched, peeled, seeded and chopped |

Combine the salt, vinegar and sugar in a bowl. Toss the chicken pieces in the mixture and set aside for 30 minutes.

Meanwhile, prepare the sauce. Put all the ingredients, except the tomatoes, in a blender and blend until smooth. Pour into a large saucepan and set aside.

Heat the oil in a large frying-pan. When it is hot, add the chicken pieces and fry until they are golden brown all over. Using tongs, transfer to kitchen towels to drain.

Set the pan containing the sauce over moderate heat and bring to the boil. Add the chicken pieces and tomatoes and reduce the heat to low. Cover and simmer for 20 to 25 minutes, or until the chicken is cooked through. Uncover and simmer for a further 10 minutes, or until about a third of the liquid has evaporated.

Transfer the mixture to a warmed serving dish and serve at once.

*Serves 6*

Preparation and cooking time: 1½ hours

# OPAR AYAM

(Chicken in Coconut Gravy)                                    (Indonesia)

| Metric/Imperial | American |
|---|---|
| 3 garlic cloves, crushed | 3 garlic cloves, crushed |
| 5cm./2in. piece of fresh root ginger, peeled and chopped | 2in. piece of fresh green ginger, peeled and chopped |
| 2 red chillis, chopped | 2 red chillis, chopped |
| 3 candle or brazil nuts, chopped | 3 candle or brazil nuts, chopped |
| 1 Tbs. ground coriander | 1 Tbs. ground coriander |
| 1 tsp. ground cumin | 1 tsp. ground cumin |
| ½ tsp. ground fennel | ½ tsp. ground fennel |
| ½ tsp. laos powder | ½ tsp. laos powder |
| 5 Tbs. peanut oil | 5 Tbs. peanut oil |
| 2 medium onions, sliced | 2 medium onions, sliced |
| 1 x 2kg./4lb. chicken, cut into serving pieces | 1 x 4lb. chicken, cut into serving pieces |
| 1 tsp. chopped lemon grass or grated lemon rind | 1 tsp. chopped lemon grass or grated lemon rind |
| 600ml./1 pint thick coconut milk | 2½ cups thick coconut milk |
| 2 curry leaves (optional) | 2 curry leaves (optional) |
| 1 tsp. sugar | 1 tsp. sugar |

Put the garlic, ginger, chillis and nuts into a blender and blend to a paste. Transfer to a mixing bowl and stir in the coriander, cumin, fennel and laos powder until they are well mixed. Add about 1 tablespoon of the peanut oil, or a little more if necessary, to blend the mixture to a smooth, thick paste and set aside.

Heat the remaining oil in a large, deep frying-pan. When it is hot, add the onions and fry, stirring occasionally, until they are soft. Add the spice paste and stir-fry for 2 minutes. Add the chicken pieces and baste with the spice mixture until they are thoroughly coated. Stir in the lemon grass or rind and half the coconut milk, and bring to the boil. Reduce the heat to low, cover the pan and simmer for 30 minutes.

Stir in the curry leaves and sugar, then pour over the remaining coconut milk and bring to the boil. Reduce the heat to low and simmer the mixture, uncovered, for 20 to 30 minutes, or until the chicken pieces are cooked through and tender.

Serve at once.

*Serves 4–6*

Preparation and cooking time: 1¼ hours

# TIMOLA

(Chicken Stew)                                                    (The Philippines)

*Pawpaw or papaya can be difficult to find in the West; if this is so, mango or guava can be substituted.*

| Metric/Imperial | American |
|---|---|
| 50g./2oz. vegetable fat | 4 Tbs. vegetable fat |
| 1 medium onion, sliced | 1 medium onion, sliced |
| 2 garlic cloves, crushed | 2 garlic cloves, crushed |
| 4cm./1½in. piece of fresh root ginger, peeled and chopped | 1½in. piece of fresh green ginger, peeled and chopped |
| 1 x 1½kg./3lb. chicken, cut into serving pieces | 1 x 3lb. chicken, cut into serving pieces |
| 300ml./10fl.oz. water | 1¼ cups water |
| 1 pawpaw, peeled and finely chopped | 1 pawpaw, peeled and finely chopped |
| 225g./8oz. spinach leaves, chopped | 1⅓ cups chopped spinach leaves |

Melt the fat in a large saucepan. Add the onion, garlic and ginger and fry, stirring occasionally, until the onion is soft. Add the chicken pieces and fry gently until they are browned all over. Pour over the water and bring to the boil. Reduce the heat to low, cover the pan and simmer for 45 minutes to 1 hour, or until the chicken is cooked through and tender.

Stir in the pawpaw and spinach and cook for a further 10 minutes. Serve at once.

*Serves 4*
Preparation and cooking time: 1½ hours

# SATAY AYAM

(Chicken Sate)                                                      (Indonesia)

| Metric/Imperial | American |
|---|---|
| 2 Tbs. soft brown sugar | 2 Tbs. soft brown sugar |
| 50ml./2fl.oz. dark treacle | ¼ cup molasses |
| 125ml./4fl.oz. dark soy sauce | ½ cup dark soy sauce |
| 2 garlic cloves, crushed | 2 garlic cloves, crushed |
| juice of ½ lemon | juice of ½ lemon |
| 2 Tbs. groundnut oil | 2 Tbs. groundnut oil |
| 3 chicken breasts | 3 chicken breasts |
| SAUCE | SAUCE |
| 225g./8oz. unsalted peanuts, shelled | 1⅓ cups unsalted peanuts, shelled |
| 2 red chillis or 1 tsp. sambal ulek | 2 red chillis or 1 tsp. sambal ulek |
| 3 garlic cloves | 3 garlic cloves |
| 1 tsp. salt | 1 tsp. salt |
| 1 onion, coarsely chopped | 1 onion, coarsely chopped |
| 50ml./2fl.oz. groundnut oil | ¼ cup groundnut oil |
| 75-125ml./3-4fl.oz. water | ⅓-½ cup water |
| 1 Tbs. soft brown sugar mixed with 2 Tbs. dark soy sauce | 1 Tbs. soft brown sugar mixed with 2 Tbs. dark soy sauce |
| 1-2 Tbs. lemon juice | 1-2 Tbs. lemon juice |

Mix the sugar, treacle (molasses) and soy sauce together in a small bowl. Stir in the garlic, lemon juice and oil and set aside.

Skin and bone the chicken breasts, then cut the meat into 1½cm./¾in. cubes. Thread the cubes on to skewers and arrange the skewers in a shallow dish. Pour over the soy sauce mixture and set aside to marinate at room temperature for 1 hour, basting occasionally. Turn the skewers in the marinade from time to time.

Preheat the grill (broiler) to high.

To make the sauce, put the peanuts in the grill (broiler) pan and grill (broil) them for 2 to 3 minutes, turning occasionally. Remove from the heat and gently rub them between your hands to remove the skins. Put the peanuts in a grinder or blender with the chillis or sambal ulek, garlic, salt, onion and 2 tablespoons of the groundnut oil. Blend to a thick paste, adding enough of the water to prevent the blender from sticking. Remove the paste from the blender, put in a bowl and set aside.

Heat the remaining oil in a saucepan. When it is hot, add the nut paste. Reduce the heat to moderately low and fry the paste for 3 minutes, stirring constantly. Stir in the remaining water and simmer gently for 5 minutes, or until it is thick and smooth. Remove from the heat and stir in the soy sauce mixture and lemon juice. Taste and add more salt and lemon if necessary. Keep hot while you cook the chicken.

Arrange the skewers on the rack of the grill (broiler). Grill (broil) the chicken for 5 minutes, turning occasionally, or until the cubes are cooked through and tender.

Remove from the heat and arrange the skewers on a warmed serving platter, or across a serving bowl. Serve at once, with the sauce.

*Serves 4-6*
Preparation and cooking time: 1½ hours

# MANGO CHICKEN

(Malaysia)

| Metric/Imperial | American |
| --- | --- |
| 1 x 2kg./4lb. chicken, cut into serving pieces | 1 x 4lb. chicken, cut into serving pieces |
| salt and pepper | salt and pepper |
| 3 Tbs. peanut oil | 3 Tbs. peanut oil |
| 1 large onion, thinly sliced | 1 large onion, thinly sliced |
| 1 mango, peeled, stoned and sliced | 1 mango, peeled, pitted and sliced |
| 1 tsp. chopped lemon grass or grated lemon rind | 1 tsp. chopped lemon grass or grated lemon rind |
| ¼ tsp. ground coriander | ¼ tsp. ground coriander |
| ¼ tsp. ground cinnamon | ¼ tsp. ground cinnamon |
| 250ml./8fl.oz. chicken stock | 1 cup chicken stock |
| 250ml./8fl.oz. single cream | 1 cup light cream |
| 2 tsp. flour, mixed to a paste with 1 Tbs. lemon juice and 1 Tbs. water | 2 tsp. flour, mixed to a paste with 1 Tbs. lemon juice and 1 Tbs. water |

Preheat the oven to fairly hot 190°C (Gas Mark 5, 375°F).

Rub the chicken pieces all over with the salt and pepper, then set aside.

Heat the oil in a large frying-pan. When it is hot, add the chicken pieces and fry, stirring occasionally, until they are evenly browned. Using a slotted spoon, transfer

the chicken pieces to a flameproof casserole. Set aside.

Add the onion to the frying-pan and fry until it is soft. Using the slotted spoon, transfer the onion to the casserole.

Add the mango slices to the frying-pan and fry, turning once, for 4 minutes. Stir in the lemon grass or rind, coriander, cinnamon and stock to the pan and bring to the boil, stirring constantly. Pour over the chicken and onion mixture in the casserole.

Cover the casserole and put into the oven. Bake for 1¼ hours, or until the chicken is cooked through and tender. Remove from the oven and, using tongs or a slotted spoon, transfer the chicken pieces to a warmed serving dish. Keep hot while you finish the sauce.

Bring the casserole liquid to the boil. Reduce the heat to low and stir in the cream and flour mixture. Cook the sauce, stirring constantly, until it is hot but not boiling and has thickened.

Remove the casserole from the heat and pour the sauce over the chicken pieces. Serve at once.

*Serves 4*
Preparation and cooking time: 2 hours

*This dish combines two favourite South-East Asian foods: mangoes and chicken. Mango Chicken is smooth, rich and spicy, without being hot.*

# AYAM BALI

(Balinese Fried Chicken)                                    (Indonesia)

| Metric/Imperial | American |
| --- | --- |
| 1 medium onion, chopped | 1 medium onion, chopped |
| 2 garlic cloves, crushed | 2 garlic cloves, crushed |
| 2½cm./1in. piece of fresh root ginger, peeled and chopped | 1in. piece of fresh root ginger, peeled and chopped |
| 2 red chillis, chopped | 2 red chillis, chopped |
| 4 candle or brazil nuts, chopped | 4 candle or brazil nuts, chopped |
| 250ml./8fl.oz. coconut milk or water | 1 cup coconut milk or water |
| 50ml./2fl.oz. peanut oil | ¼ cup peanut oil |
| 4 large chicken pieces | 4 large chicken pieces |
| 1 Tbs. soya sauce | 1 Tbs. soy sauce |
| 1 tsp. soft brown sugar | 1 tsp. soft brown sugar |
| 1 tsp. wine vinegar | 1 tsp. wine vinegar |

Put the onion, garlic, ginger, chillis and nuts into a blender with 2 tablespoons of the coconut milk or water and blend to a smooth purée.

Heat the oil in a large, deep frying-pan. When it is hot, add the chicken pieces and fry for 8 to 10 minutes, or until they are evenly browned. Using tongs or a slotted spoon, transfer the chicken pieces to a plate and keep hot.

Add the purée mixture to the frying-pan and stir-fry for 5 minutes. Stir in the remaining coconut milk or water, the soy sauce, sugar and vinegar and bring to the boil. Add the chicken pieces to the pan and baste them thoroughly with the liquid. Reduce the heat to low and simmer the chicken, uncovered, for 30 to 40 minutes, or until the pieces are cooked through and tender.

Transfer the mixture to a warmed serving dish and serve at once.

*Serves 4*
Preparation and cooking time: 1¼ hours


# KAUKSWE-HIN

(Curried Chicken with Noodles)                              (Burma)

| Metric/Imperial | American |
| --- | --- |
| ½ tsp. hot chilli powder | ½ tsp. hot chilli powder |
| 1 tsp. turmeric | 1 tsp. turmeric |
| ½ tsp. ground cumin | ½ tsp. ground cumin |
| 3 Tbs. sesame oil | 3 Tbs. sesame oil |
| 4 garlic cloves, crushed | 4 garlic cloves, crushed |
| 2½cm./1in. piece of fresh root ginger, peeled and chopped | 1in. piece of fresh green ginger, peeled and chopped |
| 4 onions, chopped | 4 onions, chopped |
| ½ tsp. chopped lemon grass or grated lemon rind | ½ tsp. chopped lemon grass or grated lemon rind |
| 1 x 2kg./4lb. chicken, cut into serving pieces | 1 x 4lb. chicken, cut into serving pieces |
| 450ml./15fl.oz. thin coconut milk | 2 cups thin coconut milk |
| 300ml./10fl.oz. thick coconut milk | 1¼ cups thick coconut milk |
| salt | salt |
| ½ tsp. lime or lemon juice | ½ tsp. lime or lemon juice |
| ½ kg./1lb. fine noodles or vermicelli | 1lb. fine noodles or vermicelli |

*Kaukswe-Hin, a delectable mixture of chicken curry and noodles topped by a variety of garnishes, is almost the Burmese national dish. It is served here with Than That, a popular cucumber pickle.*

165

| GARNISH | GARNISH |
| --- | --- |
| 4 spring onions, chopped | 4 scallions, chopped |
| 2 Tbs. chopped coriander leaves | 2 Tbs. chopped coriander leaves |
| 6 lemon wedges | 6 lemon wedges |
| 3 hard-boiled eggs, chopped | 3 hard-cooked eggs, chopped |

Mix together the chilli powder, turmeric and cumin and set aside.

Heat the oil in a large saucepan. When it is hot, add the garlic, ginger and onions and fry, stirring occasionally, until the onions are soft. Stir in the spice mixture and fry for 1 minute, stirring constantly. Add the chicken pieces and fry until they are lightly browned all over. Pour over the thin coconut milk and bring to the boil. Reduce the heat to low and simmer the mixture, uncovered, for 1 to 1¼ hours, or until the chicken pieces are tender. Stir in the thick coconut milk, salt and lime or lemon juice. Simmer for 5 minutes.

Meanwhile, cook the noodles in boiling salted water for 5 minutes. Drain and keep them hot. Arrange the garnishes in separate, small bowls.

To serve, put the chicken curry in one large serving bowl, and divide the noodles among individual bowls. Each diner should ladle the chicken and gravy over the noodles and sprinkle over the garnishes as required.

*Serves 4-6*

Preparation and cooking time: 2 hours

# AJAM GORENG

(Spicy Fried Chicken)                                              (Indonesia)

| Metric/Imperial | American |
| --- | --- |
| 1 x 1½kg./3lb. chicken, cut into 12 or 15 pieces | 1 x 3lb. chicken, cut into 12 or 15 pieces |
| 25g./1oz. tamarind | 1oz. tamarind |
| 125ml./4fl. oz. boiling water | ½ cup boiling water |
| 2 garlic cloves, crushed | 2 garlic cloves, crushed |
| 2 tsp. ground coriander | 2 tsp. ground coriander |
| 1 tsp. ground ginger | 1 tsp. ground ginger |
| 1 Tbs. wine vinegar or lemon juice | 1 Tbs. wine vinegar or lemon juice |
| 1 tsp. soft brown sugar | 1 tsp. soft brown sugar |
| 50g./2oz. flour | ½ cup flour |
| vegetable oil for deep-frying | vegetable oil for deep-frying |

Put the chicken pieces into a large, shallow dish and set aside.

Put the tamarind into a bowl and pour over the boiling water. Set aside until it is cool. Put the contents of the bowl through a strainer into the dish containing the chicken, pressing as much of the pulp through as possible.

Combine all the remaining ingredients, except the flour and oil, beating until they are thoroughly combined. Stir them into the dish containing the chicken until the mixture is blended and all the pieces are well coated. Put into the refrigerator to marinate for at least 8 hours, or overnight. Remove from the dish.

Fill a large deep-frying pan about one-third full with oil and heat until it is very hot. Dip the chicken pieces into the flour, shaking off any excess flour. Carefully lower the pieces into the oil, a few at a time, and deep-fry for 5 to 8 minutes, or until they are cooked through and golden brown. Remove from the oil and drain on kitchen towels. Serve hot.

*Serves 4*

Preparation and cooking time: 8½ hours

# FRIED CHICKEN WITH MUSHROOMS

(Cambodia)

| Metric/Imperial | American |
| --- | --- |
| 50ml./2fl.oz. peanut oil | ¼ cup peanut oil |
| 3 garlic cloves, crushed | 3 garlic cloves, crushed |
| 5cm./2in. piece of fresh root ginger, peeled and chopped | 2in. piece of fresh green ginger, peeled and chopped |
| 1 x 1½kg./3lb. chicken, cut into small pieces | 1 x 3lb. chicken, cut into small pieces |
| 8 dried Chinese mushrooms, soaked in cold water for 30 minutes, drained, stalks removed and sliced | 8 dried Chinese mushrooms, soaked in cold water for 30 minutes, drained, stalks removed and sliced |
| 1 Tbs. sugar | 1 Tbs. sugar |
| 2 Tbs. vinegar | 2 Tbs. vinegar |
| 2 Tbs. fish sauce | 2 Tbs. fish sauce |
| 175ml./6fl.oz. water | ¾ cup water |
| 1 Tbs. chopped coriander leaves | 1 Tbs. chopped coriander leaves |

Heat the oil in a large saucepan. When it is hot, add the garlic and ginger and stir-fry for 2 minutes. Add the chicken and cook for 8 to 10 minutes, stirring occasionally. Stir in all the remaining ingredients, except the coriander, and stir-fry for 10 minutes, or until the chicken is cooked through.

Transfer the mixture to a warmed serving bowl and garnish with the coriander before serving.

*Serves 4*
Preparation and cooking time: 50 minutes

# KAI TOM KHA

(Chicken with Laos Powder)                                                      (Thailand)

| Metric/Imperial | American |
| --- | --- |
| 1 x 2kg./4lb. chicken, cut into serving pieces | 1 x 4lb. chicken, cut into serving pieces |
| 450ml./15fl.oz. thin coconut milk | 2 cups thin coconut milk |
| 4 tsp. laos powder | 4 tsp. laos powder |
| 2 tsp. chopped lemon grass or grated lemon rind | 2 tsp. chopped lemon grass or grated lemon rind |
| 1 green chilli, finely chopped | 1 green chilli, finely chopped |
| 250ml./8fl.oz. thick coconut milk | 1 cup thick coconut milk |
| 1 tsp. fish sauce | 1 tsp. fish sauce |
| 1 Tbs. lemon juice | 1 Tbs. lemon juice |
| 2 Tbs. chopped coriander leaves | 2 Tbs. chopped coriander leaves |

Put the chicken pieces into a large saucepan and pour over the thin coconut milk. Stir in the laos powder, chopped lemon grass or lemon rind and chilli and bring to the boil. Cover the pan, reduce the heat to low and simmer the mixture gently for 30 minutes. Uncover and continue to simmer for a further 15 to 20 minutes, or until the chicken pieces are cooked through and tender.

Pour over the thick coconut milk and bring to the boil. Reduce the heat to low and simmer for 5 minutes. Stir in the fish sauce and lemon juice.

Transfer the mixture to a warmed serving bowl and garnish with the chopped coriander leaves before serving.

*Serves 4-6*

Preparation and cooking time: 1¼ hours

# GRILLED (BROILED) CHICKEN

(Malaysia)

| Metric/Imperial | American |
|---|---|
| 25 blanched almonds, | 25 blanched almonds |
| 2 green chillis | 2 green chillis |
| 3 garlic cloves | 3 garlic cloves |
| 1 tsp. chopped lemon grass or grated lemon rind | 1 tsp. chopped lemon grass or grated lemon rind |
| 2 tsp. turmeric | 2 tsp. turmeric |
| 1 Tbs. coriander seeds | 1 Tbs. coriander seeds |
| ½ tsp. hot chilli powder | ½ tsp. hot chilli powder |
| 1 tsp. sugar | 1 tsp. sugar |
| ½ tsp. laos powder | ½ tsp. laos powder |
| ½ tsp. salt | ½ tsp. salt |
| juice of 1 lemon | juice of 1 lemon |
| 3 Tbs. vegetable oil | 3 Tbs. vegetable oil |
| 300ml./10fl.oz. coconut milk | 1¼ cups coconut milk |
| 1 x 2kg./4lb. chicken, cut into quarters | 1 x 4lb. chicken, cut into quarters |

Put the almonds, spices, salt and lemon juice into a blender and blend, adding a spoonful or two of water, until the mixture becomes a thick paste. Scrape into a cup and set aside.

Heat the oil in a large saucepan. When it is hot, add the spice paste and fry for 5 minutes, stirring constantly. Stir in the coconut milk and chicken pieces and bring to the boil. Cover, reduce the heat to low and simmer for 40 minutes, or until the chicken is just cooked and the liquid is thick and nearly all evaporated. Cook uncovered for the last 10 minutes.

Preheat the grill (broiler) to high. Put the chicken pieces on the rack in the grill (broiler) and grill (broil) for 3 to 4 minutes on each side, or until they are golden brown, basting occasionally with the reserved cooking liquid.

Serve at once.

*Serves 6*

Preparation and cooking time: 1 hour

# KAPITAN CURRY

(Singapore)

| Metric/Imperial | American |
|---|---|
| 4 Tbs. vegetable oil | 4 Tbs. vegetable oil |
| 2 medium onions, finely chopped | 2 medium onions, finely chopped |
| 3 garlic cloves, crushed | 3 garlic cloves, crushed |

4cm./1½in. piece of fresh root ginger,
  peeled and chopped
6 green chillis, 2 finely chopped
  and 4 whole
2 Tbs. ground coriander
2 tsp. ground cumin
1 whole star anise, crushed
1 tsp. turmeric
½ tsp. grated nutmeg
½ tsp. ground cinnamon
½ tsp. ground cardamom
8 chicken pieces
600ml./1 pint coconut milk
1 tsp. salt

1½in. piece of fresh green ginger,
  peeled and chopped
6 green chillis, 2 finely chopped
  and 4 whole
2 Tbs. ground coriander
2 tsp. ground cumin
1 whole star anise, crushed
1 tsp. turmeric
½ tsp. grated nutmeg
½ tsp. ground cinnamon
½ tsp. ground cardamom
8 chicken pieces
2½ cups coconut milk
1 tsp. salt

Heat the oil in a large saucepan. When it is hot, add the onions, garlic, ginger and chopped chillis and fry, stirring occasionally, until the onions are golden brown. Stir in the spices and fry for 5 minutes, stirring constantly. If the mixture becomes too dry, add a spoonful or two of water. Add the chicken pieces and turn over in the spice mixture. Fry for 5 minutes, turning occasionally.

Pour over the coconut milk and add the salt and whole chillis. Cover, reduce the heat to low and simmer the curry for 45 minutes to 1 hour, or until the chicken is cooked through.

Transfer the chicken pieces to a serving bowl and pour over the sauce. Serve at once.

*Serves 8*
Preparation and cooking time: 1¼ hours

*Kapitan Curry from Singapore is a delightful chicken dish with a coconut-flavoured gravy. Serve with rice and a variety of chutneys for a superb meal.*

# PAPER WRAPPED CHICKEN

(Singapore)

*This dish reflects the very strong Chinese influence still present in Singapore and Malay food – it is, in fact, a standard dish in many ethnic Chinese restaurants as well as Singapore and Malaysian ones. In the Far East the chicken pieces would undoubtedly be deep-fried in rice paper, which is edible, and these can be obtained from Chinese general stores. However, if they are not available, greaseproof or waxed paper can be used instead.*

| Metric/Imperial | American |
|---|---|
| 2 large chicken breasts, skinned, boned and cut into bite-sized pieces | 2 large chicken breasts, skinned, boned and cut into bite-sized pieces |
| rice or greaseproof paper | rice or waxed paper |
| 8 dried mushrooms, soaked in cold water for 30 minutes, drained and chopped | 8 dried mushrooms, soaked in cold water for 30 minutes, drained and chopped |
| 4 spring onions, chopped | 4 scallions, chopped |
| 4cm./1½in. piece of fresh root ginger, peeled and thinly sliced | 1½in. piece of fresh green ginger, peeled and thinly sliced |
| 3 Tbs. frozen green peas, thawed | 3 Tbs. frozen green peas, thawed |
| vegetable oil for deep-frying | vegetable oil for deep-frying |
| MARINADE | MARINADE |
| 1½ Tbs. oyster sauce | 1½ Tbs. oyster sauce |
| 1 Tbs. sesame oil | 1 Tbs. sesame oil |
| 1 Tbs. rice wine or sherry | 1 Tbs. rice wine or sherry |
| ½ tsp. sugar | ½ tsp. sugar |
| ¼ tsp. ground ginger | ¼ tsp. ground ginger |

First, make the marinade. Put all the ingredients into a shallow bowl and mix until they are thoroughly blended. Add the chicken pieces to the bowl and stir them gently until they are thoroughly basted. Set aside at room temperature for 1 hour, turning and basting from time to time.

Cut the paper into squares about 15cm./6in. in diameter. Arrange a little of the filling just off centre (see the sketch below) and carefully add a little mushroom, spring onion (scallion), ginger and peas to the filling. Fold up the paper, as explained in the sketch so that the filling is completely enclosed, envelope fashion.

Fill a large deep-frying pan about one-third full with vegetable oil and heat until it is hot. Carefully lower the 'packets' into the oil, two or three at a time, and fry for 3 to 5 minutes, turning occasionally. Remove from the oil and drain on kitchen towels.

To serve, if using rice paper serve the packets to be eaten, paper and all; if using greaseproof or waxed paper, open the packets on individual serving plates and serve at once.

*Serves 4*

Preparation and cooking time: 1¾ hours

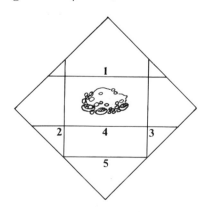

# DUCK

## GREEN DUCK CURRY

(Thailand)

*This dish can be made with either duck or chicken; the 'green' part of the title comes from the greenish tinge of the curry paste, which is effected by using green rather than red chillis and coriander leaves. The root of the coriander plant is traditionally used in Thailand as an ingredient in this curry paste but since it is virtually unobtainable in the West, the leaf has been substituted.*

| Metric/Imperial | American |
| --- | --- |
| 300ml./10fl.oz. thin coconut milk | 1¼ cups thin coconut milk |
| 1 x 3kg./6lb. duck, cut into 8-10 serving pieces | 1 x 6lb. duck, cut into 8-10 serving pieces |
| 1 Tbs. fish sauce | 1 Tbs. fish sauce |
| 2 Tbs. chopped coriander leaves | 2 Tbs. chopped coriander leaves |
| 300ml./10fl.oz. thick coconut milk | 1¼ cups thick coconut milk |
| CURRY PASTE | CURRY PASTE |
| 3 spring onions, green part included, chopped | 3 scallions, green part included, chopped |
| 2 garlic cloves, crushed | 2 garlic cloves, crushed |
| 3 green chillis, chopped | 3 green chillis, chopped |
| 2 tsp. grated lime rind | 2 tsp. grated lime rind |
| 1 Tbs. chopped coriander leaves | 1 Tbs. chopped coriander leaves |
| 1 tsp. chopped lemon grass or grated lemon rind | 1 tsp. chopped lemon grass or grated lemon rind |
| 2 tsp. ground coriander | 2 tsp. ground coriander |
| 1 tsp. ground cumin | 1 tsp. ground cumin |
| 1 tsp. laos powder | 1 tsp. laos powder |
| salt and pepper | salt and pepper |
| 1 tsp. blachan (dried shrimp paste) | 1 tsp. blachan (dried shrimp paste) |
| ½ tsp. turmeric | ½ tsp. turmeric |

To make the curry paste, put the spring onions (scallions), garlic, chillis, lime rind, coriander leaves and lemon grass or rind into a blender with a little of the thin coconut milk. Blend to a very thick purée. Transfer the purée to a bowl and stir in the remaining curry paste ingredients until all the ingredients are well blended.

Put the remaining thin coconut milk into a large saucepan and bring to the boil. Add the duck pieces and return the mixture to the boil. Reduce the heat to low and simmer for 1 to 1¼ hours, or until the duck is cooked through and tender.

Pour about half of the liquid in the pan with the duck into a second large saucepan and bring to the boil. Stir in the curry paste and fry, stirring frequently, over high heat until the milk has almost evaporated. Reduce the heat to moderate and continue frying the mixture for 3 minutes in the oily milk residue, stirring constantly. Gradually stir in the remaining coconut milk from the pan containing the duck and cook the mixture until it is thick and the oil begins to separate from the liquid.

Add the cooked duck pieces, fish sauce, half the chopped coriander and the thick coconut milk. Bring to the boil and reduce the heat to moderately low. Cook the mixture for 5 minutes, or until the liquid has thickened. Stir in the remaining coriander leaves and simmer for 5 minutes.

Serve at once.

*Serves 4–6*
Preparation and cooking time: 2 hours

# MALAYSIAN DUCK

| Metric/Imperial | American |
|---|---|
| 1 Tbs. ground coriander | 1 Tbs. ground coriander |
| 2 tsp. ground fenugreek | 2 tsp. ground fenugreek |
| 2 tsp. ground cumin | 2 tsp. ground cumin |
| 1 tsp. turmeric | 1 tsp. turmeric |
| 1 tsp. ground cinnamon | 1 tsp. ground cinnamon |
| ½ tsp. ground cardamom | ½ tsp. ground cardamom |
| ¼ tsp. grated nutmeg | ¼ tsp. grated nutmeg |
| 1 tsp. mild chilli powder | 1 tsp. mild chilli powder |
| salt and pepper | salt and pepper |
| juice of 1 lemon | juice of 1 lemon |
| 1cm./½in. piece of fresh root ginger, peeled and chopped | ½in. piece of fresh green ginger, peeled and chopped |
| 2 small onions, minced | 2 small onions, ground |
| 2 garlic cloves, crushed | 2 garlic cloves, crushed |
| 125g./4oz. desiccated coconut, soaked in 175ml./6fl.oz. boiling water | ½ cup shredded coconut, soaked in ¾ cup boiling water |
| 1 x 2½kg./5lb. duck, split through the breast bone, ribs broken at the backbone and wings and legs tied together | 1 x 5lb. duck, split through the breast bone, ribs broken at the backbone and wings and legs tied together |

Preheat the oven to fairly hot 190°C (Gas Mark 5, 375°F).

Mix all the spices together in a bowl and add seasoning, lemon juice, ginger, onions, garlic and coconut milk to form a thick paste. Spread the paste over the duck.

Put the duck on a rack in a roasting pan and roast for 1½ hours, basting every 15 minutes or so. Halfway through roasting, turn the duck over. When it is cooked through, baste once more then remove from the oven.

Serve at once.

*Serves 4–6*
Preparation and cooking time: 1¾ hours

*Barbecuing is a very popular method of cooking in Malaysia, and this simple but delicious Malaysian Duck demonstrates why. The duck is first marinated in a spicy coconut paste, then barbecued to crisp perfection.*

# FISH

## IKAN BANDENG

(Baked Spiced Fish)                                                    (Indonesia)

*Bandeng is a type of sole, found around the coast of Indonesia. Any type of fish can be substituted however – grey mullet, red snapper, even a large whiting.*

| Metric/Imperial | American |
| --- | --- |
| 2 Tbs. vegetable oil | 2 Tbs. vegetable oil |
| 1 x 1½kg./3lb. fish, cleaned and gutted | 1 x 3lb fish, cleaned and gutted |
| 3 garlic cloves, crushed | 3 garlic cloves, crushed |
| 7½cm./3in. piece of fresh root ginger, peeled and minced | 3in. piece of fresh green ginger, peeled and minced |
| 3 Tbs. soya sauce | 3 Tbs. soy sauce |
| 1½ Tbs. lemon juice | 1½ Tbs. lemon juice |
| 3 tsp. dried chillis or sambal ulek | 3 tsp. dried chillis or sambal ulek |
| GARNISH | GARNISH |
| 2 lemons, cut into wedges | 2 lemons, cut into wedges |
| 3 Tbs. chopped coriander leaves | 3 Tbs. chopped coriander leaves |

Preheat the oven to fairly hot 190°C (Gas Mark 5, 375°F).

Make some deep gashes across the fish with a sharp knife. Pour the oil into a roasting pan, then transfer the fish to the pan.

Beat the garlic, ginger, soy sauce, lemon juice and sambal ulek together until they are well blended, then pour over the fish, rubbing the mixture into the flesh and gashes.

Cover with foil then put the roasting pan into the oven. Bake the fish for 25 to 30 minutes, or until the flesh flakes easily.

Remove from the oven and serve at once, garnished with lemon wedges and coriander leaves.

*Serves 4-6*

Preparation and cooking time: 40 minutes


## VIETNAMESE FRIED FISH

| Metric/Imperial | American |
| --- | --- |
| 4 Tbs. cornflour | 4 Tbs. cornstarch |
| salt and pepper | salt and pepper |
| 4 small bream, cleaned and with the eyes removed | 4 small porgy, cleaned and with the eyes removed |
| 50ml./2fl.oz. peanut oil | ¼ cup peanut oil |
| nuoc cham (page 412) | nuoc cham (page 412) |

Mix the cornflour (cornstarch) with salt and pepper to taste and use to coat the fish lightly. Heat the oil in a large frying-pan. When it is hot, add the fish and fry for 10 to 12 minutes, or until the flesh flakes.

Serve at once, with nuoc cham.

*Serves 4*

Preparation and cooking time: 15 minutes

*Fish with Pineapple and Ginger comes from Malaysia, where fish such as mullet or snapper would be used in its cooking. But the combination is a delicious one with any firm-fleshed white fish.*

# FISH FILLETS WITH PINEAPPLE AND GINGER

(Malaysia)

| Metric/Imperial | American |
|---|---|
| 2 tsp. turmeric | 2 tsp. turmeric |
| 1½ tsp. salt | 1½ tsp. salt |
| 700g./1½lb. fish fillets, cut into bite-sized pieces | 1½lb. fish fillets, cut into bite-sized pieces |
| 3 Tbs. vegetable oil | 3 Tbs. vegetable oil |
| 2 onions, finely chopped | 2 onions, finely chopped |
| 4cm./1½in. piece of fresh root ginger, peeled and chopped | 1½in. piece of fresh green ginger, peeled and chopped |
| 2 chillis, finely chopped | 2 chillis, finely chopped |
| 1 tsp. blachan (dried shrimp paste) | 1 tsp. blachan (dried shrimp paste) |
| 1 tsp. ground lemon grass or finely grated lemon rind | 1 tsp. ground lemon grass or finely grated lemon rind |
| 1 tsp. sugar | 1 tsp. sugar |
| 4 tomatoes, blanched, peeled and chopped | 4 tomatoes, blanched, peeled and chopped |
| 1 small pineapple, peeled, cored and cut into chunks | 1 small pineapple, peeled, cored and cut into chunks |

Mix half the turmeric with 1 teaspoon of salt, then rub over the fish pieces.

Heat the oil in a large frying-pan. When it is hot, add the fish pieces and fry for 2 minutes on each side. Remove the fish to a plate. If necessary, add more oil to the pan to cover the bottom. Add the onions and fry, stirring occasionally, until they are golden brown. Add the ginger, chillis, blachan, lemon grass or rind and remaining turmeric and fry over low heat for 5 minutes, stirring constantly. Stir in the sugar, tomatoes and remaining salt, the pineapple and fish pieces. Cover and simmer for 20 to 25 minutes, or until the fish flakes easily. Serve at once.
*Serves 6–8*
Preparation and cooking time: 50 minutes

# OTAK-OTAK

(Steamed Fish Parcels)                    (Malaysia)

*In Malaysia banana leaves are used as wrappers for this dish, but foil or any other heatproof wrapping makes a good Western substitute.*

| Metric/Imperial | American |
|---|---|
| 700g./1½lb. cod or other white fish fillets, skinned and cut into strips | 1½lb. cod or other white fish fillets, skinned and cut into strips |
| SAUCE | SAUCE |
| 2 garlic cloves, crushed | 2 garlic cloves, crushed |
| 4 green chillis, finely chopped | 4 green chillis, finely chopped |
| ½ tsp. chopped lemon grass or grated lemon rind | ½ tsp. chopped lemon grass or grated lemon rind |
| 1 tsp. turmeric | 1 tsp. turmeric |
| salt and pepper | salt and pepper |
| 4 Tbs. desiccated coconut | 4 Tbs. shredded coconut |
| 250ml./8fl.oz. thick coconut milk | 1 cup thick coconut milk |

Pound all the sauce ingredients, except the coconut milk, together until they form a smooth paste. Put the milk into a saucepan and heat until it is hot but not boiling. Remove the pan from the heat and stir in the paste mixture.

Cut out four medium squares of foil. Spread some of the coconut mixture over the bottom of each one, then divide the fish between them. Cover with the remaining coconut mixture. Fold the foil into neat parcels, to enclose the filling completely.

Place the parcels in the top of a double boiler or in a heatproof plate set over a pan of boiling water. Cover and steam for 30 minutes.

Serve straight from the wrapping.

*Serves 4*
Preparation and cooking time: 45 minutes

# IKAN ACHAR

(Vinegar Fish)                                                        (Malaysia)

| Metric/Imperial | American |
| --- | --- |
| 1 onion, chopped | 1 onion, chopped |
| 1 garlic clove, crushed | 1 garlic clove, crushed |
| 2½cm./1in. piece of fresh root ginger, peeled and chopped | 1in. piece of fresh green ginger, peeled and chopped |
| 4 candle or brazil nuts, chopped | 4 candle or brazil nuts, chopped |
| 1 tsp. chopped dried red chillis or sambal ulek | 1 tsp. chopped dried red chillis or sambal ulek |
| 125ml./4fl.oz. water | ½ cup water |
| 50ml./2fl.oz. peanut oil | ¼ cup peanut oil |
| 2 Tbs. wine vinegar | 2 Tbs. wine vinegar |
| ½ tsp. soft brown sugar | ½ tsp. soft brown sugar |
| ½kg./1lb. fish fillets, skinned | 1lb. fish fillets, skinned |

Put the onion, garlic, ginger, candle or brazil nuts, chillis or sambal ulek into a blender with about 3 tablespoons of the water. Blend to a smooth purée.

Heat the oil in a large frying-pan. When it is hot, add the purée mixture and stir-fry for 3 minutes. Pour over the remaining water, the vinegar and stir in the sugar. Bring to the boil, then reduce the heat to low.

Arrange the fish fillets in the pan and spoon over the sauce to baste them completely. Cover the pan and simmer the fish for 10 to 15 minutes, or until the flesh flakes easily.

Transfer the mixture to a warmed serving dish and serve at once.
*Serves 4*
Preparation and cooking time: 35 minutes

# SAMBAL GORENG SOTONG

(Squid Sambal)                                                        (Malaysia)

| Metric/Imperial | American |
| --- | --- |
| 25g./1oz. tamarind | 2 Tbs. tamarind |
| 125ml./4fl.oz. boiling water | ½ cup boiling water |
| 4 whole almonds | 4 whole almonds |
| 4 dried red chillis, chopped | 4 dried red chillis, chopped |

2 garlic cloves, crushed
1 small onion, chopped
½ tsp. blachan (dried shrimp paste)
1½ Tbs. peanut oil
½ tsp. chopped lemon grass or
  grated lemon rind
2 tsp. jaggery or soft brown sugar
2 tsp. paprika
4 large squid, cleaned, gutted and
  sliced crosswise

2 garlic cloves, crushed
1 small onion, chopped
½ tsp. blachan (dried shrimp paste)
1½ Tbs. peanut oil
½ tsp. chopped lemon grass or
  grated lemon rind
2 tsp. jaggery or soft brown sugar
2 tsp. paprika
4 large squid, cleaned, gutted and
  sliced crosswise

Put the tamarind into a bowl and pour over the boiling water. Set aside until it is cool. Pour the contents of the bowl through a strainer into a second bowl, pressing as much of the pulp through as possible. Set aside.

Meanwhile, put the almonds, chillis, garlic, onion, blachan and about 1 tablespoon of oil into a blender and blend to a smooth purée.

Heat the remaining oil in a large, deep frying-pan. When it is hot, add the almond mixture and lemon grass or rind and stir-fry for 2 minutes. Add the tamarind water, sugar and paprika and continue to cook for 3 minutes, stirring constantly. Add the squid and cook for 10 to 15 minutes, stirring occasionally, or until the squid is cooked through and tender.

Transfer the mixture to a warmed serving dish and serve at once.
*Serves 4-6*
Preparation and cooking time: 45 minutes

# PLA NUM

(Fish in Red Sauce)                                                          (Thailand)

| Metric/Imperial | American |
| --- | --- |
| 700g./1½lb. fish | 1½lb. fish |
| 50ml./2fl. oz. peanut oil | ¼ cup peanut oil |
| 1 large onion, chopped | 1 large onion, chopped |
| 2 garlic cloves, crushed | 2 garlic cloves, crushed |
| 1 red chilli, chopped | 1 red chilli, chopped |
| 2 large tomatoes, blanched, peeled and chopped | 2 large tomatoes, blanched, peeled and chopped |
| 2 Tbs. tomato purée | 2 Tbs. tomato paste |
| 4 Tbs. water | 4 Tbs. water |
| 2 Tbs. wine vinegar | 2 Tbs. wine vinegar |
| salt and pepper | salt and pepper |
| 2 Tbs. chopped coriander leaves | 2 Tbs. chopped coriander leaves |

Clean and cut the fish if you are using a whole one; skin if you are using fillets.

Heat the oil in a large deep frying-pan. When it is hot, add the onion, garlic and chilli and stir-fry for 3 minutes. Add the tomatoes and cook gently until they have pulped. Stir in the tomato purée (paste), water and vinegar, and season to taste. Bring the mixture to the boil, then reduce the heat to low. Simmer, covered, for 10 minutes.

Arrange the fish in the sauce, basting thoroughly. Re-cover the pan and simmer the fish for 10 to 20 minutes, or until the flesh flakes easily. Just before serving, stir in about half of the coriander leaves.

Transfer the mixture to a warmed serving dish and garnish with the remaining coriander leaves before serving.
*Serves 4-6*
Preparation and cooking time: 1 hour

*Spiced Plaice (Flounder) The combination of Chinese and Malay expertise is demonstrated beautifully in Spiced Plaice (Flounder) – fish marinated in a mixture of soy sauce, sugar and chilli powder and then barbecued.*

# SPICED PLAICE (FLOUNDER)

(Malaysia)

| Metric/Imperial | American |
| --- | --- |
| 125ml./4fl.oz. dark soy sauce | ½ cup dark soy sauce |
| 2 Tbs. soft brown sugar | 2 Tbs. soft brown sugar |
| 1 tsp. hot chilli powder | 1 tsp. hot chilli powder |
| 2 garlic cloves, crushed | 2 garlic cloves, crushed |
| 4 plaice, cleaned, gutted and prepared for cooking | 4 flounder, cleaned, gutted and prepared for cooking |
| 25g./1oz. butter | 2 Tbs. butter |
| juice of 1 lemon | juice of 1 lemon |

Combine the soy sauce, sugar, chilli powder and garlic together. Put the fish in a shallow dish and pour over the soy sauce mixture. Cover and set aside for 1 hour, basting occasionally.

Preheat the grill (broiler) to high.

Arrange the fish on the rack of the grill (broiler) and grill (broil) the fish, turning them once, for 8 to 10 minutes, or until the flesh flakes easily, basting occasionally with the marinade.

Melt the butter in a small saucepan. Stir in the lemon juice and remove from the heat. Carefully transfer the fish to individual plates and discard the remaining marinade.

Pour the melted butter mixture over the fish and serve at once.

*Serves 4*

Preparation and cooking time: 1¼ hours

# IKAN GORENG

(Fried Fish in Lime Juice)                                         (Indonesia)

*Ikan Goreng (Fried Fish in Lime Juice) comes from Indonesia and is made here with mackerel. The rich yellow colour is produced by rubbing turmeric over the marinated fish.*

| Metric/Imperial | American |
|---|---|
| 300ml./10fl.oz. lime juice | 1¼ cups lime juice |
| 50ml./2fl.oz. wine vinegar | ¼ cup wine vinegar |
| 1 tsp. salt | 1 tsp. salt |
| 6 black peppercorns | 6 black peppercorns |
| 2 1k x g./2lb. mackerel, filleted | 2 x 2lb. mackerel, filleted |
| 1 tsp. turmeric | 1 tsp. turmeric |
| 4 Tbs. peanut oil | 4 Tbs. peanut oil |

Combine the lime juice, vinegar, ½ teaspoon of salt and the peppercorns together in a large, shallow dish. Place the fish in the dish and baste well. Set aside for 1 hour, basting occasionally. Remove from the marinade and dry on kitchen towels. Remove and discard the peppercorns from the marinade and reserve about 50ml./2 fl. oz. (¼ cup).

Rub the fish all over with the remaining salt and the turmeric.

Heat the oil in a large frying-pan. When it is hot, add the fish fillets and fry for 5 minutes on each side, or until they flake easily. Remove from the pan and drain on kitchen towels. Transfer to a warmed serving dish.

Pour over the reserved marinade and serve at once.

*Serves 4*
Preparation and cooking time: 1½ hours

# TAMARIND FISH

| Metric/Imperial | American |
| --- | --- |
| 25g./1oz. tamarind | 2 Tbs. tamarind |
| 125ml./4fl.oz. boiling water | ½ cup boiling water |
| 4 medium red mullets, cleaned and with the eyes removed | 4 medium red mullets, cleaned and with the eyes removed |
| 50ml./2fl.oz. peanut oil | ¼ cup peanut oil |
| 4 red chillis, seeded | 4 red chillis, seeded |
| 1 medium onion, quartered | 1 medium onion, quartered |
| 2 garlic cloves | 2 garlic cloves |
| 1cm./½in. piece of fresh root ginger, peeled and sliced | ½ piece of fresh green ginger, peeled and sliced |
| 175ml./6fl.oz. water | ¾ cup water |
| 1 tsp. soya sauce | 1 tsp. soy sauce |
| ½ tsp. salt | ½ tsp. salt |

Put the tamarind into a bowl and pour over the water. Set aside until it is cool. Pour the contents of the bowl through a strainer into a bowl, pressing as much of the pulp through as possible. Rub the fish all over with the tamarind pulp and set aside.

Heat the oil in a large frying-pan. When it is hot, add the fish and cook for 7 minutes on each side.

Meanwhile, put the chillis, onion, garlic, ginger and 50ml./2fl.oz. (¼ cup) of water in a blender and blend to a smooth purée. Transfer the mixture to a small bowl and set aside.

Remove the fish from the pan and keep them hot. Add the spice purée to the pan and cook for 2 minutes, stirring constantly. Stir in the soy sauce, salt and remaining water and bring to the boil, stirring constantly. Reduce the heat to moderately low and return the fish to the pan, basting with the pan mixture.

Transfer the fish to a warmed serving dish and pour the sauce into a warmed sauceboat. Serve at once, with the fish.

*Serves 4*
Preparation and cooking time: 1 hour

# IKAN BALI

(Balinese Sweet and Sour Fish)                                      (Indonesia)

*The fish in this dish can be as you prefer – whole (but with the head and tail removed), in fillets, or in steaks. Slightly oily fish would be best – mackerel, mullet, or halibut steaks if you are feeling rich!*

| Metric/Imperial | American |
| --- | --- |
| 1 Tbs. tamarind | 1 Tbs. tamarind |
| 50ml./2fl.oz. boiling water | ¼ cup boiling water |
| 3 Tbs. peanut oil | 3 Tbs. peanut oil |
| 1 large onion, finely chopped | 1 large onion, finely chopped |
| 2 garlic cloves, crushed | 2 garlic cloves, crushed |
| 4cm./1½in. piece of fresh root ginger, peeled and chopped | 1½in. piece of fresh green ginger, peeled and chopped |
| 1 tsp. chopped lemon grass or grated lemon rind | 1 tsp. chopped lemon grass or grated lemon rind |

| | |
|---|---|
| ½ tsp. laos powder (optional) | ½ tsp. laos powder (optional) |
| 1 tsp. dried red chillis or sambal ulek | 1 tsp. dried red chillis or sambal ulek |
| 1½ Tbs. soya sauce | 1 Tbs. soy sauce |
| 1½ Tbs. lemon juice | 1½ Tbs. lemon juice |
| 1 Tbs. soft brown sugar | 1 Tbs. soft brown sugar |
| vegetable oil for deep-frying | vegetable oil for deep-frying |
| 700g./1½lb. fish | 1½lb. fish |
| 50g./2oz. cornflour | ½ cup cornstarch |

Put the tamarind into a bowl and pour over the boiling water. Set aside until it is cool. Pour the contents of the bowl through a strainer into a second bowl, pressing as much of the pulp through as possible. Set aside.

Heat the peanut oil in a small saucepan. When it is hot, add the onion, garlic and ginger and stir-fry for 3 minutes. Stir in the lemon grass or rind, laos powder and chillis or sambal ulek and continue to stir-fry for a further 2 minutes. Add the soy sauce, lemon juice, sugar and tamarind liquid and cook, stirring constantly until the sugar has dissolved. Remove the pan from the heat and set aside. Keep hot.

Fill a large deep-frying pan about one-third full with vegetable oil and heat until the oil is hot. Gently coat the fish in the cornflour, shaking off any excess, then carefully lower into the oil. Cook for 3 to 8 minutes (depending on the type of fish and cut used), or until crisp and golden brown. Remove the fish from the oil and drain on kitchen towels.

Return the saucepan containing the sauce to low heat and heat gently until it is hot. Arrange the fish on a warmed serving dish and spoon over the sauce. Serve at once.

*Serves 4-6*
Preparation and cooking time: 30 minutes

# GULEH IKAN

(Fish Curry)                                             (Malaysia)

| Metric/Imperial | American |
|---|---|
| 1 large onion, chopped | 1 large onion, chopped |
| 1 garlic clove | 1 garlic clove |
| 2½cm./1in. piece of fresh root ginger, peeled and chopped | 1in. piece of fresh green ginger, peeled and chopped |
| 2 chillis, chopped | 2 chillis, chopped |
| 250ml./8fl.oz. thin coconut milk | 1 cup thin coconut milk |
| 1 Tbs. ground coriander | 1 Tbs. ground coriander |
| ½ tsp. ground cumin | ½ tsp. ground cumin |
| ½ tsp. turmeric | ½ tsp. turmeric |
| ½ tsp. ground fennel | ½ tsp. ground fennel |
| 1 tsp. chopped lemon grass or grated lemon rind | 1 tsp. chopped lemon grass or grated lemon rind |
| 125ml./4fl.oz. thick coconut milk | ½ cup thick coconut milk |
| 1 Tbs. tamarind | 1 Tbs. tamarind |
| 50ml./2fl.oz. boiling water | ¼ cup boiling water |
| ½kg./1lb. firm white fish steaks (cod, grey mullet, etc.), chopped | 1lb. firm white fish steaks (cod, grey mullet, etc.), chopped |

Put the onion, garlic, ginger and chillis into a blender and blend to a purée (add a spoonful or two of thin coconut milk if the mixture is too dry). Transfer the mixture to a saucepan and stir in half the thin coconut milk and the spices and lemon grass or rind.

Set the saucepan over moderate heat and add the remaining thin coconut milk and the thick coconut milk. Bring to the boil, reduce the heat to low and simmer for 15 minutes.

Meanwhile, put the tamarind into a bowl and pour over the boiling water. Set aside until it is cool. Pour the contents of the bowl through a strainer into the saucepan, pressing as much of the pulp through as possible.

Stir in the fish pieces and bring to the boil again. Reduce the heat to low and simmer for 10 to 15 minutes, or until the flesh flakes easily. Serve at once.

*Serves 3–4*
Preparation and cooking time: 50 minutes

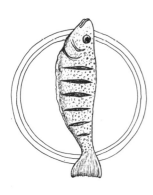

# PLA PRIO WAN

(Fried Fish with Piquant Sauce)                                    (Thailand)

*Any whole fish suitable for frying can be used in this dish; sea bream is probably the best but red snapper and jewfish could also be used.*

| Metric/Imperial | American |
|---|---|
| 1 x 1kg./2lb. whole fish, cleaned, gutted and with the head still on | 1 x 2lb. whole fish, cleaned, gutted and with the head still on |
| 25g./1oz. cornflour | ¼ cup cornstarch |
| vegetable oil for deep-frying | vegetable oil for deep-frying |
| 1 Tbs. chopped coriander leaves | 1 Tbs. chopped coriander leaves |
| PIQUANT SAUCE | PIQUANT SAUCE |
| 1 Tbs. peanut oil | 1 Tbs. peanut oil |
| 10cm./4in. piece of fresh root ginger, peeled and finely chopped | 4in. piece of fresh green ginger, peeled and finely chopped |
| 1 garlic clove, crushed | 1 garlic clove, crushed |
| 1 red chilli, seeded and chopped | 1 red chilli, seeded and chopped |
| 4 Tbs. wine vinegar | 4 Tbs. wine vinegar |
| 4 Tbs. soft brown sugar | 4 Tbs. soft brown sugar |
| 125ml./4fl.oz. water | ½ cup water |
| 3 spring onions, green part included, finely chopped | 3 scallions, green part included, finely chopped |
| 1 Tbs. soya sauce | 1 Tbs. soy sauce |
| 1 Tbs. cornflour, mixed to a paste with 1 Tbs. water | 1 Tbs. cornstarch, mixed to a paste with 1 Tbs. water |

Rub the fish, inside and out, with salt, then wash and dry on kitchen towels. Make four or five deep incisions on each side of the fish, almost to the centre bone. Coat the fish in the cornflour (cornstarch) shaking off any excess.

Fill a large deep-frying pan one-third full with oil and heat it until it is very hot. Carefully lower the fish into the pan and deep-fry it for 5 minutes, or until it is golden brown and crisp. Remove the fish from the oil and drain on kitchen towels. Keep hot while you make the sauce.

Heat the oil in a deep frying-pan. When it is hot, add the ginger and garlic and stir-fry for 2 minutes. Stir in all the remaining sauce ingredients, except the cornflour (cornstarch) and bring to the boil, stirring constantly. Reduce the heat to moderately low and cook for 3 minutes. Stir in the cornflour (cornstarch) mixture and continue to cook the sauce until it thickens and becomes translucent.

Arrange the fish on a warmed serving dish and pour over the sauce. Garnish with the coriander and serve at once.

*Serves 4–6*
Preparation and cooking time: 35 minutes

# SHELL FOOD

## PRAWNS IN CHILLI SAUCE

(Singapore)

| Metric/Imperial | American |
| --- | --- |
| 4 Tbs. peanut oil | 4 Tbs. peanut oil |
| ½kg./1lb. shelled prawns | 1lb. shelled shrimp |
| 1 garlic clove, crushed | 1 garlic clove, crushed |
| 4cm./1½in. piece of fresh root ginger, peeled and chopped | 1½in. piece of fresh green ginger, peeled and chopped |
| 2 red chillis, chopped | 2 red chillis, chopped |
| 1 green pepper, pith and seeds removed and cut into strips | 1 green pepper, pith and seeds removed and cut into strips |
| 1 Tbs. Chinese chilli sauce | 1 Tbs. Chinese chilli sauce |
| 1 Tbs. tomato purée | 1 Tbs. tomato paste |
| salt and pepper | salt and pepper |
| 2 spring onions, chopped | 2 scallions, chopped |

Heat the oil in a large, deep frying-pan. When it is hot, add the prawns (shrimp) and stir-fry for 5 minutes, or until they are cooked. Using a slotted spoon, transfer the prawns (shrimp) to a plate. Keep hot.

Add the garlic, ginger, chillis and pepper to the pan and stir-fry for 3 minutes. Stir in the chilli sauce, tomato purée (paste) and seasoning to taste and stir-fry for a further 2 minutes. Return the prawns (shrimp) to the pan and stir-fry for 1 minute, or until they are well blended with the sauce.

Transfer to a warmed serving bowl and sprinkle over the spring onions (scallions). Serve at once.

*Serves 4–6*
Preparation and cooking time: 25 minutes

## CHILLI CRAB

(Singapore)

| Metric/Imperial | American |
| --- | --- |
| vegetable oil for deep-frying | vegetable oil for deep-frying |
| 3 medium crabs, claws cracked and chopped through the shell into pieces | 3 medium crabs, claws cracked and chopped through the shell into pieces |
| 3 red chillis, chopped | 3 red chillis, chopped |
| 1cm./½in. piece of fresh root ginger, peeled and chopped | ½in. piece of fresh green ginger, peeled and chopped |
| 2 garlic cloves, crushed | 2 garlic cloves, crushed |
| 2 tsp. sugar | 2 tsp. sugar |
| salt and pepper | salt and pepper |
| 250ml./8fl.oz. chicken stock | 1 cup chicken stock |
| 2 tsp. cornflour, mixed to a paste with 2 tsp. water | 2 tsp. cornstarch, mixed to a paste with 2 tsp. water |
| 1 egg, lightly beaten | 1 egg, lightly beaten |
| 1 tsp. vinegar | 1 tsp. vinegar |
| 2 Tbs. tomato purée | 2 Tbs. tomato paste |

Fill a large deep-frying pan one-third full with oil and heat it until it is very hot. Carefully lower the crab pieces, a few at a time, into the oil and deep-fry for 1 minute. Using tongs or a slotted spoon, remove the pieces from the oil and drain on kitchen towels.

Reserve 3 tablespoons of the oil from the pan and pour it into a deep frying-pan. When it is hot, add the chillis, ginger and garlic. Fry, stirring occasionally, for 3 minutes. Return the crab pieces to the pan and add sugar, salt and pepper to taste, and stock. Bring to the boil, reduce the heat to low and cover the pan. Simmer for 15 minutes, or until the crab pieces are cooked through. Stir in the cornflour (cornstarch) mixture and cook until the liquid thickens and becomes translucent.

Stir in all of the remaining ingredients and cook gently for 2 to 3 minutes, or until the egg 'sets'.

Transfer the mixture to a large warmed serving bowl or deep serving platter and serve at once.

*Serves 4*
Preparation and cooking time: 1 hour

# KARI BONGKONG LASAK

(Curried Shrimps and Cucumbers)                                        (Cambodia)

| Metric/Imperial | American |
|---|---|
| 2 garlic cloves, crushed | 2 garlic cloves, crushed |
| 2 spring onions, chopped | 2 scallions, chopped |
| 4cm./1½in. piece of fresh root ginger, peeled and chopped | 1½in. piece of fresh green ginger, peeled and chopped |
| 1 tsp. ground fennel | 1 tsp. ground fennel |
| 2 tsp. ground coriander | 2 tsp. ground coriander |
| ½ tsp. turmeric | ½ tsp. turmeric |
| 2 tsp. hot chilli powder | 2 tsp. hot chilli powder |
| 4 Tbs. peanut oil | 4 Tbs. peanut oil |
| ½kg./1lb. shelled prawns | 1lb. shelled shrimp |
| 450ml./15fl.oz. coconut milk | 2 cups coconut milk |
| 1 cucumber, quartered lengthways, seeds removed and cut into thick slices | 1 cucumber, quartered lengthways, seeds removed and cut into thick slices |
| 2 tsp. chopped lemon grass or grated lemon rind | 2 tsp. chopped lemon grass or grated lemon rind |
| juice of 1 lemon | juice of 1 lemon |
| 1 tsp. sugar | 1 tsp. sugar |
| 1 Tbs. fish sauce | 1 Tbs. fish sauce |

Put the garlic, spring onions (scallions) and ginger into a blender and blend to a purée. Scrape the mixture from the blender and transfer to a mixing bowl. Stir in the ground spices.

Heat the oil in a deep frying-pan. When it is hot, add the spice purée and stir-fry for 3 minutes. Add the prawns or shrimp and stir-fry for 5 minutes. Stir in the coconut milk and bring to the boil. Reduce the heat to low, add the cucumber and remaining ingredients and simmer gently for 5 minutes, or until the cucumber is translucent.

Serve at once.

*Serves 6*
Preparation and cooking time: 25 minutes

*The cuisine of Cambodia tends to be overshadowed by its neigbours Vietnam and Thailand, but it has many unique features of its own. One of the most popular dishes is Kari Bongkong Lasak, a refreshing mixture of curried shrimps and cucumbers cooked in coconut milk flavoured with lemon.*

# TOM VO VIEN

(Shrimp Cakes) (Vietnam)

| Metric/Imperial | American |
|---|---|
| ½kg./1lb. shelled prawns | 1lb. shelled shrimp |
| 1 Tbs. fish sauce | 1 Tbs. fish sauce |
| ½ tsp. sugar | ½ tsp. sugar |
| 2 spring onions, chopped | 2 scallions, chopped |
| 3 Tbs. chopped coriander leaves | 3 Tbs. chopped coriander leaves |
| salt and pepper | salt and pepper |
| 125ml./4fl.oz. peanut oil | ½ cup peanut oil |

Put the prawns or shrimp, fish sauce, sugar, spring onions (scallions), half the coriander leaves and seasoning into a blender and blend to a smooth paste. Shape into little cakes with floured hands and chill in the refrigerator for 15 minutes.

Cover the bottom of a frying-pan with half the oil. When it is hot, add about half the cakes and fry for 5 minutes on each side, or until they are golden and cooked through. Cook the remaining cakes in the same way. Drain on kitchen towels and serve hot, with nuoc cham (page 412).
*Serves 4-6*
Preparation and cooking time: 30 minutes

# GULEH UDANG DENGAN LABU KUNING

(Prawn [Shrimp] and Marrow [Squash] Curry) (Malaysia)

*If you prefer, courgettes (zucchini) can be used instead of marrow (squash) in this recipe. If you do use them, do not peel – the green skin will make the dish look particularly attractive.*

| Metric/Imperial | American |
|---|---|
| 1 large onion, chopped | 1 large onion, chopped |
| 2 red chillis, chopped | 2 red chillis, chopped |
| 1 tsp. chopped lemon grass or grated lemon rind | 1 tsp. chopped lemon grass or grated lemon rind |
| 1 tsp. turmeric | 1 tsp. turmeric |
| ¼ tsp. laos powder (optional) | ¼ tsp. laos powder (optional) |
| ½ tsp. dried basil | ½ tsp. dried basil |
| 250ml./8fl.oz. water | 1 cup water |
| 1 tsp. lemon juice | 1 tsp. lemon juice |
| 350g./12oz. marrow, peeled and cut into cubes | 2 cups peeled and cubed winter squash |
| ½kg./1lb. peeled prawns | 1lb. peeled shrimp |
| 175ml./6fl.oz. thick coconut milk | ¾ cup thick coconut milk |

Put the onion and chillis into a blender and blend to a smooth purée. Transfer the purée to a saucepan, then stir in the lemon grass or rind, turmeric, laos powder and basil until they are thoroughly blended. Gradually stir in the water and lemon juice.

Set the saucepan over moderately low heat and cook the mixture until it comes to the boil, stirring constantly. Reduce the heat to low and add the marrow (squash) cubes. Cook the mixture gently for 5 minutes, or until the cubes are half cooked. Add the prawns (shrimp) and coconut milk and continue to cook gently for a further 5 minutes, or until the prawns (shrimp) are cooked through and tender.

Transfer the mixture to a warmed serving bowl or large serving platter and serve at once.

*Serves 4*
Preparation and cooking time: 20 minutes

# UKOY

(Shrimp and Sweet Potato Cakes)                                      (Philippines)

| Metric/Imperial | American |
| --- | --- |
| 10 medium shrimps, in the shell | 10 medium shrimp, in the shell |
| 300ml./10fl.oz. water | 1¼ cups water |
| 125g./4oz. plain flour | 1 cup all-purpose flour |
| 125g./4oz. cornflour | 1 cup cornstarch |
| 1 tsp. salt | 1 tsp. salt |
| 1 large egg, beaten | 1 large egg, beaten |
| 2 sweet potatoes, peeled | 2 sweet potatoes, peeled |
| 4 spring onions, chopped | 4 scallions, chopped |
| salt and pepper | salt and pepper |
| vegetable oil for deep-frying | vegetable oil for deep-frying |
| DIPPING SAUCE | DIPPING SAUCE |
| 2 garlic cloves, crushed | 2 garlic cloves, crushed |
| 1 tsp. salt | 1 tsp. salt |
| 125ml./4fl.oz. malt vinegar | ½ cup cider vinegar |

First make the dipping sauce. Stir the garlic and salt into the vinegar until all the ingredients are thoroughly combined. Set aside.

Put the shrimps and water into a small saucepan and bring to the boil. Cook for about 5 minutes, or until the shrimps are cooked through. Remove from the heat and transfer the shrimps to a plate. Strain the cooking liquid and reserve it. Remove the shells and veins from the shrimps.

Put the flour, cornflour (cornstarch) and salt into a mixing bowl. Gradually beat in the egg, then the reserved shrimp liquid until the mixture resembles a slightly thick pancake batter. Grate the sweet potatoes into the mixture, then stir until it is completely blended. Beat in the spring onions (scallions) and seasoning to taste.

Fill a large deep-frying pan about one-third full with oil and heat until it is hot. Carefully slide about a heaped tablespoonful of the batter mixture into the oil and arrange a shrimp in the centre. Cook the cakes in this way, two or three at a time, pressing down lightly on them with a slotted spoon and spooning oil over occasionally. Cook for about 3 minutes, then carefully turn over and cook for a further 3 minutes, or until the cakes are crisp and golden brown. Remove from the oil and drain on kitchen towels.

Serve at once, with the dipping sauce.
*Makes 10 cakes*
Preparation and cooking time: 50 minutes

# VEGETABLES & ACCOMPANIMENTS

## CABBAGE WITH SHRIMP

(Malaysia)

| Metric/Imperial | American |
| --- | --- |
| 3 Tbs. vegetable oil | 3 Tbs. vegetable oil |
| 225g./8oz. prawns, shelled | 8oz. shrimp, shelled |
| 2 medium onions, sliced | 2 medium onions, sliced |
| 4cm./1½in. piece of fresh root ginger, peeled and shredded | 1½in. piece of fresh green ginger, peeled and shredded |
| 2 red chillis, finely chopped | 2 red chillis, finely chopped |
| 1 medium white cabbage, shredded | 1 medium white cabbage, shredded |
| 1 tsp. salt | 1 tsp. salt |
| 1cm./½in. slice of creamed coconut, dissolved in 1½ Tbs. boiling water | ½in. slice of creamed coconut, dissolved in 1½ Tbs. boiling water |

Heat the oil in a large frying-pan. When it is hot, add the prawns or shrimp and fry for 3 to 5 minutes, or until they are pink and firm. Transfer to a plate and keep hot.

Add the onions, ginger and chillis to the pan and fry, stirring occasionally, until the onions are soft. Stir in the cabbage and stir-fry for 2 minutes. Stir in the salt and coconut mixture and cook for 5 minutes, stirring frequently. Stir in the prawns or shrimp. Serve at once.

*Serves 6*
Preparation and cooking time: 30 minutes

## SAMBAL I

(Potato Sambal)                                                              (Indonesia)

| Metric/Imperial | American |
| --- | --- |
| 225g./8oz. potatoes, boiled in their skins, peeled and coarsely mashed | 8oz. potatoes, boiled in their skins, peeled and coarsely mashed |
| 4 spring onions, finely chopped | 4 scallions, finely chopped |
| 2 green chillis, finely chopped | 2 green chillis, finely chopped |
| ½ tsp. salt | ½ tsp. salt |
| 1 Tbs. lemon juice | 1 Tbs. lemon juice |
| 2 Tbs. thick coconut milk | 2 Tbs. thick coconut milk |
| 1 Tbs. chopped coriander leaves | 1 Tbs. chopped coriander leaves |

Combine all the ingredients, except the coriander, in a shallow serving bowl. Taste the mixture and add more salt or lemon juice if necessary. Sprinkle over the coriander.

Chill in the refrigerator until ready to use.

*Serves 3–4*
Preparation and cooking time: 25 minutes

# SAMBAL II

(Chicken Liver Sambal)                                                    (Indonesia)

| Metric/Imperial | American |
| --- | --- |
| 3 Tbs. vegetable oil | 3 Tbs. vegetable oil |
| 2 medium onions, very finely chopped | 2 medium onions, very finely chopped |
| 2 garlic cloves, crushed | 2 garlic cloves, crushed |
| 700g./1½lb. chicken livers, cleaned and halved | 1½lb. chicken livers, cleaned and halved |
| 2-4 red chillis, finely chopped | 2-4 red chillis, finely chopped |
| 1 tsp. chopped lemon grass or grated lemon rind | 1 tsp. chopped lemon grass or grated lemon rind |
| ½ tsp. laos powder | ½ tsp. laos powder |
| 1 tsp. sugar | 1 tsp. sugar |
| 1 tsp. salt | 1 tsp. salt |
| 2 curry leaves (optional) | 2 curry leaves (optional) |
| 350ml./12fl.oz. thick coconut milk | 1½ cups thick coconut milk |

Heat the oil in a large saucepan. When it is hot, add the onions and garlic and fry, stirring occasionally, until the onions are golden brown. Add the chicken livers and fry until they lose their pinkness. Stir in all the remaining ingredients and bring to the boil, stirring occasionally. Reduce the heat to low and simmer for 20 minutes, or until the sauce is thick.

Spoon the sambal into a warmed serving dish and serve at once.

*Serves 4–6*
Preparation and cooking time: 35 minutes


# SAMBAL GORENG TELUR

(Egg and Chilli Sambal)                                                  (Indonesia)

| Metric/Imperial | American |
| --- | --- |
| 4 eggs | 4 eggs |
| 1 large onion, chopped | 1 large onion, chopped |
| 2 garlic cloves | 2 garlic cloves |
| 1 Tbs. dried chillis or sambal ulek | 1 Tbs. dried chillis or sambal ulek |
| 3 Tbs. peanut oil | 3 Tbs. peanut oil |
| ½ tsp. blachan (dried shrimp paste) | ½ tsp. blachan (dried shrimp paste) |
| 1 tsp. sugar | 1 tsp. sugar |
| ½ tsp. laos powder | ½ tsp. laos powder |
| ½ tsp. chopped lemon grass or grated lemon rind | ½ tsp. chopped lemon grass or grated lemon rind |
| 250ml./8fl.oz. coconut milk | 1 cup coconut milk |

Hard-boil the eggs, then shell and halve them. Set them aside. Put the onion, garlic and chillis into a blender and blend to a rough purée.

Heat the oil in a large, shallow saucepan. When it is hot, add the onion puree and fry, stirring frequently, for 2 minutes. Stir in the remaining ingredients and bring to the boil, stirring constantly. Reduce the heat to very low and carefully add the egg halves. Simmer gently until the mixture thickens slightly.

Serve at once.

*Serves 6–8*
Preparation and cooking time: 20 minutes

# THAN THAT

(Cucumber Pickle)                                              (Burma)

| Metric/Imperial | American |
| --- | --- |
| 2 cucumbers, peeled and cut in half lengthways | 2 cucumbers, peeled and cut in half lengthways |
| 50ml./2fl.oz. vinegar | $\frac{1}{4}$ cup vinegar |
| 250ml./8fl.oz. water | 1 cup water |
| Pepper and salt | Pepper and salt |
| 75ml./3fl.oz. sesame oil | $\frac{1}{3}$ cup sesame oil |
| 1 large onion, finely chopped | 1 large onion, finely chopped |
| 6 large garlic cloves, crushed | 6 large garlic cloves, crushed |
| 2 Tbs. sesame seeds | 2 Tbs. sesame seeds |

Remove the seeds from the cucumbers and cut into strips. Put into a saucepan and add all the vinegar except 1 tablespoon, the water and seasoning and bring to the boil. Reduce the heat to low and simmer for 5 minutes, or until the strips are translucent. Drain and transfer the strips to a shallow serving bowl to cool to room temperature.

Heat the oil in a frying-pan. When it is hot, add the onion and garlic and fry gently for 5 minutes, or until they are lightly browned. Transfer to a plate. Add the sesame seeds to the pan and fry gently until they are lightly toasted. Tip the sesame seeds and oil into the onion and garlic, add the reserved vinegar and mix. When the cucumber strips are cool, pour over the sesame oil mixture and toss gently. Serve at once.

*Serves 6–8*
Preparation and cooking time : 1 hour


# ROJAK

(Mixed Salad)                                              (Malaysia)

| Metric/Imperial | American |
| --- | --- |
| $\frac{1}{2}$ cucumber, diced | $\frac{1}{2}$ cucumber, diced |
| $\frac{1}{2}$ small pineapple, peeled, cored and diced | $\frac{1}{2}$ small pineapple, peeled, cored and diced |
| 1 green mango, peeled, stoned and diced | 1 green mango, peeled, pitted and diced |
| 2 dried red chillis, crumbled | 2 dried red chillis, crumbled |
| DRESSING | DRESSING |
| 2 tsp. dried chillis or sambal ulek | 2 tsp. dried chillis or sambal ulek |
| $\frac{1}{2}$ tsp. blachan (dried shrimp paste) | $\frac{1}{2}$ tsp. blachan (dried shrimp paste) |
| 1 Tbs. sugar | 1 Tbs. sugar |
| 1 Tbs. vinegar | 1 Tbs. vinegar |
| 1 Tbs. lemon juice | 1 Tbs. lemon juice |

Put the cucumber, pineapple and mango in a shallow bowl. Combine all the dressing ingredients in a blender, then pour over the salad. Toss gently, then scatter over the crumbled chillis.

Set aside at room temperature for 10 minutes before serving.

*Serves 6*
Preparation and cooking time : 15 minutes

# GADO-GADO

(Indonesia)

| Metric/Imperial | American |
| --- | --- |
| ½ small white cabbage, shredded | ½ small white cabbage, shredded |
| 225g./8oz. French beans | 1⅓ cups green beans |
| 125g./4oz. bean sprouts | ½ cup bean sprouts |
| ¼ small cucumber, chopped | ¼ small cucumber, chopped |
| 2 potatoes | 2 potatoes |
| 2 hard-boiled eggs, sliced | 2 hard-boiled eggs, sliced |
| PEANUT SAUCE | PEANUT SAUCE |
| 2 Tbs. peanut oil | 2 Tbs. peanut oil |
| 2 garlic cloves, crushed | 2 garlic cloves, crushed |
| 2 red chillis, crumbled | 2 red chillis, crumbled |
| 1 tsp. blachan (dried shrimp paste) | 1 tsp. blachan (dried shrimp paste) |
| ½ tsp. laos powder | ½ tsp. laos powder |
| 1 tsp. soft brown sugar | 1 tsp. soft brown sugar |
| 4 Tbs. peanut butter | 4 Tbs. peanut butter |
| 250ml./8fl.oz. coconut milk | 1 cup coconut milk |
| 2 tsp. lemon juice or vinegar | 2 tsp. lemon juice or vinegar |
| GARNISH | GARNISH |
| prawn crackers | shrimp crackers |
| 2 Tbs. chopped spring onions | 2 Tbs. chopped scallions |

Cook all of the vegetables lightly but separately. Drain and arrange in layers on a serving platter. Set aside until cold.

To make the sauce, heat the oil in a small saucepan. When it is hot, add the garlic and chillis and stir-fry for 3 minutes. Stir in the blachan, laos and sugar and cook until they have dissolved. Stir in the peanut butter and coconut milk and blend thoroughly. Bring to the boil. Remove from the heat and stir in the lemon juice or vinegar.

Pour the sauce over the top of the vegetables and garnish with the crackers and chopped spring onions (scallions).
*Serves 6*
Preparation and cooking time : 40 minutes

# NUOC CHAM

(Prepared Fish Sauce)                                                                 (Vietnam)

| Metric/Imperial | American |
| --- | --- |
| 4 Tbs. fish sauce | 4 Tbs. fish sauce |
| 2 garlic cloves, crushed | 2 garlic cloves, crushed |
| juice of 1 lemon (use a little flesh as well) | juice of 1 lemon (use a little flesh as well) |
| ½ dried chilli, crumbled (optional) | ½ dried chilli, crumbled (optional) |
| 1 tsp. sugar | 1 tsp. sugar |
| 2 Tbs. water | 2 Tbs. water |

Mix all the ingredients, except the water, together and beat well. Add the water and stir well. If you prefer the sauce less strong, dilute it with more water to taste.
*Makes 1 table serving*
Preparation time : 5 minutes

# YAHM CHOMPU

(Savoury Fruit Salad) (Thailand)

| Metric/Imperial | American |
|---|---|
| 1 large tart apple, diced | 1 large tart apple, diced |
| 1 small pineapple, peeled, sliced then diced | 1 small pineapple, peeled, sliced then diced |
| 225g./8oz. lean cooked pork, diced | 1⅓ cups diced lean cooked pork |
| 125g./4oz. prawns, shelled | 4oz. shrimps, shelled |
| 2 Tbs. chopped spring onions | 2 Tbs. chopped scallions |
| 1 cos lettuce, shredded | 1 romaine lettuce, shredded |
| DRESSING | DRESSING |
| 6 Tbs. olive oil | 6 Tbs. olive oil |
| juice of 1 lemon | juice of 1 lemon |
| 2 Tbs. soya sauce | 2 Tbs. soy sauce |
| 1 Tbs. soft brown sugar | 1 Tbs. soft brown sugar |

To make the dressing, combine all the ingredients in a small bowl and set aside.

Put the fruit, pork, prawns or shrimp and spring onions (scallions) in a large bowl. Pour over the dressing and mix well.

Arrange the lettuce around the edges of a dish and pile the salad into the centre. Serve at once.

*Serves 6*
Preparation time: 10 minutes

*Fruit is often served as a salad, or is included in salads in South-East Asia, and Yahm Chompu from from Thailand is no exception. This particular version is made more substantial by the addition of pork and shrimps.*

# CHA GIO

(Vietnamese Spring Rolls)

*In Vietnam, these rolls are wrapped in special rice paper called banh-da and then deep-fried; spring roll wrappers, however, are a good substitute. If you prefer, minced (ground) pork or shrimp may be substituted for the crab.*

| Metric/Imperial | American |
| --- | --- |
| 225g./8oz. crabmeat, shell and cartilage removed and flaked | 8oz. crabmeat, shell and cartilage removed and flaked |
| 1 small onion, finely chopped | 1 small onion, finely chopped |
| 1 carrot, grated | 1 carrot, grated |
| 50g./2oz. bean sprouts | ¼ cup bean sprouts |
| 1 egg | 1 egg |
| 10 spring roll wrappers | 10 spring roll wrappers |
| vegetable oil for deep-frying | vegetable oil for deep-frying |

Put the crabmeat, onion, carrot, bean sprouts, and egg in a bowl and combine thoroughly. Put about 2 tablespoons of the filling in the centre of one spring roll wrapper and carefully roll up diagonally to make a neat parcel, making sure that the filling is completely enclosed.

Fill a large deep-frying pan one-third full of oil and heat it until it is very hot. Carefully lower the rolls (on a spatula or slotted spoon), a few at a time, into the oil and fry until they are golden brown and crisp. Remove from the oil and drain on kitchen towels. Serve hot with nuoc cham (see recipe on page 412)
*Serves 8*
Preparation and cooking time: 20 minutes


# MASAK LEMAK

(Cabbage Curry)                                                                 (Malaysia)

| Metric/Imperial | American |
| --- | --- |
| 1 onion, sliced | 1 onion, sliced |
| 2 red chillis, chopped | 2 red chillis, chopped |
| ½ tsp. blachan (dried shrimp paste) | ½ tsp. blachan (dried shrimp paste) |
| 1 tsp. turmeric | 1 tsp. turmeric |
| 250ml./8fl.oz. thin coconut milk | 1 cup thin coconut milk |
| 1 potato, cut into large cubes | 1 potato, cut into large cubes |
| 1 small white cabbage, shredded | 1 small white cabbage, shredded |
| 125ml./4fl.oz. thick coconut milk | ½ cup thick coconut milk |

Put the onion, chillis, blachan, turmeric and thin coconut milk into a saucepan. Bring to the boil. Reduce the heat to moderately low and add the potato pieces. Cook for 10 minutes, or until the potato is half-cooked. Stir in the cabbage and cook for 5 minutes. Pour over the remaining thick coconut milk and bring to the boil, stirring constantly.

Serve at once.
*Serves 4*
Preparation and cooking time: 30 minutes

# URAP

(Mixed Vegetables with Coconut) (Indonesia)

| Metric/Imperial | American |
|---|---|
| 2 celery stalks, cut into 2½cm./1in. lengths | 2 celery stalks, cut into 1in. lengths |
| 225g./8oz. bean sprouts | 1 cup bean sprouts |
| 225g./8oz. French beans, cut into 2½cm./1in. lengths | 1⅓ cups green beans, cut into 1in. lengths |
| 125g./4oz. Chinese cabbage, shredded | 1 cup shredded Chinese cabbage |
| ½ fresh coconut, grated | ½ fresh coconut, grated |
| 2 spring onions, finely chopped | 2 scallions, finely chopped |
| 1 tsp. sambal ulek or 2 dried red chillis, crumbled | 1 tsp. sambal ulek or 2 dried red chillis, crumbled |
| ½ tsp. blachan (dried shrimp paste) | ½ tsp. blachan (dried shrimp paste) |
| 1 Tbs. lemon juice | 1 Tbs. lemon juice |

Steam or boil the vegetables, separately, until they are just cooked through. Set aside and keep hot.

Combine all the remaining ingredients in a mixing bowl until they are well blended. Stir into the vegetables until all the vegetable pieces are coated.

Serve at once, either as a vegetable dish or as an accompaniment.

*Serves 6*
Preparation and cooking time: 15 minutes

# SERUNDENG

(Coconut and Peanut Garnish) (Indonesia)

| Metric/Imperial | American |
|---|---|
| 1 Tbs. peanut oil | 1 Tbs. peanut oil |
| 1 small onion, chopped | 1 small onion, chopped |
| 1 garlic clove, crushed | 1 garlic clove, crushed |
| 1 tsp. blachan (dried shrimp paste) | 1 tsp. blachan (dried shrimp paste) |
| 1 Tbs. ground coriander | 1 Tbs. ground coriander |
| 2 Tbs. sugar | 2 Tbs. sugar |
| 1 tsp. salt | 1 tsp. salt |
| 125g./4oz. coconut, freshly grated | 1 cup freshly grated coconut |
| 225g./8oz. shelled salted peanuts | 1⅓ cups shelled salted peanuts |

Heat the oil in a saucepan. When it is hot, add the onion and garlic and fry, stirring occasionally, until the onion is soft. Stir in the blachan and cook for 5 minutes, stirring frequently. Reduce the heat to low. Stir in the coriander, sugar, salt and coconut and fry, stirring constantly, until the coconut is golden brown. Stir in the salted peanuts and mix until the ingredients are thoroughly blended.

Remove from the heat. Set aside to cool completely, then transfer the serundeng to a storage jar. Store in a cool, dry place until you are ready to use.

*Serves 6–8*
Preparation and cooking time: 25 minutes

*Kachang Bendi Goreng is a Malaysian dish of fried mixed green vegetables with shrimps. It can be served as part of an Oriental meal, as a fairly substantial vegetable accompaniment, or even as a light snack dish on its own.*

# KACHANG BENDI GORENG

(Fried Mixed Green Vegetables with Shrimps)                    (Malaysia)

| Metric/Imperial | American |
|---|---|
| 3 Tbs. peanut oil | 3 Tbs. peanut oil |
| 2 onions, finely chopped | 2 onions, finely chopped |
| 1 garlic clove, crushed | 1 garlic clove, crushed |
| 2 green chillis, finely chopped | 2 green chillis, finely chopped |
| 4cm./1½in. piece of fresh root ginger, peeled and chopped | 1½in. piece of fresh green ginger, peeled and chopped |
| 1 Tbs. ground almonds | 1 Tbs. ground almonds |
| 2 Tbs. soya sauce | 2 Tbs. soy sauce |
| ½ tsp. black pepper | ½ tsp. black pepper |
| 350g./12oz. prawns, shelled | 12 oz. shrimp, shelled |
| 1 green pepper, pith and seeds removed and sliced | 1 green pepper, pith and seeds removed and sliced |
| 175g./6oz. French beans | 1 cup green beans |
| 2 courgettes, sliced | 2 zucchini, sliced |

Heat the oil in a large frying-pan. When it is hot, add the onions, garlic, chillis and ginger and fry, stirring occasionally, until the onions are golden brown. Stir in the ground almonds, soy sauce and pepper and cook for 2 minutes. Add the prawns or shrimp and stir-fry for 3 minutes. Add the vegetables. Reduce the heat to low and simmer the mixture for 10 minutes, or until the vegetables are cooked through.

Serve at once.

*Serves 6–8*
Preparation and cooking time: 30 minutes

# SAJUR LODEH

(Mixed Vegetables Cooked with Coconut)  (Indonesia)

*Almost any vegetable can be used in this soupy dish although, traditionally, there would be a mixture of at least three or four different types. Chinese or white cabbage, courgettes (zucchini) or pumpkin, French (green) beans, bamboo shoots, aubergine (eggplant), onion or even leeks, would all be successful.*

| Metric/Imperial | American |
| --- | --- |
| 1 medium onion, chopped | 1 medium onion, chopped |
| 2 garlic cloves, crushed | 2 garlic cloves, crushed |
| 1½ tsp. dried chillis or sambal ulek | 1½ tsp. dried chillis or sambal ulek |
| 1 tsp. blachan (dried shrimp paste) | 1 tsp. blachan (dried shrimp paste) |
| ½ tsp. laos powder | ½ tsp. laos powder |
| 3 Tbs. peanut oil | 3 Tbs. peanut oil |
| 700g./1½lb. mixed vegetables, cut into bite-sized pieces | 1½lb. mixed vegetables, cut into bite-sized pieces |
| 1 large tomato, blanched, peeled and chopped | 1 large tomato, blanched, peeled and chopped |
| 725ml./1¼ pints coconut milk | 3 cups coconut milk |
| 1 tsp. soft brown sugar | 1 tsp. soft brown sugar |
| 1 Tbs. peanut butter (optional) | 1 Tbs. peanut butter (optional) |

Put the onion, garlic, sambal ulek and blachan into a mortar and pound to a paste with a pestle. Alternatively, purée in a blender. Stir in the laos powder.

Heat the oil in a large saucepan. When it is very hot, add the spice paste and stir-fry for 2 minutes. Add the tomato and stir-fry for 3 minutes, or until it has pulped. Gradually stir in the coconut milk and bring to the boil. Add the veget-

ables to the pan, in the order in which they should be cooked (longest cooking vegetable first). Reduce the heat to moderately low and cook until they are just tender but still crisp. Stir in the sugar and peanut butter and simmer for 1 minute longer.

Transfer to a warmed serving bowl and serve at once.

*Serves 6*

Preparation and cooking time: 30 minutes

# BAKED BANANAS

(Malaysia)

| Metric/Imperial | American |
|---|---|
| 50g./2oz. butter | 4 Tbs. butter |
| 50g./2oz. soft brown sugar | $\frac{1}{3}$ cup soft brown sugar |
| $\frac{1}{4}$ tsp. ground cloves | $\frac{1}{4}$ tsp. ground cloves |
| 2 Tbs. orange juice | 2 Tbs. orange juice |
| 1 tsp. lemon juice | 1 tsp. lemon juice |
| 2$\frac{1}{2}$cm./1in. piece of fresh | 1in. piece of fresh green |
|    root ginger, peeled and finely diced |    ginger, peeled and finely diced |
| 6 bananas, sliced in half lengthways | 6 bananas, sliced in half lengthways |

Preheat the oven to fairly hot 190°C (Gas Mark 5, 375°F).

Cream the butter and sugar together until they are pale and soft. Beat in the cloves, orange and lemon juice and ginger.

Lay the bananas on a well-greased medium baking dish and spread the butter mixture over them. Put the dish into the oven and bake for 10 to 15 minutes, or until the top is bubbling and the bananas are cooked through and tender.

Remove from the oven and serve at once.

*Serves 6*

Preparation and cooking time: 30 minutes

*One of the very best of the traditional rijsttafel accompaniments, Baked Bananas have the refreshing tang of oranges and lemons to counteract the slightly dense taste of the bananas.*

198

# GLOSSARY

**Ajar**
An Indian-style pickle, very popular throughout Malaysia and Indonesia. It is closely related to the Indian *achar*.

**Annatto**
Small red seeds used for flavouring throughout Latin America and in the Philippines. Obtainable from Latin American stores or better supermarkets. If unobtainable use a blend of paprika with a dash of turmeric for the same colouring effect. No flavouring substitute.

**Blachan**
A form of dried shrimp paste used extensively as a flavouring all over South-East Asia. It has a variety of names depending on its origin – in Malaysia, for instance, it is called *trasi* and in Thailand *kapi*. For ease of reference in this book it is always referred to as blachan (dried shrimp paste). Sold in plastic bags, in dry cakes or slabs, or even in cans. When opened always store in a covered container – as much to keep in the very strong taste as to keep it fresh! Keeps indefinitely. Available in oriental, especially Indonesian, stores.

**Candle nuts**
A hard, oily nut used extensively in Malay and Indonesian cooking, especially in curries. Virtually unobtainable in the West, so substitute brazil nuts, or even unsalted peanuts if necessary.

**Coconut milk**
The milk of the coconut fruit is a popular cooking gravy throughout the Orient. If fresh coconut milk is unavailable, make your own using 75g./3oz. creamed coconut slice and about 450ml./15fl.oz. (2 cups) of boiling water. Stir or blend until the liquid is white and has thickened. Increase the amount of coconut to make thick coconut milk, decrease slightly to make thin. If creamed coconut is not available, desiccated (shredded) coconut in the same quantities can be used instead.

**Coriander**
Many parts of the coriander plant are used in oriental cooking – the seeds and a ground version of the seeds are used in curries, and the leaves are used extensively as a garnish in all types of dishes; in Thailand and Burma coriander leaves are sprinkled over practically everything! Since it is a member of the parsley plant, chopped parsley can be used as a substitute, although the taste will not be nearly so pungent. Available from Indian, Greek and Mexican stores.

**Daun pandan**
Long, green leaves which are used as a flavouring all over Malaysia and Indonesia. The leaves are crushed and boiled before using. Virtually unobtainable in the West and no substitute. Omit if unavailable.

**Fish sauce**
A thin, brownish liquid made from fermented dried shrimp paste and used with great enthusiasm in many parts of South-East Asia. Thailand, Vietnam, Burma and Cambodia all have their versions – the Vietnamese, in fact, use it as a garnish in much the same way as the Chinese use soy sauce and Westerners would use salt and pepper. When used in cooking, it should be measured straight from the bottle; when used as a dipping sauce or condiment, it is usually diluted with water to which lemon juice and flesh has been added – and perhaps garlic too (see recipe for *nuoc cham*). Available from most Chinese stores, or other oriental stores and from any shop stocking Vietnamese specialities. If unavailable, an acceptable substitute can be provided by mixing equal portions of anchovy paste and light soy sauce together.

**Jaggery**
The raw sugar of the palm tree, used in curried dishes throughout the Orient. Available from Indian or other oriental stores. If unobtainable, substitute the unrefined dark sugar available in health food stores, or refined dark brown sugar.

**Kapi**
See under blachan

**Kha**
See under laos

**Laos**
A fragrant spice made from the tuberous galingal plant, which is somewhat similar in flavour to ginger, although more delicate. Found throughout South-East Asia but known by different names in each country. Laos is the Indonesian name; in Malaysia it is called *lengkuas*, in Thailand *kha*. For ease of reference, in this book, it is always referred to as laos powder. Obtainable from Indonesian stores and some better spice chains.

| | |
|---|---|
| **Lemon grass** | A citron-smelling, bulbous plant somewhat similar in appearance to a small spring onion (scallion). A popular seasoning in South-East Asia, lemon grass is known as *serai* in Malaysia, *sereh* in Indonesia and is also found in Thai and Burmese cooking. For ease of reference, in this book it is always referred to as lemon grass. Sold fresh and in powdered form from Indonesian or oriental stores, but if unavailable in any form, then grated lemon rind can be substituted. |
| **Lengkuas** | See under laos |
| **Lotus seeds** | Small, fresh-tasting seeds used both in cooking and as a digestive in South-East Asia. Virtually unavailable in the West. No substitute. |
| **Peanuts** | Widely used as a garnish in Indonesian cooking and forms the basis of the famous *sate* sauce, used as an accompaniment to pork or chicken kebabs or *sate*. In this latter case, usually roasted then ground and mixed with the other sauce ingredients. To cut out some of the work, an acceptable short-cut is to use crunchy peanut butter for *sate* sauces. |
| **Rambutan** | An exotic oriental fruit, often eaten as a dessert. Available throughout Indonesia, Malaysia and Thailand. Virtually unobtainable in the West, though lychees make a near substitute. |
| **Rijsttafel** | Literally, rice table in Dutch, and in reality a series of contrasting and complementary dishes served together to make a complete Indonesian meal. The centre is always rice but the other dishes can range from six or eight up to thirty or forty, depending on the grandness of the occasion (and the quantity of the servings). Usually contains at least one *sate* dish with sauce, several different meat dishes (at least one curried), a fish dish, some pickle or sambal dishes and of course the garnish dishes of peanuts and *serundeng*, a mixture of ground peanuts and grated coconut (see recipe). A fuller description of rijsttafel is given in the introduction. |
| **Serai or serah** | See under lemon grass |
| **Sambal ulek** | A pungent mixture of ground red chillis and salt used both in cooking and as a condiment in Indonesian cooking. Available in jars or cans from better oriental or any Indonesian store. If unavailable commercially, substitute dried red chillis or make your own paste by grinding red chillis and salt to taste, then adding water until it forms a thick purée. |
| **Tamarind** | Acid-tasting seeded fruit. Tamarind is sold in thick slabs, usually dried, in Indian and other oriental stores. The juice from the pulp is used more often in recipes than the dried flesh itself. To make tamarind juice, put the tamarind into a bowl and pour over boiling water. Set aside until cool. Pour the contents of the bowl through a strainer and press through as much pulp as possible. It is now ready to use. |
| **Trasi** | See under blachan |

# RECIPE INDEX